Jenny Dawson

As If Nothing Would Be Wrong Again

Limited Special Edition. No. 3 of 25 Paperbacks

Jenny Dawson was a radiographer in the NHS for most of her working life. She lives in Lincolnshire, England.

Jenny Dawson

AS IF NOTHING WOULD BE WRONG AGAIN

AUSTIN MACAULEY PUBLISHERS™

LONDON • CAMBRIDGE • NEW YORK • SHARJAH

A CIP catalogue record for this title is available from the British Library.

ISBN 9781528937252 (Paperback)
ISBN 9781528937269 (Hardback)
ISBN 9781528969031 (ePub e-book)

www.austinmacauley.com

First Published (2019)
Austin Macauley Publishers Ltd
25 Canada Square
Canary Wharf
London
E14 5LQ

Thank you, everyone who has asked after the progress of this book and helped it on its way. Thank you, anyone who has the grace and patience to read it. Thank you, all the wonderful people at the Lincolnshire Archives, where I became interested in post-war England. And, finally, thank you to my unfailingly kind and conscientious publishers.

Part 1 – 1945

Chapter I

Meanwhile, at the other side of the square, two people were trying to get married. Lola saw them climbing the four steps to the door of the chapel, he in his demob suit and she in a pale mauve dress. The left arm of his jacket hung limp and empty by his side. In her right hand she carried a bunch of garden flowers, orange marigolds and pink carnations, already drooping in the hot smoke sun of the early morning.

If they were to change places one with the other, Lola thought, and if the bride were to transfer her flowers to the other hand, they could have helped each other up the steps. But they didn't. She watched as they went through the open door of the chapel and were embraced by its dark Methodist interior.

She remained standing in front of the shoe shop, leaning on the window frame and inhaling its smell of melting paint. The sun, in the few moments it had taken the bride and groom to emerge from the gathering crowd and climb the nine steps into the rest of their lives, had leapt high above the bank and the grocer's, turning the drab square suddenly into a magical place, engulfing everything in a golden mist and laying long shadows across the flag stones.

A man threw his cap into the air. Then another did. And another. And another. Until the whole of the Market Square was a sea of hats, flat caps, trilbies, felt, tweed, feathered, plain, and in the midst, rising out of a crescendo of cheers, the thin voice of a mouth organ.

The crowd fell silent and listened as *The Lambeth Walk* sounded, tentatively, from its midst. Then someone shouted, something inaudible, which was nevertheless interpreted as an invitation to begin. And all at once everyone was dancing, in a line, in a circle, kicking this way and kicking that way, singing perfectly the cockney words in a northern town where the only daily event was the buzzer bleating for the start and end of work.

A woman at the edge of the line of dancers had noticed her and beckoned with a wide sweep of her arm, mouthing the words, 'Come on, little girl.'

Lola shook her head and retreated farther into the doorway of the shop. The woman called again, and again. Lola shook her head, looking down at the thick turned-up hem of the skirt that had been her mother's, the brown shoes laced with string, and the pull of the blouse across her shameful chest. The woman persisted, still dancing, her skirt flying up at each kick to reveal a flannel petticoat underneath. But Lola wouldn't. She couldn't.

'As you please, then.'

The dance continued until the song came to an end. Then it started again, breaking into separate dances as more people joined. Until the whole of the Market Square was a dance, and a song, and cheers, and gales of laughter, and nothing would ever be wrong again.

At the other side of the square the doors of the Methodist chapel were opening, not by themselves, but pushed from the inside by Mr Parnell, who came out from behind them and lodged each one open with a brick, then, without a glance at the scene in the square below, went back inside.

Presently, the married people appeared, rising up into the dark rectangle of the doorway as if they had come out of a well. Standing there, framed and illuminated together, she with her left arm through his right, the gaudy orange and pink flowers resting tiredly over the other arm. His left arm, Lola saw now, was there, but in some kind of a brace under the double-breasted jacket. A war wound. He had been demobilised early. For some obscure reason, she felt reassured; how else could this man show his face at the chapel door? They stood there, side by side, his hand slightly clenched, a wisp of a smile on her face.

'A penny for them,' a voice said, hot and near.

Lola started, and turned away. She didn't know the speaker. There was liquor on his breath.

'No offence, darling, I won't bite you.'

The man moved off. The married people were still at the door of the chapel, looking down on the dance below, until someone noticed them, and another cheer rose out of the crowd, and more hats and caps flew up into the fitful smoke of the sun.

And then they were gone, overwhelmed, as Lola thought, by the occasion, by the whole of the world at their feet celebrating the ending of the war in this corner England, by the beginning of the long peace, overwhelmed more than anything by this outrageous celebration of their union.

The chapel door remained open but no one else came out. Could it be possible that there were no others, that the woman in her mauve crepe dress with an armful of wilting marigolds and carnations, and the man in his early demob suit had married with so few witnesses – only Mr Parnell who was the doorkeeper in the house of the Lord, and the Methodist minister and the rest of the world? Lola felt desperately and unaccountably lonely. She had to get home, away from this raucous and jubilant crowd.

Suddenly, the married people were in front of her on Durne Street, facing her, the woman with her arm in the man's, still carrying the flowers, and he with his good arm in hers, the other a difficult shape under the double-breasted jacket. Lola felt the blush creeping up from under the collar of her too small blouse and spreading over her face.

'I'm sorry. I didn't mean to…' she said. 'I was going home.'

'Have we got anything for her, Pip? Look at her shoes,' the woman said to the man.

'We might have.' The man released his arm from the woman's and dug in his pocket, bringing up a shiny threepenny bit. He dug again. 'What's this? Hey presto, and another one!' Then, stooping down to bring himself level with Lola, 'A little bird told me you might have a sister or brother at home.'

'Don't be ridiculous, Pip,' the woman said, 'she's far too old for talk like that. How old are you, dear?'

'Thirteen.'

The woman was pretty, in a film star way. Her mauve dress was patterned with tiny sprigs of flowers.

'She's thirteen. Where do you live, dear?'

'Barratt's Place.'

'There are probably half a dozen more like her at home,' the woman said.

'There aren't,' Lola said. 'I mean, there would have been, but…' Her voice trailed away. She didn't know how to put it, not with a man there.

The corners of the woman's mouth began to quiver.

'Oh, you poor dear. Your poor mother. Here, darling, give these to your mam.'

Lola found herself holding the bouquet of limp marigolds and carnations, cradling them in the crook of her arm like a baby.

'Thank you.' Nothing more than a murmur came out. There were now four threepenny bits in the man's outstretched hand.

'But I can't. Mother would kill me.'

'Don't force her, Pip. These people are sometimes proud.'

The man's face crumpled.

'I'm sorry,' Lola whispered. The whole, unusual day, with its raucous dancing and glittering sunlight crashed around her and lay in broken pieces at her feet.

'Now look what we've done,' the man said. Then, to Lola, 'We never could do anything right. But we've got a whole life-time to practise,' he added, turning her suddenly from a small girl into a confederate of his own age. 'I'm Pip.' He held out his hand. 'And this lady is Jean.'

Lola shook hands with the man called Pip.

'Lola,' she said.

The woman called Jean stooped to kiss her forehead. She smelt of powder and lipstick.

'We have only been married a few minutes,' she said. 'Whether we'll last the year out is anybody's guess.'

'I like your dress,' Lola said. She didn't know what else to say to the married people who were suddenly taking her into their confidence. She blushed. 'It's nice.'

The woman smoothed the fabric over her neat figure. 'Thank you.' She must have been wearing a corset and a brassiere.

All at once, the dance rounded the corner into Durne Street, separating her from the married people, who had introduced themselves as Jean and Pip, and who had talked to her like the child she had left behind and the adult she hadn't yet reached. She could see them, melting into the crowd, swept along on a tide of other people's happiness. The man waved. The woman blew her a kiss. Then they were gone.

Lola glanced at the flowers folding themselves wearily into the crook of her arm, yet still smelling of themselves, the orange marigolds of pepper and the carnations of cloves, and very faintly of powder, red lipstick and of the dark bibleness of the Methodist chapel.

They were for her mother, for whom the married people's faces had pleated in dismay. For her mother, who would have had more children but for some unspeakable calamity she had not questioned. Neither more did Lola herself, knowing only that at random times in her childhood her mother had said the words to her almost in passing, 'You would have had a brother or sister by now but it was not to be.' And then she would cast her mind back to the closed bedroom door and the loud presence of a neighbour called Audrey, and the clanking sound of pails being carried down the stairs brimming with blood-soaked rags.

Lola watched as the dance swept along Durne Street, leaving in its wake a scattering of children as drab as herself, turned up at the hem and held together with string; leaving the high sun skittering in and out of the clouds; glancing on the road and pavement, on doors and windows like so many eyes, glassy and open wide in disbelief that it should all have come to an end.

'Yer mam's looking for yer, duck,' a voice said.

'Where is she?'

'Where d'yer expect? Gallivanting? Nay. Yer pa's there. Might as well warn yer.'

'I thought...'

'Well, yer thought wrong, duck. Yer'll have yer work cut out. I sez t'yer mam, don't be too reticent to ax my missis and me. An' I'll tell yer the self-same thing, duck, don't be too reticent to ax for help. Folks is there for yer, duck. She's a good lass is yer mam. What yer got there?'

'They were given to me for mother.'

'Given t'yer, eh? Put 'em in water and they'll come up a treat.'

The man, who was called Hudson as if he had no other name, moved off.

Somewhere inside a front room, the national anthem was playing. People in the crowd stood still. A boy giggled, followed by others and yet others, until the man with the name of Hudson, reappearing from nowhere and everywhere, strode into their midst with his fists flying.

'Are yer ignorant or what that yer mek light of the peace, eh? Yer oughta know better, yer ragamuffins. An' yer'll give an ear ter Mr Attlee, yer rapscallions.'

One boy stuck his tongue out. The tongue boy fled and the rest followed, leaving in their wake the smell everyone had, compounded of sweat and dust, green soap for occasions and the clinging aroma of old meals and dark front rooms.

They all had it, Lola reflected, as she stood still in the street, the captive of Mr Attlee, who was about to speak, or had spoken, she didn't know which. She carried the smell herself: all that, as well as the other female aroma that came at the time of the monthly. Doors were opened. The voice of Mr Attlee came out, trim and unlikely, spilling into the crowd where the men stood holding their hats in their hands, the women with their hands folded as if they were in the Methodist chapel; some suffering their menstrual period for all that she knew, with the cramps and the shameful damp, and making nothing of it because it was theirs. For thirty-seven years. Her mother had been quite certain of that. Thirty-seven years, and then it will stop, and then you will be an old woman, Lola, with your best years behind you. So cherish this moment in time, with the voice of Mr Attlee falling out of the sun, and the flags, and the first day of the long peace. Cherish it, Lola Robertson.

'What does he say, duck?' The woman was chewing and still had in her hand a half crust with a scraping of margarine. 'An' I awful, duck, the prime minister an all.' She put the crust in her pinafore pocket. 'What's he say, duck?'

'It's the peace,' Lola said.

'I ha thought yon peace were declared a time back,' the woman said, still chewing. 'Yer'll forgive me, duck.'

'This is Japan,' Lola said. 'The other was Germany.'

'Aye,' the woman said. 'Japan. Ta, duck.'

Mr Attlee had finished, but the doors of Durne Street remained open, the women standing there, the men hatless, the dust hanging in the middle air and the sun blistering the road.

'But at what cost,' a voice said.

Lola looked around. The same dark front rooms, the same women, the same men. No one different. It was no voice she knew, neither was it her own. She tried to bring it back but it had gone, far away into the populated country of grown-up thoughts she sometimes had and couldn't say.

There was now no end to the red, white and blue, coming out in the early afternoon like so many flowers under the high dusting of sun: flags and streamers and rags of bunting. Everyone in Durne Street had something, kept in closets and attics and storerooms under the stairs in the case of another patriotic event.

But not Barratt's Place, as if the news had not yet picked its way across the difficult space that defined its northern edge, and where doors and windows stood stubbornly closed, like mouths declining to speak or eyes refusing to see. Only Barry Green sat on the step in front of his house rolling marbles disconsolately into the gutter.

'Yer mam's looking for yer, Lola Robertson.'

'She probably is, Barry Green.'

'What'll yer give me for telling yer? She axed me to tell yer, Lola Robertson.'

'It's "asked", A-S-K-E-D.'

'Axed. What'll yer give me?'

'I've given you a spelling lesson, so I have, Barry Green.'

'Yer pa's back.'

Lola stopped walking. It was true then. She felt suddenly cold and was aware of the damp under her arms and inside her knickers. She almost certainly smelt of the monthly. She probably had done when she met the married people, Jean in her sprigged dress and Pip with his kind crumpled face.

'How do you know?'

'Yer ma said. Yer got a ha'penny?' Barry Green wiped his nose with the back of his hand. He stood up. 'God's truth, Lola Robertson, honest.' A trail of mucus gleamed on the back of his hand.

'Give me the clean hand, then. Not that one, the other one.'

'Yer got a ha'penny then?'

'I might have…no I haven't.'

'Oh.' The corners of the boy's mouth drooped.

'I've got something else. It has been given to me. Mother would kill me if she knew so you've not got to tell. Close your eyes.' She placed a bright three-penny bit in the outstretched hand. 'You can open them now. What do you say?'

'Thank you, Lola Robertson.'

'You've not got to tell your mam it was me. God's honour?'

'Yes.'

'Give it to your mam. The war's over. Did your mam know?'

'We knowed that already, Lola Robertson. Where yer been?'

'Up town, Barry Green. Japan has surrendered, Mr Attlee says so. They're dancing up town.'

'Dancing?' The boy's eyes sparkled. 'Yer coming, Lola?'

'I've just come back, Barry.'

'Nah, yer too old anyway. Yer mus be pushing sixteen. Me mam says yer developed.'

Lola blushed. 'I'll have that threepenny bit back, Barry Green, if you please.'

'Nah, I didna mean nowt, Lola Robertson.'

The front room was different. It didn't look different. It was the same dark cube with a pencil of light coming in through a gap in the curtains. It had the same blank hearth and the same print on the wall of Jesus suffering the little children, which Lola Robertson knew vaguely at the corner of her mind was not suffering in the way she suffered the affronts of Barry Green and his kind but something better and incomprehensible.

There was the same sideboard, there were the same chairs, the same triangles of dust lodged in the corners of the windowsill. But it was different. Someone had passed through the living room. No. Someone was still here, seated in what most nearly approximated to an ingle, obscured by shadow. There was only an extended leg to indicate that anyone was present. There was a sickly smell, of something festering.

'Aren't yer speaking then?'

'I didn't see you, father.'

'It's "father" now, is it? What's up wi yer?'

'Barry Green said you were back.'

'So yer mam's been blabbing again. I'll kill her. What's them?'

'Flowers. For mother. They need a drink.'

'Swiped um, did yer? If yer swiped um I'll give yer the back of me hand.'

'They were given to me for mother. I just said so.'

'I'll believe yer, duck. Plenty wouldn't. Give yer pa a kiss.'

Lola drew back the curtains.

'Yer didn't need to do that, duck. An' yer can tek that look off yer face for a start.'

'What's happened to your leg, father?'

'Ever heard of Dunkirk?'

'Yes.'

'Well, it weren't Dunkirk, but it were summat like. It's gone to bad, yer ma says. Ain't it, Lil?' – raising his voice – 'Draw them curtains to again, will yer.'

'Your father's back, Lola.' Her mother replaced the curtains, pulling them tighter so that the pencil of light was no longer visible. 'What have you got there?'

'If she swiped um I'll give her the back of me hand, I telled her.'

'They're for you. The lady who got married at the Methodists gave them to me. For my mother.'

Tears brimmed up in her mother's eyes and flowed over, rolling down her cheeks. She had rouge on. And lipstick.

'Yer need to crush them stalks,' her father said. 'They'll tek up watter.'

'Here, let me do them,' said her mother.

'She's a great girl, Lil, she can do them.'

Lola's face burned. Here was her father, returned from who knows where, looking at her body.

'I'll do them,' she said.

She went into the scullery, listening to the silence that hovered between her parents. Her mother was waiting for her to go back.

'Lola knows why she hasn't seen you these last three years, Cyril.' Her mother began as soon as she was back in the front room. 'She knows that you've been with another lady, behaving as if you were married to her.'

'Chrissake, Lil, the girl knows the word, don't she? Look at her, for God's sake. She's nigh on a woman.'

Then Mrs Green was in the room, a threepenny piece shining in her open palm, and at arm's length as if it were something contaminated. 'We don't take charity, Lil. I know it's well meant, but we can't accept it.'

'The gentleman who had just got married put it in my pocket when I wasn't looking,' Lola said. 'I gave it to Barry because mother would kill me.'

'Put it on the mantle shelf to go to the poor, Lola,' her mother said. 'And you might as well get the kettle on. Least said soonest mended.'

But Mrs Green wouldn't stay.

'That's took the wind out of her sails,' said her father when she had gone.

'Your father's leg's gone to bad,' said her mother in a low voice as if Mrs Green was still standing outside the closed door. 'We don't know what the Army will pay, but likely it won't be enough.'

'Why not?'

'Never you mind.'

'Yer might as well tell her, Lil,' said her father, 'or I will.'

Lola looked down at the string laces in her shoes, and then at her parents. The crack in the curtains had opened when Mrs Green banged the front door; the pencil of light fell across the threads of the carpet and climbed her father's extended leg, showing the yellowed dressing.

'It isn't the child's fault,' her mother said. 'It didn't ask to be born into shame and filth. Because that's what it is. Filth and shame.'

'What…' Lola began the sentence, not knowing how it would end.

'Never you mind,' said her mother. 'The least said, soonest mended. Your father can tell you the rest.'

'When's yer birthday, duck?'

'Four weeks today.'

'And remind yer ma and pa of yer age.'

'I'll be fourteen.'

'Don't beat about the bush, Cyril. Tell her.'

'Yer got to leave school and earn yer keep, duck. There's plenty does the same at fourteen.'

A lump lodged itself in the back of Lola's throat.

'Why?'

'On account of the bairn, duck.'

'Why?'

'Leave it, Cyril,' said her mother. Then, to Lola, 'Your father has to maintain the child, that's why. He hasn't done anything decent yet, but he's agreed to do that.'

'Yer mother was allus one for playing the martyr, duck,' said her father.

Lola went up to her room and sat by the window looking out at the last of the day. The musician had long gone from the square and the dancing had stopped in the town. The doors of Barratt's Place stood open. Tatters of bunting had appeared in one or two windows, a flag on a stick in a milk bottle here and there. In her own house, nothing. Only a bunch of orange and pink flowers straightening and unfolding in a dark airless room. A martyred mother. A father who had committed who knew what outrage against her mother, against Mr Attlee and against the married people Jean and Pip, whose leg had gone to bad, and who had come home. And here Lola experienced her second adult thought of the day, that some other husband had come back from the war and her father had nowhere to go but home.

An aeroplane flew high overhead. The people still in the street squinted up into the bright sky and waved. Then the bell of a fire engine was in the neighbourhood, beckoning every child to run after it as if it were the Pied Piper. She saw Barry Green come out of his front door wearing his pyjamas, too short and tight in the arms and legs, and big slippers with the loose soles tied on with string and flapping against the cobbles. Everything and everyone in Barratt's Place was tied together with string.

She would lie on her bed and read *Jane Eyre* until the church clock struck midnight, until her mother had come up to bed and until the tap in the back yard had finished and the lavatory had been used for the last time and the summer exhalations of the drains had sunk back into the earth. She would hold on to this unusual day as long as possible, the first day of the long peace.

The door opened an inch and her mother's voice came through.

'Tidy the drawer, dear.'

'It is tidy, mother.'

'Nevertheless, see to it.'

'However, it is tidy, mother.'

'None of your cheek, dear.'

Two brown paper packets had been placed on top of her folded nightdress. Tied up with string, with scraps of paper attached. From Mother x. From Father x (in her mother's writing). Her father's present was a pair of brown shoelaces. Her mother's was a brassiere. She pulled the curtain across and put it on over her blouse, standing in front of the flyblown mirror looking at herself. Then she threaded the laces into her shoes.

And so the day ended and the doors of Barratt's Place closed. And Lola Robertson stood in front of the glass far into the night, looking at herself, not believing herself.

Chapter II

A stone flew past his head. And then another, narrowly missing him and coming to rest with a commonplace thud some inches ahead. A third stone, lobbed above his head, crashed through the lower branches of a lime tree, sending a debris of small twigs and tired leaves cascading to the ground.

A commonplace event.

'Good shot,' he said under his breath. 'Better luck next time.'

Stefan Czerniak carried on walking, waiting for the usual word. But it didn't come. 'Conchie,' he said to himself. He didn't know what he was. I searched myself and I found nothing.

'You ought to leave that book,' his mother had said before he came out. 'It's bad for you. And you may call me Ruth. "Mum" is childish. How old are you?'

A rhetorical question.

'How old are you?'

'Sixteen. What shall I call father?'

'You'll have to ask him.'

Stefan picked up the leavings from the tree: a cluster of small nodular fruits and a trailing papery bract. Conchie.

Across the park, they were fastening bunting to the railings of the bandstand, setting out chairs on the grass, heaving the kettledrum and double bass. A woman and two children stood by the pond throwing pieces of bread from a paper bag to brown ducks. A man was standing at the edge smoking. He finished his cigarette and threw the end into the water, where it fizzed briefly and remained floating on the sparkling surface. Isn't that what we all do, fizz briefly and then float aimlessly on the sparkling surface of…

'You ought to leave that book. It's bad for you.' His mother's voice echoed in the empty rooms of his mind. Seats were being carried into the bandstand, trombones, cornets, the tuba, up the steep steps, sweeping aside the fallen leaves of all the autumns of the war.

Stefan stood by the edge of the pond, looking down into the lapping water. The park was filling with summer. God. There was no end to this.

'Conchie!'

Contrary to what you assume, I'm nothing. In particular. My father might well have been sent to the mines. I was told that I was old enough, then being twelve, to absorb this knowledge. But Stefan wouldn't say it. He wouldn't have thought it, except that it was there, written indelibly between the lines of the volume of the volume of Sartre he ought not read.

'Conchie!'

They didn't talk about it at home, not in so many words. It merely informed every waking thought.

But what do the neighbours think?

That my father...He didn't know. The neighbours didn't talk about it either.

'Sorry, sir! Didn't mean it.'

The brackish level of the pond was suddenly coming up to meet him, with all its flashing clouds and wisps of leaves, its insects and morsels of half-beaked bread.

The man he had noticed was still standing there, lighting another Players; the woman with the children was throwing fistfuls of bread for the brown ducks, tipping the bag upside down and shaking out the last of the crumbs.

The park was filling with the peace.

Sitting on a bench in Congreve Park on the morning of the commemoration, Stefan Czerniak pulled off his shoes, emptied the water out of them and peeled off his socks. Then he stood to go home, having asked nothing of the day and having received nothing more and nothing less than a headful of green water, the seeds of the lime tree and a mouthful of words: familiar enough and of no particular consequence.

Across the park, the band was tuning up, sending bright metallic spurts in his direction; single notes at first, and then runs of notes, chasing each other across the pond, fastening themselves in his head. The man smoking removed the cigarette from his mouth. The woman with the children screwed up the paper bag and put it in her pocket, then, brushing the children down and settling the bows in their hair, shook them into straightness holding each one by the hand. The man no longer smoking stood tall, the cigarette in his hand, dripping ash onto the ground. All the park was standing for the peace. The band rose collectively to its feet. Stefan Czerniak, the only moving entity in a still and peaceful world, slipped out of the gate, over the road into the alley behind Golen Avenue and home, gaining the back garden before the first verse of the anthem had finished.

The neighbours' French windows were open and another verse was beginning on the wireless. He could sense the standing and straightening and the folding of hands in their room. Bazal was in the garden decimating his mother's cabbages.

'Hello.' He picked up the tortoise and peered at the pleasant face and astonishing sculptured shell, at the little legs paddling in the shining air. 'Hello.'

The anthem finished and glasses clinked in the room next door. The voice of Clement Attlee wandered out of the French windows and hung about among the roses.

'Oh, Stefan dear, what happened?' Mrs Beaumont's puckered face was at the fence.

'It's all right. Bazal was helping us out with the cabbages.'

'He's a naughty fellow. But I meant you, dear. You've had a calamity.'

'I fell into the pond.'

'That's too bad. Lad's home. Let us know if you have any more trouble, dear.'

'Thank you, Mrs Beaumont.'

'I mean it, dear. Shall I take Bazal?' She reached over the fence. A bracelet of glass beads slipped up to her elbow. 'Did I ever tell you we found him in the foul drain? That's why we called him Bazal, after Mr Bazalgette, you know.' She lowered her voice and edged nearer to the fence, glancing towards the open windows. 'It might sound as if we're making merry, but it's not what everyone wanted. In Japan, dear. What a terrible cost.' She raised her voice. 'We're about to toast Pip's wedding. In absentia, you know.'

'Pip?'

'Yes, dear. She seems a nice little thing. From somewhere in the north. Methodist. We haven't seen her, of course, with the war on. I don't know what she'll make of us but no doubt we'll all do our best.'

'Yes.'

'We are all of us called upon to do our best, isn't that so? How's your father, dear?'

Mr Attlee was finishing. Stefan heard the wireless in the room next door being turned off, choking briefly on the remaining words and swallowing them.

'Freda?'

'Coming! They want me to go in for the toast. How's your father these days, dear?'

'Freda!'

'I suppose he's coming home. Some time.'

'Your father's coming home.' Ruth Czerniak held the letter in her hand, shedding dry tears. 'Your father's coming home, Stefan,' she said again. 'Haven't you anything to say?'

'When?'

'It doesn't say. Here.' His mother handed him the letter.

'It's dated the twelfth of May. It's been read.'

'Of course it's been read. What do you expect?'

'I've been in the park.' He still couldn't call her Ruth.

'So I see.'

'I had an adventitious encounter with the pond.'

'So I see. What do you expect?'

'Nothing. In particular.'

'Do you know who it was?'

'No, not really.' He handed the letter back to his mother.

'Keep away from them in future. What was Mrs Beaumont saying?'

'That Bazal was named after Mr Bazalgette because they found him in the foul drain.'

'Yes. I hope they washed him. Who is Mr Bazalgette?'

'I'll find out and let you know.' Stefan turned to go.

'Don't go. I was talking to you. About your father.'

'He's coming home. That's all, isn't it?'

'Isn't that enough?'

'I suppose so.'

'What's got into you, Stefan?'

'Nothing much, mother. About a gallon of pond water and a couple of minnows.'

'You would go. I told you what it would be like.'

'No you didn't, mother. You didn't know I was going. I went in a spirit of enquiry. Pip's getting married.'

'It wasn't all about Bazal then. Who to?'

'I don't know. "A nice little thing".' He'd said too much. He'd repeated Mrs Beaumont's words and in repeating them had distorted them. In the eye of his mind, her soft rumpled face had twisted into the *risus sardonicus*. 'She'll be round later with a cabbage. Two cabbages.'

'We must be kind to the young lady, Stefan. And we must try to look decent for Mrs Beaumont.'

'Pip isn't here, only Lad. Will a chap be expected to call his father by his Christian name?'

'What an odd question to ask. Who's the chap?'

'You said I should call you by yours.'

'Did I? When?'

'I don't remember.'

'Neither do I. You'll do as you please, I expect, Stefan. Try and look decent for Freda coming, dear.'

Stefan stood at the door.

'And another thing, dear. We don't let your father know.'

'Know what?'

'That you fell in the pond or suffered any other mishap on account of…you know. He's had enough, I expect. And it won't necessarily go away even now the war's ended. It will follow us. One gets used to it.'

'You as well?'

'Yes, you might as well know. I don't talk about it, that's all, and neither will you talk about it. You may call me Ruth, dear.'

The morning sun balanced on the windowsill of his room, spilled over and spread across the floorboards, climbing the opposite wall and stopping there. Illuminating the haywain, making the dark summer trees darker and the louring sky more louring.

Stefan didn't know if he had got used to the painting. It was merely there. It had been there for as long as the house had been visited for a weak cup of tea and a perfunctory look around. We don't like doing this, Mrs Zerniack. Churnick. It's the job, you see. Needs must. Ah, Constable, a fine painter of the English school. That'll do. The usual all clear. No need to worry, Mrs Zerniack. Churnick. Husband well? Good, good. One gets used to it.

As he would no doubt to the shirt drying on him and to the faint patina of evaporating pond water and its detritus of leaf parts and crawling things. He removed an insect from his sleeve, opened the window and let it go. Glen Miller came in, and, farther away and fainter, *The Lambeth Walk* from the bandstand in the park. They would be dancing. In another life, he, Stefan Czerniak, might have been dancing. For the laying down of arms. For the long peace stretching ahead into his life. For the two mushroom clouds rising and hovering and sinking in dismay on some distant land. Now look what we've done.

Mrs Beaumont was attaching bunting to the garden fence, but not to the Czerniaks' side. Mr Beaumont was cutting the grass, rasping the mower haphazardly back and forth, at right angles and every other angle in between until Lad took the machine and mowed in straight lines up and down and along the edges. For the rest, the garden sank into the arms of the gathering heat, the leaves of the cabbages losing their sheen, the beans folding in on themselves under the brassy tunes of the distant bandstand.

Mrs Beaumont finished the bunting and went in. A card table was brought out, and chairs, sinking clawed feet into the green velvet of the lawn. More glasses and a jug of something pale and green. Mr Beaumont looked up and waved. Stefan continued to sit at the window in his room, his arms on the sill, drugged by the sun and the rancid smell of his drying shirt, by the green pond water in the jug on the table next door, the tinny voice of the sun and by the sweet shorn grass, and the long peace. Which on this fifteenth day of August in the year 1945 had no meaning for him, nor, he assumed, for his mother or for his father in absentia, because the Czerniaks had been objectors in the first place. His head sank onto his arms and he drifted into the difficult word, conchie, letting it fall into the empty caverns of his sleep, where only the dried pond and the burning white of the sky existed.

'Stefan.' His mother was in the room. She hadn't knocked. She wanted him to call her by her name, Ruth, and yet she had entered his room without his leave. 'I knocked but you didn't hear.' The first shining day of the peace which had no relevance was passing in the well-worn pattern of every other day, a descent into oblivion and a contention with his mother. 'So I had to come in. Mr and Mrs Beaumont are downstairs, dear. I'll tell them you are on your way. Here…' Handing him a pressed shirt, one of his father's.

'Not that.'

'There's nothing wrong with it.'

'It's not mine.'

'Since when has ownership been so important to you?'

'It hasn't.'

'Then put it on, please.'

Mr and Mrs Beaumont were seated at the table with the teapot between them and cups and saucers in front of them.

'I hope we're not running you short,' Mr Beaumont said.

'No, indeed you're not,' said his mother. 'You shouldn't have troubled with this.' Passing her hand lightly over the textured crown of the cabbage.

'It was the least we could do, dear. We were meaning to have a talk with you and Bazal has unexpectedly provided us with an opportunity. After Mr Bazalgette, you know. We found him in the foul drain.'

'I hope you washed him.' Stefan, standing at the door, mouthed at his mother and saw a flicker of amusement pass across her face.

'What a delightful story,' she said. 'I'll have to ask my husband to inspect ours.'

Mr and Mrs Beaumont looked at one another.

'Ken has something to say.'

Mr Beaumont stirred his tea. 'No, no sugar, thank you, Ruth, my dear. Bad for the waistline.'

'Go on, Ken, say what we have to say.'

'Is the young man coming?'

'He's just behind you, Mr Beaumont. Sit down, Stefan.' His mother pulled out a chair. 'He was reluctant to wear his father's shirt.'

'Of course you were,' said Mrs Beaumont. 'But it becomes you, dear. You have the fine looks of your father and his shirt becomes you. Go on, Ken.'

Mr Beaumont took a sip of tea, grimaced slightly and drank the whole down as if it were a draught of physic. 'Ah, that's done me a power of good.' The sun glancing through the high pane of the window rested on his domed head, as if conferring a benediction for some sacrificial deed.

'Go on, Ken.'

'I will, Freda, when I can get a word in edgeways.' Then, clearing his throat, 'Pip got married today. At least, we presume that's the case.'

'In absentia, of course,' said Mrs Beaumont.

'My wife's the scholar, more so than I. That's not what we came to talk about,' before Ruth could wish Pip…happiness, anything. 'The long and the short of it is…How old are you, Stefan, if I might be so bold as to ask?'

'Sixteen, sir.'

'And what plans have you for your – er – life, sir? Since we are all of us thrown into this troublesome world to make of it what we will.'

'Don't talk that way, Ken.' Mrs Beaumont laid a soft hand on her husband's arm.

'To cut a long story short, Mr Czerniak, sir, dear Freda and I came to – er – inform you that the firm has done rather well in recent years, and the growth we have experienced lately looks likely to continue well into the future. In brief, we have a position going for a young man to undertake clerical duties, and we would like to offer it to you, Mr Czerniak, sir. We don't ask for your answer right now because no doubt you will wish to talk it over with your parents. But the offer is there and the post is yours for the asking. Shall we say forty days, Mr Czerniak?' Ken Beaumont looked at the face of his watch as if it would add forty days to fifteen, subtract sixteen for the remaining days of the month of August and work out the difference. 'Give or take a day or two, Mr Czerniak?'

'September the twenty-ninth, sir.'

'Good man, the feast of St Michael and all the angels.' Mr Beaumont held out his hand and withdrew it almost immediately. 'As a man of the world, young Mr Czerniak will know that we shake hands when a deal is done. Until then, he is at liberty to decline the proposal, with no hard feelings on either side. Mrs Czerniak, my dear?'

'Thank you, Mr Beaumont; we will discuss it with his father.'

Stefan went out of the front door and down the chequered path to the gate. On either side, the hydrangeas had escaped the planting of vegetables, dawn blue hydrangeas, and every shade to dusk, there for as long as he could remember, coming back every year, with their impossibly bright leaves and paper flower heads. He went out, and up the shallow hill to the park. Measuring the steps of his – er – life in flags and bunting. There was no end to the bunting, skeltering and looping across windows and across gardens, fences, walls, stopping only to draw breath at number 20 and then continuing, pushing itself under a gate and climbing a flagpole where it terminated in a knot.

'What does the firm do?' he had said to his mother after Mr and Mrs Beaumont had gone, and his mother said, 'We will discuss it with your father.'

In the park, they were folding down deck chairs and picking up litter. The same man stood smoking by the edge of the pond. The same brown ducks dibbling in the water. The same water. The sun sinking into it. The man threw down his cigarette end, raised his hat and moved off.

Then they were unravelling the bunting from the sides of the bandstand, rolling it up, and piling it into heaps. And already there were the scents of the end of summer, the rust on the leaves and the dried and trodden grass.

Far off the dust of a distant war hung over London.

And at the end of the day, Stefan sat at the window of his room looking out, to where the shadows gathered in the Beaumonts' garden, where the chairs and table were being taken in, and the bunting was being unhooked from the fence and rolled up for the next patriotic occasion.

He didn't know the nature of the post he had been offered by Mr Beaumont.

Nor did he know when his father would be back to discuss the matter; or from what place his father might be making the journey home. Or how it would be to find themselves, his parents and by extension himself he supposed, to be walking on nothing; since this was the long peace and the ground on which they walked had vanished as surely as if the black and white chequered path leading to the gate had been replaced by a bottomless pit.

And at the end of the day, Stefan Czerniak was full of unknowing. Hearing nothing in the dark silence of the night but the muffled closing of a door on his – er – life, a sound he recognised as disappointment.

Chapter III

There was no end to Stefan Czerniak's unknowing. It walked in front of him as his shadow did in the mornings, and followed him in the evenings. It clung to him as the wartime smoke still hovered, insistently, over towns and cities. It was the curtain across the window of his room. It was the mask he wore, and the words he spoke, or didn't speak.

Suddenly, the word "mother" sounded incomprehensible.

'Ruth.' His mother was at the table cutting beans, the bright flicker of the knife dancing across the wall as she worked.

'Yes?' Her shoulders tensed. She wouldn't mention it. There would be a hiatus while she arranged her expression, before she turned to face him. 'You were going to say something, Stefan.' Her back was still towards him. She was waiting for his words, scooping up the beans and dropping them into the colander.

'When is father coming back?'

'You know the answer to that as well as I do.'

'Is there no one we can ask?'

'No. No, there isn't.'

'There must be.'

'There isn't. Anything else?'

'No.'

His mother turned round.

'We don't know, dear. That's all. There's something else.'

'There isn't anything else.'

'If your father hasn't returned by the time you have to give your answer to Mr Beaumont, we will just have to explain as well as we can. They have been good to us and asked no questions. We must be good to them. We can do no less.' Then, when he was at the door. 'What did you want to do with your life if not…that?'

A rhetorical question.

'What did you want to do, Stefan?'

Still rhetorical.

'If you have nothing more pressing on your agenda, the garden needs attention. You've been neglecting it, dear, no doubt because you wish to avoid Mr Beaumont. What else did you want from your life, Stefan?'

Not rhetorical.

'Not that.'

'You don't know what it is yet.'

'He said the firm had done well out of the war.'

'Not in those words.'

'"Done rather well in recent years".'

'That's different. What do you think he's been doing?'

'You and father didn't support the war, Ruth. You told me I was free to decide for myself when I was older. Well, I've decided. I don't support the war.'

'The war's over, Stefan.'

'But their firm's done well out of it.'

'Discuss it with your father, dear. Now, if you would kindly attend to the garden. And wash your hands when you come in. You don't know where that creature's been.'

Bazal was nowhere to be seen. Stefan cast a sideways glance into the garden next door. There was no one there. He hoed round the greens and unwound a skein of bindweed from the tall runners. There was still no one in the garden next door. No one visible, but a blue spiral of cigarette smoke rose from behind the fence.

Somewhere a page turned.

His thoughts wandered yet again to the young man required to take up clerical duties for a firm that had been rather successful in recent years. Seated at a desk. Wearing cufflinks and armbands. Certainly wearing armbands. And he was not alone. There were others there, vaguely delineated, yet there nevertheless, and similarly occupied. In the corner, a coat stand, its arms full of government-issued raincoats. Another page turned. 'That's it,' he said. Out loud. 'So that's it.' Behind the fence, the thrap of a magazine being thrown down.

'Gosh, I'm so sorry. I must have been eavesdropping.'

'No, you weren't. Only on my thoughts.'

'A penny for them.' The young woman was pretty, like a film star. She reached over the fence, offering a cigarette.

'No, really, thank you.'

'I'm Jean, Pip's wife.'

'Stefan.'

'Stephen?'

'No, Stefan, with an "f". It doesn't matter, though.'

'But it does.' She hesitated. 'Freda thought I would be a "nice little thing". I'm not, am I? Don't think you have to answer that question. You must forgive me. It's all a bit of a shock.' She whimpered a little. 'It shouldn't be but it is. We've been through a war, for heavens' sake.'

'I'm sorry.' He didn't know what else to say. 'I'm sorry.'

'It's not your fault.' She dabbed at her eyes with a man's bordered handkerchief. 'Look at this, for heavens' sake. It's like a tablecloth.' She laughed. 'You must be the young gentleman who's going to work in Ken's office.'

Another page turned, a different one.

'We're waiting to discuss it with my father. He's not back yet.'

'Oh. I'm so sorry. These things happen.' She folded the tablecloth back into its creases and tucked it up her sleeve, then looked at him enquiringly as if searching for some kind of response. He would always, from now on, be in the presence of others who required words from him. He could imagine it, an endless march of conversations until his life's end.

'It's not your fault either,' he said, immediately wondering if he'd been ill mannered.

She laughed, untucking the tablecloth from her sleeve and dabbing at her eyes again.

'Maybe you can think of better things to do with your life than sit at a desk all day,' she said. 'But it's a start. We all have to start somewhere. It doesn't mean we have to stay. Pip will do clerical work. There are worse things.'

'How's Pip?'

'As well as can be expected. Getting used to being married to a nice little thing. We might both have married other people if there hadn't been a war on. Pip would have found a sweet uncomplicated girl and I would have found a nice steady boy from the next street. But there you are.'

'My father was an objector.' He didn't know why he'd said it. Probably he hadn't said it.

She picked up the magazine. 'I'm looking forward to meeting him,' she said. 'He'll be back soon.'

And she was right. Paul Czerniak returned. Not in the sense that he walked through the gate of 20 Golen Avenue and up the chequered black and white path to the front door. But in the other sense, that he had become a visible entity, most often to be seen walking away, travelling more rapidly than Stefan in spite of the disparity in their ages, the cap pulled forward on his head and the dark coat flapping as if attempting to keep up with him. The red bandana flying. He was there, at all times and in all places made festive by the long peace.

One day, Pip looked over the fence, wearing his hair in tufts as if he had forgotten to comb it down.

'Nice,' he said, to the garden more than Stefan. His innocent grey eyes wandered over the manicured grass and hoed beds. 'Good job you've done there. Jolly good job, chief. We're going today.'

'Oh.'

'Yes. Not going well.'

'I'm sorry, Pip.'

'Nice of you to say so, old chap.' Pip remained at the fence and lit a cigarette. 'Like one?'

'No, no thank you.'

'Quite right. Doesn't do to get into bad habits. Not going well, as I said. Mother and the wife don't hit it off. Women, you see.' He punched the fence half-heartedly.

Stefan didn't see. 'I'm sorry, Pip,' he said again.

'Not your fault, old chap.'

'It might be better next time.'

'Dad took a shine to her. That didn't help.' Pip still didn't go. 'Have to be off soon. Just came out to say cheerio.'

'Ruth and I think she's lovely.' Stefan blushed. He had jumped in, saying something he only hoped was true, and would no doubt come up covered in detritus and reeking of pond water.

Pip transferred the half-smoked cigarette with difficulty to the other hand. 'Appreciate that, Stefan, old chap. To tell you the truth, I'm of the same opinion myself. Your dad back yet?'

'No, not yet.'

'Thought I saw him, that's all.'

'Where?'

'A few times. Must have been mistaken.'

'Where did you see him, Pip?'

'Filthy habit, this.' Pip stubbed the cigarette out on the sole of his shoe and threw the end down onto the garden. 'Makes the sprouts grow. Getting on the trolley bus, in the park, Woolworths, usual places.'

'What did he look like?'

'Pretty much like himself, old chap. Mind you, I wasn't that near. Wearing a cap and a dark coat on the long side. Plenty of chaps around again now. Could have been anyone. Good chap, your dad.'

Pip was still doing his bit for the sprouts, grinding the end of his cigarette into the soil. 'I suppose you've heard?'

'I don't know.'

'Of course you don't know, not unless a chap tells you. Dad's lined you up for the office.' Pip leaned over the fence and lowered his voice. 'Can't advise you one way or the other, but between you, me and the gatepost, I'd say...Now look what I've done, spilt the beans good and proper.'

'I did know. Mr Beaumont mentioned it,' Stefan said. 'He said he'd ask again after forty days, give or take a day or two.'

Pip lit another cigarette. 'Filthy habit. Here, try it.' He passed the cigarette over the fence. 'How is it?'

Stefan gave it back. 'Not bad.'

'Here, for your dad.' Pip passed the packet over. It was nearly full. 'A good chap, your dad.'

'Thank you, Pip.' The occasion to ask had gone, dissipated on the mild September air as completely as the blue spiral of cigarette smoke. Pip was making moves to go in, looking at the French window and at the shadows moving around inside, getting ready for a farewell.

What does the firm do? But he couldn't say it now. He couldn't ever have said it. He ground the words into the earth with the toe of his shoe.

The French windows were opening and Mrs Beaumont was coming out, arm in arm with Jean, already in her hat and coat.

'I've come to say good-bye.' She looked in her handbag. 'Here, for your mother. I hope it's her colour.' She leaned over the fence and kissed him on the cheek, then pressed a crumpled paper bag into his hand.

'Did you say thank you?' Ruth held the lipstick in her hand.

He couldn't remember. It had all happened quickly. He couldn't bear to look at her tears.

'I suppose I did.' They didn't want to be thanked.

'Mr Beaumont came, Stefan. While you were in the garden.'

'It's not the middle of September yet. Father isn't back.'

'It wasn't that. Pip and Jean went home earlier than Mr and Mrs Beaumont were expecting.' His mother's voice was rising in some awful crescendo of obligation. 'We'll have to go. There's nothing else for it.' She looked up. 'I'm sorry, but we have to go. I said yes. It's an orchestral concert.'

'We can't afford it, Ruth.'

33

'It's not a case of affording it, Stefan. They're complimentary tickets, or something of the kind.'

'Complimentary what for?'

'Do mind your grammar, dear. And don't let your speculations run away with you.'

'They aren't doing.'

'Grammar!'

'Complimentary for assisting the war effort, Ruth. It might as well be said.'

'We don't know…'

'What's that but speculation?'

'Do I have to give your apologies or will you come?'

'Yes.'

'I have to give your apologies?'

'No, I'll come. I'm sorry, Ruth.' The pattern of his – er – life. Being sorry. Over and over again.

'You have nothing to be sorry about.'

The day had turned to an early dusk and an incessant penetrating drizzle. He could sense his mother moving about upstairs, getting ready, rolling her hair into a pleat, putting on lipstick. Pressing her white blouse and grey skirt, finding the least worn pair of stockings and darning them. Twice her steps approached the door of his room and stopped. Then went away. He opened the door. As he expected: his father's jacket and his father's tie; the tin of shoe polish and a brush; mended socks. Mr Beaumont was in the garden smoking, wearing his hair like a black bathing cap, dripping water. He finished his cigarette and ground it into the soil. Good for the sprouts. He lit another, examined it and stubbed it out on his shoe. Mrs Beaumont's voice was at the French windows. 'We'd better take the Rover, dear.'

'What's wrong with the you-know?'

'In this weather, dear? Poor Ruth would get drenched.'

Mr Beaumont went in.

Then they were at the front door, not ringing the bell but hovering there behind the glass, two amorphous shapes, inspecting their watches and adjusting their hats.

His mother was still moving around upstairs. 'Answer the door, please, dear. I'm on my way.'

'Ken suggested we take the Rover.' Mrs Beaumont looked up from under her hat. 'On account of the weather, you know. I hope you don't mind if I sit in the back, dear. I feel sick in the front,

34

especially if I have to…what's that nautical word, Ken? Navigate. With a map, you know. I'm told it's something to do with the ears, unlikely though it may seem.'

'Left standing, sir.'

Stefan could see his mother in the mirror, looking out of the side window. Mrs Beaumont's eyes were closed.

'We were left standing, sir.'

'Don't, dear.' Mrs Beaumont had woken up. 'Ken means the firm, Stefan.'

'It's on our way, Freda.'

'It isn't the only way, dear. There are others.'

But Mr Beaumont wasn't listening. He was edging the Rover into the warren of back streets at the eastern edge of the city, negotiating depressions in the road and bumping up and down kerbs in order to get there, the thin yellow light from the street lamps running in slow sheets down his face. He brought the car to a sudden halt.

'We were left standing, you see, Mr Czerniak.'

On one side, the ground was open in a great howl of pain. On the other, the buckled and agonised skeleton of another building. The brass plate bearing the name of the firm was still visible, glistening in the rain.

'Left us standing, sir. Thank God it was night. Other poor buggers weren't as fortunate, Mr Czerniak.'

'That's enough, dear,' Mrs Beaumont said presently, from the back. 'And do mind your language, Ken. Remember that we're in distinguished company.' Then, to Ruth, 'You'll know Brahms and Smetana, dear, of course you will.'

In the mirror saw his mother turn away into the side window of the car, so that her face was reflected there, wanly smiling. He could see her brimming eyes, and she didn't know.

'Yes, Freda, yes of course. Smetana. How wonderful.'

As the tenth day in September closed, Stefan Czerniak was given an additional two words in the Latin language, those being the title of the song quoted at the end of the *Academic Festival Overture*. *Gaudeamus igitur*.

And Mr Beaumont had said, 'Crusty old chap, Brahms. My wife will tell you what it means, Mr Czerniak, sir. She's the scholar.'

And Mrs Beaumont, 'I handed in my school books, you know. We all had to. Heaven knows what those poor little ragamuffins would make of a lot of Latin mumbo-jumbo. It means let us therefore be joyful, Stefan dear, or something of the kind.'

Not only two words, but the land of Smetana also, where a river called the Vlatava wound its way through the quiet woods and fields in a Europe where they were coming up from bunkers and out of prisons, looking again in astonishment at the whole shining world. For this was the year 1945, the beginning of the long peace, and there was no reason why they should not therefore be joyful.

Chapter IV

The new school year of 1945 started and Lola Robertson wasn't there.

She thought of the classroom, her classroom, the heated September air drifting in through the hopper windows, the jam jar on the windowsill full of wilting hips and haws, and conkers falling from the tree outside, splitting as they hit the ground, and she thought of the autumn smell of them. She thought of her desk with its dried up ink well and its grained-in grime, the chair, slightly sticky to the touch and bearing the faint aromas and stains of other girls who were too embarrassed to ask to leave the room.

Soon a letter arrived from the headmaster, addressed to her mother on the understanding, she thought, that her father was still serving with the army somewhere. Lola knew the handwriting, a beautiful copperplate, which elevated Lilian Robertson to a person of consequence. Her mother removed her headscarf and apron and washed her hands in green soap before she read it.

'From the King, duck?' Her father was still there, seated in the chair in the dark corner of the room as if he had not moved from it since he came home on VJ Day. His leg with its malodorous dressing was still stretched out in front of him.

'No.' Her mother took the letter over to the window.

'You could have fooled me, duck,' said her father, 'by the looks of yer, dolling yerself up like. Who's the lucky feller then?'

Lola saw the frown gather on her mother's face, and her lips move as she read the letter. After she had finished reading, she turned the paper over as if some clue to its contents might be found on the back.

'Here.' She made to hand it to her father. 'See what it is.'

'If yer would shove them curtains back, duck, I might.'

'And have all the neighbourhood gawping in? You don't think we like having an adulterer perched in the corner, do you?'

'Leave the lass out of it, Lil. Give it here, duck, and I'll construe it for yer.'

Lola watched as her father's eyes moved across the lines.

'Well?' Being the one hundred and fifteenth word her mother had said to her father in the three weeks since he had been back. For the most part, they had been silent. 'What does it say?' One hundred and nineteen.

'It says, duck…' He stopped.

'Well, what does it say?' One hundred and twenty-four.

'Hold yer horses, Lil, I'm coming to it. "Dear Mrs Robertson".'

Her mother huffed in expectation.

'It says, duck, that Miss Lola Robertson has not returned to school following the vacation. And it says about summat of 1944, and it says under it…are yer follering, duck? It says that under it Miss Lola Robertson should rightly…are yer follering, duck? Should rightly be in school. However…' Here her father drew a breath. 'However, the provisions of the Act have yet to be implemented. Nevertheless, I (meaning the headmaster, duck) would strongly urge that Miss Lola Robertson stays at school, being a pupil of great promise. Reckon they say that to all and sundry, duck. There was never no great promises came out of Barratt's Place, that's all I can say. Here, duck.' He gave the letter to Lola. 'What yer got to say for yerself? Promises, eh? What yer promised? Yer not told yer ma and pa.'

'It doesn't mean that, father.'

'I weren't born yesterday, duck. It means potential. D'yer know that word, duck?'

'Yes, father.'

'Promise or no promise, she's got to bring in a wage,' her mother said. The words were coming thick and fast. Lola crossed her fingers behind her back. She folded the letter without looking at it.

'Go on, read it, duck,' her father was saying. 'Since it pertains to yerself like. Yer mother's right, lass. Promise or no promise et cetera.'

Lola handed the letter back to her mother.

She saw it again later, in the cupboard when she was putting back the plates after dinner, torn into neat oblongs for ration lists, side by side with the larger oblongs of newspaper and bread paper for the privy.

Her mother was behind her, 'Your father will make up something,' reaching in front of her and removing one of the oblongs of Mr Brumby's letter. She could feel the heat of her mother's body at her back. She was too near.

'Make up what?'

But her mother didn't answer.

'Make up what, mother? Is he going to write back to Mr Brumby?'

'Certainly not. We're not kowtowing to a teacher.'

'Then what...?'

'Never you mind. Your father's spun enough tales in his time. Likely, he can spin another one.'

A plate slipped from Lola's hand and broke on the tiles.

'Right, my girl, that's the first penny out of your wages. You might as well know. Your father's going to put a notice for you in Summerskill's.'

'What kind of notice?'

'A young lady seeking a situation. That's what kind of notice.'

Then her mother was opening the door of her room, standing there in her good coat, and the hat with the hatpin, and bringing with her the combined mother aromas of cabbage and green soap and powder.

'Will I do?' Her mother's pinched face lit up.

'Where are you going?'

'You'll know when we get there.'

'We?'

'Yes, dear.' Her mother took a sixpence out of her purse and slipped it inside her glove. 'You're old enough now. We're going to see a woman in a tent.'

'A fortune teller? But that's naughty, mother!'

'Do grow up, Lola.'

There wasn't a tent. Nothing resembling one. Only a back room in an ordinary house a long way away, more respectable than Barratt's Place, and with blackout curtains across the window. The man who had shown them into the room disappeared, leaving Lola and her mother in the company of someone else, not a gypsy with gold loops in her ears and a coloured shawl round her shoulders, but an ordinary woman wearing a maroon dress and beads.

Lola's mother took the sixpence out of her glove and gave it to the woman, who looked at it, bit it and nodded towards the other chair.

'One can't be too careful these days,' she said. 'Not much around, and a girl has to make a living. Been caught out many a time, you see. Yes, caught out many a time.'

'I think you'll find that one genuine,' Lola's mother said.

And the woman said, 'No offence, dear. What can I do for you? Cards or palm?'

'Palm, please, dear.' Her mother took off both gloves, straightened them and laid them on her knee, then turned her hands palm upwards.

Lola remained standing. There was a smell of something exotic and foreign in the room and she felt faint. She moved her feet, and the woman said, 'Keep still there,' then continued, in a low voice, to read her mother's palm. Her voice seemed to be coming from a great distance, from farther and farther away, and the room was getting darker and darker in spite of the glaring overhead bulb.

Suddenly, she found herself seated on a front wall in the cold wind with her mother there beside her. The pungent mist of *sal volatile* was in her eyes and nose and mouth. She looked around. It was a different house. And a different street.

'Was she a nice lady?' she said to her mother.

Her mother said, 'Never you mind,' and continued to wave the bottle of *sal volatile* in front of her face.

'Did she say anything nice?'

'What do you think?'

'Did she tell you you're going to meet a tall dark stranger?' Lola suddenly felt better.

'What ridiculous nonsense,' her mother said. Then she laughed, a mirthless, terrible laugh. 'She did say that. And other things.'

'But you're married. Why did she say that?'

Her mother pulled off the glove of her left hand, tugging at the fingers one by one. The wedding ring wasn't there.

'Where's your ring, mother?'

'Never you mind.' Then, presently, 'It's in my pocket. And your father's watch.'

'No! You're not! Mother, please don't!'

Her mother laughed the same grim laugh. 'Just you wait, my girl. You've got a lot to learn before your time's out.'

'Where are we going?'

'You'll know soon enough.'

But Lola knew already. She had passed by the pawnbroker's shop on occasions, always quickly, but always glancing into its window as if her eyes were drawn to the misery there: the trifling keepsakes, the tarnished jewellery, the jackets frayed at the cuffs, and the lacquered boxes, cutlery with bone handles yellowed in decrepitude and misery. Each item bearing a minutely written ticket.

She stood outside while her mother went in, standing with her back to the window, swallowing the salt fluid that flooded her mouth. The door of the shop blew open in the wind, letting out a dark smell of dirt, and cigarette smoke – and shame. She could hear her mother's voice inside, and that of the man who kept the shop. The door closed, and opened again. Her mother came out.

'Did you see anyone we know?'

'No, mother.'

'Good.' Her mother slipped some coins inside her glove.

Lola followed her. 'Where are we going?'

Her mother didn't answer.

'Where are we going now?' Lola said again, risking, as she knew, either one of two parental answers: Never you mind. To see a man about a dog. 'To see a man about a dog?' she said, hopefully.

'Less of your cheek,' her mother said. 'We're going to see what your father's been up to.'

Lola shivered. A sharp pain sliced through her middle. 'I think I'll have to go home soon, mother.'

'The sooner we get done, the better then.' Her mother handed her the bottle of *sal volatile*. 'And no more of that kind of talk in the street, dear. Or in front of your father. We keep such matters to ourselves. Even film stars have monthlies. Have you finished with that, dear?' Taking back the *sal volatile*.

Lola could see her mother's face reflected in the window of Summerskill's, her lips moving as she read the advertisement. 'That'll do.'

'But I'm fourteen, mother!'

'And who on earth do you think's going to give you a post at fourteen?' her mother said. 'Have some sense.'

'It's a fib, mother.'

'Read me what it says, dear.'

'"Reliable girl seeks work. 15 years of age. Anything considered. Answers to Mr and Mrs C Robertson". But I'm only fourteen, mother. What father's written isn't true.'

'It'll do. The mirthless smile flickered across her mother's face and was gone. 'It'll do. Now I don't want to hear any more about it, dear.'

There was someone else there when they got back to the house in Barratt's Place. Someone unobtrusively present, who on entering had closed the door and was conducting what conversation there was in a low voice. Lola could hear her father's laugh. Her mother told her to go straight up to her room and not to come down in case it was the Assistance Board and she opened her big mouth, 'About you know what,' her mother said.

Then presently Lola heard her mother's voice, climbing up through the wall spaces and arriving, muffled and equable, in her room. Her father's laugh again, and the third voice, like none she had heard before, the consonants and vowels making a music of their own. She opened her room door. She could hear her mother in the scullery putting the kettle on the hob. Not the Assistance Board, then.

'Lola, bring the work basket if you would, dear.' Her mother's voice was at the bottom of the stairs. 'And tidy your hair, please.'

The visitor rose to his feet when she entered the room. A tall, foreign-looking man wearing a long dark coat. With no shoes. The toes of one of the socks were in holes.

'Our daughter,' her father said.

The visitor held out his hand and looked down at her. He had dark brown eyes and black hair beginning to go grey.

'What do you say, Lola?' her mother said.

Lola said, 'How do you do?' and blushed.

'I am honoured to meet you, Lola. Paul Czerniak. Your father helped me. I have come to say thank you.'

There was a bunch of flowers on the table, Michaelmas daisies and golden rod. Her mother brought in a jug of water and began to arrange them, breaking off the ends of the long stems and removing the lower leaves. 'They're beautiful,' she said. 'Help me with the teapot, Lola, and then we have a job for you.'

Lola followed her mother into the scullery, wondering to whom the word "we" referred. Surely, her mother had not used it in the same sense that her father had when he said "our" daughter. Otherwise, "we" was her mother and the tall dark stranger.

'That lady was right,' she ventured.

'Don't be so ridiculous.' Her mother's face was suddenly pretty.

'What did father do?'

Her mother huffed. 'That's anyone's guess.'

The visitor declined milk and sugar.

'I couldn't drink it like that,' her father said, then to Lola, 'Yer ma's got a job for yer, duck. Mr Czerniak here's got a tale to tell yer, and don't yer believe a word of it.'

Lola started darning the sock, moving from the small holes to the large, making a warp and weaving the wool in and out.

'She won a competition at school,' her father said.

Lola blushed. 'Only a little competition.' Then, still concentrating on the complicated needlework, she whispered, 'What did father do, sir?'

'Once upon a time…' her father began. 'That's right, isn't it?'

The visitor turned to Lola. 'I was an objector in the war and some objectors had to work in the mines. When the war was over and I was discharged, I was on a train where some chaps were the worse for drink and were abusing the objectors. They were about to open the door and throw us out onto the track, but a corporal from the army intervened. He was your father, Lola.'

'Don't yer believe a word of it, duck,' her father said.

'So I made it my duty to come back and thank him,' the visitor went on.

Lola stopped darning. 'How did you find him, sir?'

'I noticed that his leg was injured, and I saw the station where he got off and asked around. They told me in the canteen at Retford that an army fellow with a bad leg had passed through.

'It could have been anyone, sir.'

'Yes, I was lucky.'

Her mother's face had resumed its grim smile.

'The chappy who swabbed the floor said a corporal had asked him to mind a haversack for five minutes, and that he went off on the branch line.'

Her mother's face softened.

A sudden thought swept over Lola and she felt herself blushing. She leaned over the sock, making unnecessary stitches here and there, giving the thought time to go away. But it didn't go. It stayed, hammering insistently inside head. A strange, inconsequential thing, which nevertheless gained in plausibility the longer it was there. Suddenly, she knew, beyond any doubt. Her father's "fancy woman" had worked in the canteen on Retford station.

She was being spoken to. She looked up. No. No one had spoken.

A crack of sunlight fell across the floor, picking out her father's bad leg, from which he was unwinding endless ravels of yellowed bandage, yanking at it when it was stuck, knitting his brow, grimacing. The smell was unbearable.

'MO says it's going along champion,' her father said.

'Surely. Seeing the MO again?' The visitor, whose unusual name she had forgotten as soon as he said it, was bent over the disgusting wound, touching the edges of it. 'Seeing the fellow again?'

'Yes,' her mother said. The day was full of confusion.

'Good, good. We'll bind it up.'

'Get that sheet, Lola,' her mother said.

'No need, Mrs Robertson.' He had bandage in his satchel.

Then he was gone, saying a gracious farewell, and collecting his shoes at the door. Followed by the questioning eyes of all the adults of Barratt's Place, and the skittering feet of the children. Through the waste land where the end house had once been, his dark coat flapping behind as if it were following him, and his beret pulled down, a red bandana round his neck.

Lola leaned out of her window. He turned to wave. She waved back. At the door of their house, her mother and father waved. On the cobbled road below, all the grubby, shoeless, runny-nosed children waved. He waved back.

And at the end of the day, she had gained a year in her age, and a mysterious foreign name she couldn't remember. And she had given, to the owner of the name, an extensive and complicated darn with all her pains and confusions and wonderings sewn into it.

Chapter V

Mr Brumby was in the library.

'Ah, Lola Robertson.'

'At least you don't have spots,' her mother had said. But today there was one, and she felt the headmaster's eyes gravitating towards it. She cast her eyes around for a means of escape.

'I was meeting my father here,' she said. 'In the reading room.'

Mr Brumby said, 'Ah well, Lola Robertson. We won't forget you. To be sure we won't. It is pleasing to see you in the library.' And he went, without a book, she noticed.

Then the miserable thought overwhelmed her, that her confusion had driven him away. That, or her untruth. She wasn't meeting her father in the reading room, or anywhere else. He was at home in his usual place with his bad leg stretched out into the crack of sunlight coming through the blackout curtains.

Lola ruminated on her untruth, trying to make it less bad, trying to make it true. She took *Northanger Abbey* off the shelf and put it back, then took it down again. She didn't know how to say the word Northanger in her mind. She took it to the desk and whispered, 'How do you say that word, please?' And was advised by the librarian to split it into its constituent parts.

'Didn't they tell you to do that at school?' They might have done, but she had already forgotten.

She made for the way out, glancing, as she went, through the open door into the reading room. Her father was there. He was half turned away, standing reading the local paper, leaning on the stand and taking his weight on his good leg. He didn't notice her. She could make out the small blocks of print and the heading "Vacancies" at the top of the page. She went back to the librarian at the desk and asked if she might go into the reading room.

'How old are you?'

Lola thought. The married people she had met on VJ Day talked to her as if she were an adult, and the tall dark stranger also had made no concession to her youth when he was talking to her. Her mother and father had blithely added a year to her age when they placed the advertisement in Summerskill's. And Barry Green had passed on the shameful information that she was considered to be "developed".

'My father says I'm fifteen.' She blushed.

'And what do you think, Miss Robertson?'

'I...don't think very much.'

'You have borrowed *Northanger Abbey,* therefore you think, dear. You may go into the reading room, but don't make a noise.'

Her father was jotting down details on a scrap of paper, another fragment of Mr Brumby's letter, she noticed. His writing sloped slightly backwards and he did it with his left hand. She stood beside him, reading the advertisements. He winked at her. Her mother didn't like people to wink; she said it was common. Eventually, he finished and lodged the pencil behind his ear, which her mother also said was common. Lola followed him out of the library.

He patted his pocket.

'Plenty there to be going on with,' he said, without specifying for whom the "plenty" might be. Lola didn't ask. 'And as you're here, duck, you might as well come with me to the hospital. I'd be much obliged, duck. Yer not yer ma, but yer'll do.'

'I'm not old enough, father.'

'They're not going to ask yer to do an operation duck.'

'Operation?'

'Only a manner of speech, duck.'

'You haven't got to have an operation, have you, father?' Lola felt suddenly sick.

Her father didn't answer.

'Have you, father?'

'No, duck.'

The outpatients' waiting room was full. Lola was frightened of it, with its smells of disinfectant and suppurating wounds and clammy clothing, and its sounds of retching and coughing.

'I'll wait outside, father.'

'No, duck. You'll come in. Yer'll thank yer pa for it one day, duck. Nowt like facing up to yer fears, as the big-wig chaps said in the army.'

'I'm not in the army, father.'

All the time, her father was advancing into the waiting room.

'D'yer have to check in?' He addressed no one in particular.

'There, duck.' A woman pointed to the desk. 'Yer'll be wanting a seat, duck. Sit yerself here when yer come back.'

'Nah, duck, thanking yer.' Her father touched a hat that wasn't there. 'And let a lady stand? Nah, duck.'

Suddenly, her father had become a gentleman, and the seated woman a lady. 'My beautiful daughter,' he said.

'Ah, ducky,' the woman said, 'yer going inter nursing one day?'

The negative filled Lola's mouth like a piece of gristly meat she could neither swallow nor spit out.

'She don't know yet, duck. Only fifteen.' Her father had become so accustomed to his fib that he believed it.

'Plenty of time yet,' the woman said.

Her father gave his name and went to lean against the wall. She went with him.

'Yer'll need yer book,' he said. '*Northanger Abbey*, eh?' He pronounced the word with a hard g. 'Let me know if it's a good'un.' His voice was too loud in the murmuring waiting room.

'Mr Robertson, please.' Her father's name was being called.

'Can my lovely daughter come in, sister?'

'How old is she, sir?'

'Going on sixteen, sister.'

'Come in then, dear. There's nothing to be frightened of. What's your name, darling?'

'Lola Robertson,' she whispered.

The nurse was terrifyingly starched and clean, as if she never had to deal with the time of the month. She removed the bandage from her father's leg, and asked how long it had been on and who had put it on.

Her father said, 'The MO tells me it's coming along champion.' The wound was leaking thick yellow fluid and the smell was unbelievable.

The nurse said it didn't look like an army dressing, the likes of which she knew well enough in her job. She said she thought he would need an x-ray, and opened an adjoining door, saying something in a low voice that Lola couldn't hear. A gentleman came in, dressed in a suit and waistcoat and wearing a bow tie. He shouted at her father as if he were deaf. 'It's likely to be in the tibia and it'll be in the blood next if we don't do something.'

Her father said, 'Very good, doctor,' and was helped into a bath chair and taken away.

Lola carried his shoe and jacket with the fragment of Mr Brumby's letter and details of vacancies crackling in the pocket;

following until her father was taken into another room and she was told to wait outside. She was still holding the jacket and shoe.

Presently the door opened, and she could hear the voice of the doctor with the bow tie, 'The little girl can come in now. Bring her in, someone.' Lola suddenly lost the extra years her father had credited her with, and several more besides.

'Are you there, little girl?' He had his back towards her, and was looking at a wet x-ray picture in a frame propped up against a lighted box. Her father was seated in the bath chair, facing the x-ray picture.

'Are you there, little girl?' The doctor still didn't turn to look at her.

'Yes, sir,' she whispered.

'Have you seen one of these before? No, neither have I.' He replied to his own question before she could find her voice. 'Coming along champion, my foot. I'll have to have a word with that MO. Some superannuated fossil from the Great War, no doubt. This…' he produced a stick similar to Mr Brumby's when he was pointing out things on the blackboard. 'This, little girl, is the worst case of osteomyelitis I have seen.'

The nurse, standing behind him, mouthed something like, 'And I've seen the lot.'

'And I've seen the lot,' the doctor with the bow tie said. 'Is the little girl still there? She is? Good. What was that word, little girl?'

'Osteolitis?'

The doctor turned to look at her. 'Say that again, please.'

'Osteolitis.'

'Osteomyelitis. You were very nearly correct, young lady. How old is she, father?'

'Going on sixteen, sir.'

'When she's seventeen send her back and we'll see what we can do with her. Young lady,' he turned back to her father's x-ray picture, 'the thick bone is called the tibia. What is the thick bone called?'

'The tibia, sir.'

'And the thin bone is called the fibula. What is the thin bone called?'

'The fibia, sir.'

'Fibula. F-I-B-U-L-A.'

'Fibula, sir.'

'That's right. Learn a bone every day and you can't go wrong. Nurse, arrange a domiciliary visit from the district. What kind of a home is it?'

Lola blushed.

'It's a lovely home,' the nurse said, and when the doctor with the bow tie had gone, 'Who does he think he is?' Then, to Lola, 'Don't worry. He says that to everyone.'

And she wanted to ask what he always said, whether it was the question about the home, or whether it was the names of the bones, or whether it was to invite them back when they were seventeen. And she wanted to ask his name. But she didn't. She gave her father his shoe and his jacket, and they left the hospital, forgetting *Northanger Abbey*.

It was a grey day spitting rain. Her father dragged his bad leg through the flat colourless streets.

'Feels champion now,' he said. 'Good chap, that doctor.'

'What was his name, Father?' she said, and he told her chaps like that didn't have names.

'They're not like you and me, duck.'

They passed Summerskill's and her father stopped to look at the notice he had placed. It had been moved to make way for a larger one.

'Can't have that, duck.' He went into the shop and Lola waited outside.

Presently, he came out. 'Rectified, duck,' he said. 'Just a temporary relocation.' He had two white envelopes in his hand. 'Yer look as if yer've lost sixpence and found thruppence, duck. What's up?'

'I've left my book, father.'

'Well yer best go back forrit it, duck. *Northanger Abbey*, weren't it? Let me know if it's a good'un.'

Lola returned to the hospital. She went into the outpatients and asked at the desk if she might go back to the room. The receptionist indicated a bag on the counter and said, 'There, dear.' Lola thanked her and went away. She almost asked the name of the doctor. But in the end, she didn't.

When she arrived home, there were three envelopes on the table. Her father was seated in his customary chair and her mother was coming in from the scullery, her sleeves rolled up and her hair tucked into a scarf.

'Yer mother's not communicating, duck,' her father said. 'Yer need to tell her what yer pa's been up ter.'

Her mother was wearing her grim face.

'Go on, duck,' her father said. 'Tell her yer pa's been gallivanting with his fancy woman.'

'Father went to the hospital, mother. I saw him in the reading room and went with him.'

Her mother coloured.

'An' yer might as well tell yer ma the rest, duck,' her father said.

'The doctor said father's leg's bad and he's sending a nurse here to see to it.'

'Here! You stupid child!'

Lola could feel her mother's fury coming towards her like a deafening black wave. She stepped backwards. When she opened her eyes, she was on the floor, half under the table. She could hear her father's voice coming from somewhere near the ceiling.

'Yer lay a finger on that lass again, Lil, and yer'll get what's coming to yer.' Her mother was seated on one of the upright chairs and her father was standing in front of her.

'Get your hands off me, Cyril.' Her mother was crying dry tears.

Audrey was standing in the doorway, her bare arms covered in suds, wearing her apron and slippers. 'What's up, Lil?'

Lola heard her father say that it was nothing they couldn't resolve themselves.

'Oh.' Audrey turned to go away. 'I weren't after being a busybody, Cyril, to be sure.'

''Course you weren't, duck,' her father said.

Then she found herself seated on a chair, facing her mother across the table. Between them lay the three letters, two replies from Summerskill's and an envelope the postman had brought. There was also the copy of *Northanger Abbey* she had rescued from the hospital. Her father was filling the kettle in the scullery.

Her mother said, 'I don't know what came over me.'

'Yer got ter say the magic word, Lil.' Her father's voice came in from the scullery. 'What yer got ter say ter her?' As if her mother was suddenly a child.

'Mother thinks we can't pay for the nurse,' Lola said.

Her father was in the room again. 'If yer ma don't say sorry, she'll allus be in yer debt, duck, and yer knows it, and that's not right neither.'

Afterwards, Lola couldn't remember if the word was said or not. All she knew was that her mother dabbed at the cut on her head with the corner of a dishrag and that her father told her to open the letters from Summerskill's.

'But they're not addressed to me, father.'

'They're concerning you, duck, and that's as good as.'

So she opened them. The first was for domestic duties. The second was for general assistance around the home. She handed them to her mother. She could see her mother's lips moving as she read them.

'Ask your father,' her mother said, giving them back to her. 'Ask him which one you should go for.'

And her father said, 'Well, I'll be hanged. They're the same, Lil. Looks like the lass'll be going for a skivvy.'

'If it's good enough for her mother, it's good enough for her.'

Lola didn't know if her mother's remark was addressed to her father or not. It didn't matter.

She put her coat back on, pulling it tight at the front to fasten it.

'You'll need to let those buttons out,' he mother said. 'Where are you going?'

'Nowhere.'

Lola went out of the door and shut her mother's voice inside the house. She went to the library and handed in *Northanger Abbey.* She wouldn't go back to the library. Not ever. She would turn into her mother wearing a scarf over her hair and always carrying on her person the scent of cabbage and green soap.

When she got back to Barratt's Place, the neighbour Audrey and Barry Green's mother were in conversation in the middle of the road. Waiting for her.

'What happened to yer head, duck?'

'It's my monthly and I fainted.' Lola didn't know if she had fainted or not. She crossed her fingers.

'That's what they all say. I'll get my old man to yer pa next time, duck, if yer likes.'

Lola felt the blush creeping into the roots of her hair. 'It wasn't father.'

'Well, it wasn't yer ma, that's fer sure. We know our Lil.'

'It wasn't father.'

'If yer need owt, let us know, darling.'

She went in. She could hear her mother upstairs. Her father was sitting in the chair with his bad leg stretched out, gleaming in its new swaddling of bandage. The third letter, the one the postman had brought, was open on the table.

'Tek a look at un, duck,' her father said.

Lola read the letter. She read it again.

'What does demolition mean, Father?'

'What d'yer think it means, duck? Yer the one with yer head allus in a book.'

'But not Barratt's Place. Not where we live.' Lola read the letter a third time. 'What does mother think?'

'If yer can elicit an opinion from yer ma, yer a better chap than I am,' her father said.

'When is it?'

'Yer read the letter, duck. It don't give no date. Yer mother's up yonder packing. I tell her it won't be tomorrer, but yer know yer ma.'

And it came to Lola, suddenly and from what place she couldn't say, that she didn't know her mother. Not now. Not anymore.

Chapter VI

The slight figure of his mother glimmered crimson and ultramarine through the coloured glass of the landing window. Stefan Czerniak watched her as she walked down the chequered path with a pail of water in her hand.

He ran down the stairs and out of the door. His mother had vanished in the space of seconds, leaving the steaming pail at the gate with a scrubbing brush floating on its surface, and the word scrawled on the pavement: CONSHY.

'Can't you bloody spell?' The word sounded alien, as if it wasn't at home in the interstices of his brain. He said it again, louder.

'Can't you bloody spell?' That was better.

And again, a third time, with embellishments.

'Can't you spell, you bloody bastard?' Pitch perfect.

He started to scrub, inundating the offending word with steaming water. 'Can't you bloody spell, you bastard?'

Language, Stefan.

He looked up. There was no one there, only a couple at the top of the avenue, and Mrs Beaumont upstairs next-door dusting windowsills. She waved. Stefan waved back, and returned to the word on the pavement. A line of *Ma Vlast* played in his mind, a shining river winding out of a distant Prague. He didn't bear the scribe any ill-will. He couldn't even swear with any degree of efficiency. The couple were approaching. He would finish and go in before he had to step aside and wish them a good day.

Was there such a thing, he asked himself. Did anyone, truly, have a good day in this grey and uneventful peace? And what would a good day be? He continued scrubbing at the mildly offending word. A good day would not, for instance, mean sitting at the desk in a firm the nature of whose business he didn't know, empty except for others similar, yet not similar, to himself and their collective raincoats clothing the coat-stand in beige anonymity. The line from *Ma Vlast* came back. For all his scrubbing, the unoffending word was still visible on the pavement, thrown into sharp relief by the presence of the water.

He threw the brush back into the pail and looked up. The shadows of the couple he had seen at the top of the avenue were standing there, arm in arm. Mrs Beaumont had finished the sills and was leaning out of the window waving.

'It won't come off,' he said, uselessly, scuffing at the misspelt word with the toe of his shoe. 'It won't come off. I'm sorry, dad. Sorry, mother.' He couldn't call her Ruth now. 'Good to have you back, dad. It's spelt wrong anyway.'

'Grammar, dear,' his mother said. 'That was an adverb.'

He still hadn't looked at them. They would be as they were in the photograph that stood on the mantle-shelf in the front room. Foreign, ecstatic, beautiful. They would be like that again.

'It doesn't matter. It's only a word,' his father said. And then, 'Where's Stefan Czerniak? I haven't seen him yet.'

'I will call him for you, darling,' his mother said. 'Stefan, aren't you going to welcome your father? Leave that. It's only a word.'

He looked up. Foreign, ecstatic, beautiful. But they weren't. His mother was as she had been when she walked out of the house and down the chequered path to the front gate that morning, pale and thin. His father had the same pallor, with the disfigurement of a knotted scar running up into the hairline. Only their eyes were…ecstatic and beautiful. He hadn't noticed before. His mother carried a bunch of red roses.

He shook hands with his father. 'You go in,' he said. 'I'll finish this.'

'As you wish,' his father said.

'No, Stefan…' his mother began. But he already had the scrubbing brush in his hand, dribbling grey water onto the misspelt word.

It wouldn't come off. The more water and the more scrubbing only served to make it worse. CONSHY, a sky-bright word against the dark rain-grey of the pavement. There was a possibility that it would never go away, not until years had passed and people came along to resurface the pavement. He continued scrubbing, with diminishing conviction, until his father came out.

'It doesn't matter,' his father said. 'It's a word, that's all.'

Stefan dropped the brush back into the pail. He said nothing, waiting for his father to go back in. But his father didn't. He remained standing there, his long shadow stretching out down the avenue.

'It's a word, that's all,' his father said again. 'A word is nothing.' He wasn't going to go. Mrs Beaumont would be out in a moment offering an avalanche of goodwill and some concoction Mr Beaumont used for cleaning the Rover.

But Mrs Beaumont didn't come out. Stefan cast about in his mind for words; what to say to a father who had returned in a reduced version of himself, to whose clothes the smoke of the mines still clung, and whose breath was delivered in short difficult rasps. Who had gone away as an objector and come back as a...there was no other word for it, yet it was a word so shameful and intimate he would not say it to himself, even in the secrecy of his thoughts.

Still his father stood there, his unkempt greying hair lifted on the breeze.

Stefan looked around: to his right the avenue leading up to the park; to his left the same avenue leading down to the traffic lights and, eventually, to an office standing in the middle of a bomb site. Behind him, the chequered path leading to the front door, and the faded, whispering flowers of the hydrangeas of a summer that would never return. Standing in front of him, his father.

'We can make an attempt at it later. If you're assuming your mother and I would prefer to be alone, then you're wrong, Stefan.'

'That's what one would assume, father.' This wasn't going well. 'Thank you for the loan of the shirt.'

'Shirt?'

'Mr and Mrs Beaumont took us to the Albert Hall.'

'Ah.'

'Brahms and Smetana.'

'Smetana, ah.'

'*Ma Vlast*. They played *Ma Vlast*. How are you, dad? Good to see you.'

'And you, Stefan. And you. Are you coming in?' His father picked up the pail.

'I guess...'

'Your mother wouldn't like that.' His father's eyes sparkled. 'She sure wouldn't.'

Dregs of tea stood in shallow ginger pools at the bottom of their cups. His father offered his mother a cigarette. Stefan intercepted the question that passed between them. He wished he hadn't come in.

His mother shook her head. 'Not yet, darling. He's only sixteen. Where are you going, Stefan?'

'To fetch something.'

'It will do later.'

He would forget later.

When he got back, the words said in his absence hung on the air, dense and silent, like cigarette smoke.

'From Pip, dad. I'd almost forgotten. He left these for you. He sends his best regards.' He couldn't remember if Pip had said that. 'He got married somewhere up north. She's called Jean. She's nice, isn't she, mum?'

'Pip?'

He saw with horror that the sparkle in his father's eyes was not, as he had thought, the result of merriment, but tears. It suddenly became necessary to fill the room with vacuous chatter.

'He brought her down to see Mr and Mrs Beaumont. She's called Jean, did I say that? Mrs Beaumont thinks she's a nice little thing.'

'We shouldn't really be talking about our neighbours like this, Stefan,' his mother said. She turned to his father. 'They have been very good to us, darling. There's something we have to tell you.'

So they hadn't discussed the – er – life yet.

His mother continued. 'Mr Beaumont said there was an opening for a young man in his office. He has offered it to Stefan and has asked him to consider it over a period of forty days, which ends on the twenty-ninth.'

'There's something else, mother. That wasn't all he said.'

'Mr Beaumont said that the firm had enjoyed some success during the war, or words to that effect. It was decided that we should defer the decision until his father came home. That's you, darling,' she added.

His father rested his elbows on the table and made a steeple of his fingers.

'We must first ask Stefan what his wishes are,' he said presently.

'There's something before that, father. Ask mother.'

'We do not know the nature of the business, darling.'

'We must find that out, certainly,' his father said.

'Mr Beaumont asked if I had any thoughts on what I would do with my – er – life.'

'Stefan, please. Mimicry is hurtful and rude. I'm afraid we've fallen into bad habits, darling,' his mother said.

'I must go to see Ken.' His father got up to leave the table.

'There's no hurry, father. We have six days.' Then, before he could reel back the words, 'Why were you so long?'

'Stefan, please.'

'I'm sorry, mother.'

'But I will tell you,' his father said. 'A corporal in the British Army did a good turn on a train and I wished to thank him. I made a journey to a town on the Nottinghamshire border, and I found him.'

'What happened, father?' The road at the bottom of the avenue suddenly lengthened and narrowed into a country lane lined with elms and crowned with blue sky and stacks of white cumuli.

'A few guys...'

'Darling!'

'...the worse for drink saw I came from the mines and deduced that I was an objector, and as such should be thrown out onto the line. The corporal stood up to them and I guess (his father's eyes sparkled) I owe him my life. He had a bad leg and left the train at Retford. I stayed on the train as far as King's Cross and took the underground to come home. I got off at Gant's Hill, but I knew I couldn't come home until I'd found him and thanked him. So I went back, and to the canteen on Retford station where, by some chance, one of the WVS helpers knew of a corporal with a badly damaged leg and directed me to a branch line. And I found him, some days later, in the most reduced circumstances, living in a slum and, as the neighbours were not unwilling to inform me, with his army pension gone to maintain a child born out of wedlock.'

'Darling, not at the table.'

'Stefan's sixteen, sweetheart. He's a grown man. He knows the ways of the world. The corporal was called Cyril Robertson. He had a poor embittered slip of a wife, and a daughter.' His father pulled off a boot. 'The dear girl mended my sock.'

His mother looked as if she was going to cry. But she didn't. Instead, she left the table and returned with a rose-patterned china thimble on her finger. 'We must send her something, darling, to say thank you. We can write a letter. What about the corporal's leg?'

'Pretty awful.'

Stefan watched the unwelcome question of his life draining away, as the grey pail water had run down the avenue minutes before. His mother brought a sheet of writing paper and the blotter, and the bottle of ink, crusted and recalcitrant around the top.

'Do we have a pen?'

No, neither of his parents did. His father had given his fountain pen away. To the heroic corporal on the train? No, not to Cyril Robertson, but he couldn't remember to whom. His mother's pen had a crossed nib.

'You can use mine.' Somewhere at the little visited interior of his soul, Stefan was aware of the dubious generosity of giving away the key to the door of his life's prison.

'You'll need it in the future, dear, if you are to work in an office,' his mother said. 'If your father uses it, the nib will be spoilt.'

The key fell back into his hand. His father used the pen and asked him to test it afterwards. There was no damage.

'What have you written, darling?' his mother said. His father had written a formal letter, beginning it, "Dear Miss Lola Robertson", reiterating his gratitude, and explaining that his wife had wished to make a small gift to her for use in her workbox. The letter ended with kindest regards to her parents, and assurances that the timely help from her father would never be forgotten.

'Darling, is that a letter for a young girl?' his mother said. 'Surely those are adult sentiments?'

'She was a rare young lady,' his father said. 'It was a rare family. Unhappy and pitiably poor, but endowed each one in their separate ways with the gifts of the spirit, though they didn't know it.' Tears stood in his father's eyes.

Stefan couldn't bear to look. He would have to take the key that lay hotly in his palm and throw open the door of his future prison.

His mother was wrapping the thimble in a handkerchief and folding the letter around it. His father lit another cigarette. Stefan looked out of the side window at the chequered path leading to the front gate. A passer-by stopped to look at the word, glanced at the house, and went on.

'Someone has seen the word.'

'We were considering your future,' his mother said. 'It's only a word, dear. It will no doubt go away and if it doesn't, we will live with it.' Then, turning to his father, 'We would do best to find out the nature of the business, darling. They must assume we know.'

'I will go and see Ken.'

'He won't be there at this time of day, darling. We'll have to work out a way of asking tactfully.'

The key was hot and sticky in Stefan's hand. He was at the door of his prison, which had somehow metamorphosed into the door of Mr Beaumont's premises, still standing, alone and fractured, on a bombsite in the city.

'We've been there. Mother and I.'

'Been there?'

'When we went to the concert. Mr Beaumont drove past the building. The one next to it had been bombed. I think I know what they do.'

'You haven't said that before, Stefan. How do you know?'

'I just think I do.'

His mother and father exchanged glances.

'Are you going to tell us?' his father said.

'There were demob raincoats hanging on a stand and a lot of chaps at desks in demob shirts.'

'When did you see that, dear?'

'I didn't. I just imagined it.'

'Then you don't know, Stefan.'

'No, but I'm sure I'm right.'

'I hope you don't say these things to anyone else, dear.'

'I have no one else to say anything to. Have I?'

And it was true. Half true. There was Bazal.

His mother and father exchanged glances again. As if he wasn't there.

'What has Stefan been doing since school, sweetheart?' his father said. 'I'm afraid he's had to pay a heavy price for our principles.'

'Gardens,' said his mother. 'Several gardens in the avenue. He does them beautifully. Freda tells me.'

'Digging for victory.'

'Don't, Stefan,' his mother said. 'Your father's trying to talk to you.'

'No, he's talking to you, mother.'

'That's true,' his father said. 'I was talking to your mother about you in front of you, and that's reprehensible. I'm sorry. We'll work something out. For all of us.'

All of us. His mother went out and returned with the brass plaque, as it had been when it was taken off the wall four years before, with a wisp of ivy and the tatters of a cobweb clinging to it. The surface had dulled, the letters darkened. "Paul Czerniak. Professor of Mathematics". It lay on the table along with the other paraphernalia of his father's homecoming: a packet of cigarettes from Pip; a white jug of red roses; finished cups of black tea.

At the front gate a word that didn't matter, that was spelt wrongly and couldn't be washed away. On the mantle shelf a packet, wrapped in brown paper and tied with string, addressed to a girl on the borders of Nottinghamshire, who had nothing but the gifts of the spirit and didn't realise.

Chapter VII

'I'll post the letter,' he said

His mother took a shilling from her purse.

'No need,' he said. 'Won't the thimble break?'

No, it wouldn't break. His mother said it had survived a hundred years and many hundreds of miles over land and sea, so it wouldn't break merely travelling to the border of Nottinghamshire. His father said it was sent with their blessing and therefore it would not break. Heaven would not permit it. Stefan had almost forgotten the embarrassing tendency in his father. Either that, or his father had become worse. He decided that his father had become worse. He had heard of it, how chaps who had gone away in 1939 or 1940 as themselves had come back – and the earlier expression nudged into his consciousness – as reduced versions of themselves.

The pavement had dried and the word was less obtrusive. But it hadn't gone away. Instead, it had acquired a metallic sheen. CONSHY. Faintly luminescing under a high white sun that had come out while he was inside the house. It would show up in the night. It would collect the first light of the dawn and the last red flash of the sun.

Stefan went to the post office. He waited in the queue, edging away from the customers behind him, who looked curiously like the chap in the park who had launched him into the pond on VJ Day. Whom he had not seen, only heard. The first counter clerk looked the same, as did the second counter clerk. He turned round and caught the eye of the chap behind him, who raised his eyebrows. Stefan turned away.

'Next, please.' He went to the counter.

'What's in the package, sir?'

'A thimble and a handkerchief and a letter.'

Ah, to a lady love. The counter clerk didn't say the words, but raised an eyebrow. 'Then we must take care of this package, sir, mustn't we?' A rhetorical question.

Stefan came out of the post office and stood in front of the stationer's next door, not looking into the window but watching the reflections of people passing by behind him: women in headscarves, the odd GI washed up on the hinterland of London and not yet recalled home, men not long out of the war in demob raincoats and hats as uniform as if they were still serving. The more he looked, the more certain he became that Mr Beaumont's firm, which had enjoyed some measure of success in recent years, had something to do with this beige peacetime uniform.

In front of him, in the window of the stationer's, an arm was reaching from somewhere inside the shop and removing a jar of pens from the display. He watched as it was lifted and taken away into the darkness; then he went into the shop and hovered near the door as a customer looked at the pens, taking one after another out of the jar and laying them side by side on the counter.

'Maybe I can help this gentleman while you're deciding, madam.'

Gentleman. Sender of a careful package to a girl who lived on the border of Nottinghamshire, who possessed the gifts of the spirit but did not know it. Conchie.

'May I help you, sir?'

'Thank you, I was also looking for a pen.' His voice sounded unfamiliar in the dim cube of the shop. 'I don't mind waiting.'

'This good lady visits us often and she doesn't mind if other customers come in.'

The woman smelt of the war, of dust and smoke and cigarettes, and cabbage and sweat. Stefan took his place beside her at the counter. She eyed him sideways and smiled a toothless smile. Maybe he smelt the same. Maybe his mother and father did. And Mr and Mrs Beaumont, and Pip and Jean. The pens were all the same. They were eleven-pence each.

'I'd like two, please. Thank you.' Outside the home, away from his parents, he was suddenly civil.

The doorbell jangled. The other customer had gone.

'The lady comes in to look,' the stationer said. 'That'll be one and ten-pence, please. *Writing War and Peace*, sir?'

'They're for someone else.'

'Ah, I see. Someone else writing *War and Peace*. Remind them to rinse the nibs in cold water after use. Should last a lifetime with good care. So to speak, sir. So to speak.'

A lifetime.

His mother and father were still seated at the table. The jug of roses was still there. The teacups had gone. Instead, there was a sealed envelope addressed to his parents, of the type that arrived every year after the end of the summer term.

'You've taken a long time, Stefan,' his mother said. 'Your father has been to see Mrs Beaumont.'

He sat down.

'Take your coat off, dear,' his mother said presently. 'Your father has had a word next door.'

'I went to the stationer's. There was a lady who just goes in to look. She hadn't changed her clothes since the war.'

'Try not to judge others, dear. It was probably Mrs Temple. She can't help it.'

'Do we smell like that?'

'Stefan! That's something a child would say.'

'It's merely a question, mother. I'm not judging anyone.'

'The answer is probably yes,' his father said. 'And now we've settled that…'

'You've been to see Mrs Beaumont, Father.'

'Yes.'

'You were going to ask the nature of the business.'

'When she opened the door, Freda didn't know whether to laugh or cry, and it wasn't appropriate to ask. I'll speak to Ken later. But we still have to discuss the future. All our futures.' His father picked up the sealed envelope. 'We'll talk about you first, Stefan, if we may.'

He didn't have any choice.

'May we?'

If you must. He said nothing.

'Open it, darling,' his mother said. She reached behind her and took the letter opener out of the sideboard drawer. Stefan watched his father's face, the crosshatch of the frown and the swift eyes leaping down the page. He finished reading and handed the report to his mother.

'Do take your coat off, dear,' she said. 'Your father and I will begin to think you don't like the present company.'

He stood and shrugged off his coat. The pens from the stationer's clattered to the floor. He had forgotten them. The nibs would be bent now.

But they weren't. The pens lay on the floor beneath the table, as neat and orderly as if they were under scrutiny on the counter. Last a lifetime. So to speak.

'Welcome home, dad. Thanks for putting up with me, mum.'

He looked on, amazed, as his parents' faces broke into laughter. Foreign, ecstatic, beautiful. As his mother brought a piece of paper, and tore it in half, and as they began to practise with their new pens. He watched their names appear, again and again. Paul Czerniak. Ruth Maria Czerniak. As the half pages became covered with the filigree of their merriment. The lazy dogs jumped over the fence after the quick brown fox. His mother said the sentence, though not a nice one, contained all the letters of the alphabet. They would make up another sentence, a less cruel one, less suggestive of the pursuers and the pursued.

'And now to your report, dear.'

Stefan's hand tightened around the key to his prison. 'What does it say, mother?'

'Your father will tell you, dear.'

'You have to rinse the nibs in cold water. I'll do it.'

'Then we will discuss your report when you come back,' his father said. 'We sure know how to procrastinate.'

'Darling!'

'Procrastinate?'

'No, sure.'

'Ah, indeed.'

Stefan could hear his parents from the scullery. Discussing linguistics now. He went back in.

'The report is good in most respects,' his father said. 'Where it is not good, your mother and I only have ourselves to blame, and we are deeply sorry. The report uses the expressions "self-contained", "unwilling to circulate, participate in outdoor activities". If I were to ask if you were given a hard time by the other chaps, you would say no, Stefan Czerniak. Therefore, we will pass on to the academic side of things.' His father sounded like a headmaster. 'All good, some exceptionally so. Biology, excellent. English language excellent. Latin. Mathematics. So what are you going to do with your life? What do you not want to do with your life?'

His father had turned over the page of practice paper, had dipped the pen into the ink and written "1". In the top left-hand corner.

'I don't know.'

His father laid down the pen. 'You don't know?'

Stefan said nothing. His mother brought in more tea. His father said he was fine without milk and his mother raised an objection to the word "fine". Procrastinating.

'We will consider all your options,' his father went on. 'Do you wish to pursue your education?'

'No, dad.'

'If that is because you are unwilling to be a financial drain on the family, forget it. We would manage.'

'It's still no, dad.'

His father wrote "Studies" by the side of question 1 and put a cross against it.

'Any other vocational training?'

'What's that, dad?'

'To have a worthwhile skill, like that of a plumber or a doctor.'

'Not really.' A question mark went down on the page.

'Non-vocational. That is doing a job you don't necessarily have to train for, like office work, or travelling sales, hospital orderly, gardening and so on.'

'The last one.'

'Why?' His mother and father exchanged glances.

'Shall we go on to you and mum?'

'We'll finish you first, Stefan, and then you will help us. Why the last one?'

He didn't answer. His father drew a large and elaborate question mark and laid down the pen.

'Would you consider pursuing your education at night school? Bearing in mind that the other chaps would be from all walks of life and there solely for the pursuit of knowledge. Would that suit you?'

'What would I pursue?'

'Knowledge, it is to be hoped,' his father said.

'Darling, don't,' his mother said. 'He's had enough. He said gardening because it's what he knows and what he excels in. And for that other reason you have touched on, for which we only have ourselves to blame, in setting him apart from the rest.'

'For which we are truly and deeply sorry, Stefan,' his father said. 'Please forgive us.' He picked up the pen again. 'The best writer I ever had. And I must rinse the nib in cold water after each use. In a word, we are mortified,' he added. The colour fled from his father's face and the scar stood out as if it were painted there, a thick and jagged red line travelling up into the hair.

'What did you do to your head, dad?'

'Stefan, not yet, please.'

'I was trying to change the subject, mum.'

His father was about to become embarrassing again. Maybe his mother didn't mind. Maybe she didn't notice. Maybe she was used to it.

'You don't need forgiveness.'

Bad move. In a moment, his father would say that everyone stands in need of forgiveness. But he didn't. He dipped his pen into the ink and wrote down "Ruth". 'That's you, sweetheart.'

'So it is,' said his mother. 'I will be…a chemist. And you will be a teacher of mathematics, darling. A very fine teacher, with a sound intellect and a wealth of patience. You will be that again. We will polish up the plaque and put it up, and people will see it.'

Stefan found himself in the garden, retrieving Bazal and looking into the passive prehistoric face. He had a vague image in his mind of his mother, with her head on the table and her arms stretched out across the cloth – and (horrors) convulsed with weeping. After that, there was nothing, not until he came to himself in the garden communicating with the tortoise, who, he was suddenly and inconsequentially very certain, was a creature of no defined gender, with no defined purpose but to be.

Then his mother was there, standing beside him, looking herself again. He didn't know how long she'd been there.

'You had better come in, Stefan. Mrs Beaumont's here.'

There were new cups on the table and a new pot of tea. A plate of cakes.

'Look what Mrs Beaumont's made,' his mother said. 'Aren't they lovely?'

'Don't say thank you until you've had one, dear,' Mrs Beaumont said. 'I never was much good in the kitchen.'

She had come bearing gifts for a homecoming: iced cakes, a tin of some concoction her husband kept for removing rust from the Rover. A folded piece of paper.

'Ken keeps this in for the Rover,' she said. 'I thought it might do for…you know. It works on most things. Don't thank me until you've tried it. It might be quite useless. And Ken wished for you to read this, Stefan dear.' The prison door clanged shut. 'You don't have to make any comment at all, dear, or even read it until I've gone. It's what you might call the *modus operandi* of the firm of Beaumont. I'm not certain if that's the correct expression, dear. No doubt it'll do for the present until we come up with another one. See what you think, dear.' After which, having unravelled her string of

66

words, Mrs Beaumont rested her elbows on the table and her chin in her hands and gazed beatifically at his parents.

'Such a blessing, my dears,' she said. 'Thank God.'

Oh no.

'How's Pip?'

'He's well, as far as we know, Stefan dear. It's a trunk call from the border of Nottinghamshire of course. But he has a job as a clerk in an engineering firm, which we have to be thankful for.'

Oh no, not more thankfulness. His father seemed to have passed on his tendency to be embarrassing to Mrs Beaumont. Probably the condition was infectious.

'Bazal was in the garden, Mrs Beaumont.'

'Then he's a naughty boy.'

Mrs Beaumont turned to his father. 'We found him in the foul drain. Named after Mr Bazalgette, you know.'

His father knew but said, 'Extraordinary. A happy landing indeed.'

'Oh yes,' Mrs Beaumont continued. 'One could say that Bazal had a good war, with all those vegetables around.' She stopped suddenly. 'Dear me, what have I said? Do forgive me.'

'Why, Freda, you were talking about a small domestic reptile, that's all,' his father said.

But Mrs Beaumont wouldn't be pacified and went away soon, crushed and mortified, leaving the *modus operandi* on the table. 'Now look what I've done.'

'Did we thank Freda?' his mother said presently.

No one knew.

'The answer to that is probably no,' his father said.

'We should look at it,' his mother said. She slid the folded *modus operandi* across the table to his father.

'It concerns Stefan. He should look at it,' his father said. 'Will you look at it, please, Stefan. It's the least we can do.'

Stefan unfolded the page. It was a letter in Mr Beaumont's handwriting, with the address in Golen Avenue in the top right hand corner and dated two weeks previously. His eyes travelled down, tripping on the crossings out and leapfrogging the blots until he came to the end: "Ken, your loving father-in-law". He then went back to the top: "My dear Jean…Unfortunately, there seem to have been problems. No one regrets this more than I." The rest swam before his eyes, the black words and scratchings out and blots floating on a sea of white. He folded the paper.

'It's a letter. To Jean from Mr Beaumont. Mrs Beaumont brought the wrong paper.'

His mother had already opened the sideboard drawer and was looking for an envelope.

'Put it in here, Stefan. You didn't read it, I hope.'

'It didn't make any sense, Mother. I couldn't read the writing. It's nothing we didn't know.'

"We". He was suddenly making himself equal with these foreign, ecstatic, beautiful parents, who shortly before had been practising their names like children. They exchanged glances. Glances, forgiveness, thankfulness. Another glance.

'I'm not going to say anything, mum. What shall I do with it?'

'We'll put it in an envelope and seal it up to begin with,' his mother said.

'If it's in Ken's writing we must give it back to him,' his father said. 'Freda need know nothing about it.'

The *modus operandi* drifted far away, down the chequered path to the front gate. It leapt over the word written on the pavement and glided in the Rover to the still standing premises of the firm of Beaumont on the east of the city. It stopped in front of the door, facing the plaque: "Beaumont", and other words, blackened in the assault that had decimated the adjoining building.

'Textiles.'

'What was that, dear?' his mother said.

'Textiles. They deal in textiles. I saw it on the plaque.'

'When we went to the concert, darling,' his mother said. 'Stefan was sitting in the front of the car. Mrs Beaumont travels more comfortably in the back.'

His father nodded slowly. 'We must ask Ken. We must remember to be thankful, whatever the outcome.'

Chapter VIII

Lola Robertson was on her way back to Barratt's Place. It was raining, a steady, grey, piercing rain. Her shoes were filled with water and a blister had opened on her heel where a stocking was torn. She felt a ladder creeping up the back of her leg and above the hem of her skirt, insistent and rude, like fingers. If she lifted her head she could see the bombed house that designated the entrance to Barratt's Place, its rooms open to the sky, the wallpaper hanging off and sodden.

The shambling, half-made figure of Barry Green came round her left shoulder as if he had come around a corner, unexpectedly and from nowhere.

'Where yer going, Lola Robertson?' He stood in front of her.

'I'm going home, Barry Green,' she said. Suddenly, he was no longer a child. She could smell strong liquor on his breath. A cigarette hung loosely from his mouth.

'Give us a light, Lola.' He moved closer to her.

'I haven't got a light, Barry Green. You know I haven't.'

'Liar. Yer a liar, Lola Robertson.' He was in her space, his face level with hers. In one deft movement, he tore open her coat. His hands were on her chest, gliding between the buttons of her blouse. She could feel them under her brassiere, clammy and obscene. Down below she was aware of a hot flood. It wasn't time for her monthly.

'Give us a light, Lola Robertson.'

'Ask your mother.'

All at once, he was gone, leaving nothing to suggest that he had ever been there apart from a crowd of footprints quickly filling with water.

Lola pulled her coat across her chest and fastened it as best as she could. Ahead of her, the bombed out house still guarded the entrance to Barratt's Place, the secrets of its rooms uncovered. She would tell no one what had happened. She would forget it.

She continued walking, watching the scuffed toes of her shoes and her thick ankles progressing over the waste ground. A lace snapped. She stopped to make a knot, and went on, the dripping hem of her coat wrapping around her legs. She stopped again, to unravel it. And it was then that she saw a ration book all but submerged in a puddle of rain. She picked it up and shook the water off.

GREEN. The ink swam across the cover. Amelia. She hadn't known Mrs Green's Christian name. It sat oddly with Barry's mother. Miss. Miss? Maybe it belonged to someone else. She would leave it for them to find. But there was an address in Barratt's Place. She had to do something. She would return it to Mrs Green without entering into conversation, without enduring her scrutiny, without the inevitable observation that it was time to let the buttons out. She didn't know why, but she ran her finger across the rain-soaked designation "Miss", obliterating it.

A notice had been posted on the broken house informing residents of imminent slum clearance. On the wall underneath it, someone had chalked, "GOOD RIDDANCE TO BAD RUBBISH".

The blackout curtains were drawn across Mrs Green's front window. Lola went through the snicket and round to the back, where the curtains were also drawn. She went to the front again and tried to push the ration book through the letterbox. It wouldn't go. A strange smell hung around the house, somehow as if the privy was blocked, but not quite that. She would ask her father. She folded the ration book and pushed it with difficulty into the wet well of her pocket.

Her father was seated in his customary place, his bad leg outstretched. Osteomyelitis. She had rehearsed the strange word every day, until it had become familiar; part of her father; something he dragged around with him, as he did his spoilt reputation, the aroma of it following him wherever he went. Affecting the bone called the tibia.

Her mother came in from the back and took two envelopes out of her apron pocket.

'Hang your coat up,' she said. 'Heaven knows when that'll be dry. Why didn't you stand up somewhere until the rain had passed?' And then, 'Aren't you going to open them? Your father says they're for you.' Her mother put the letters, one small and one large, on the table by the side of another, opened, letter.

'Yer ma wants ter know if yer've got a young feller, duck.' Her parents must have been communicating.

Lola took her coat off. She caught sight of her front, the blouse scarcely meeting in the middle, the skirt with the cobbled hem. The smell of perspiration rose from her body. A young feller. No.

'I found Mrs Green's ration book,' she said.

Her mother told her to leave it on the table. Her father would take it round when the rain had stopped.

'A woman who spreads ill report,' her mother added, but that shouldn't prevent her father from doing a neighbourly act.

'I tried to put it through the letterbox but I couldn't,' Lola said. 'There was a funny smell.'

She went up to her room. She heard the front door open as her father went out, and heard the drag of his leg until it was drowned in the clatter of rain. She sat on the bed and looked at the envelopes.

One didn't have a stamp. Or an address. Just her name. The other had been brought by the postman, and was thicker, as if something else was inside. The writing was alarmingly like Mr Brumby's. She put it to one side and opened the other.

"Dear Miss Robertson", it said. "I enclose a letter for you which was found by a subsequent borrower inside the library copy of *Northanger Abbey*. Please rest assured that, although we were obliged to open it to ascertain for whom it was intended, the contents will remain confidential.

Yours faithfully,

Bridget O'Rourke (Miss)

Librarian"

Lola ran her finger over the script. It was lovely. The words shimmered in front of her eyes. She had lost the habit of writing. She copied the words, "Yours faithfully" at the bottom of the page, trying to emulate Bridget O'Rourke's elegant loops and flourishes.

The other piece of paper, the one enclosed, smelt faintly of the hospital. She unfolded it. Downstairs she could hear the front door open as her father returned, and the unequal sound of his feet as he went through to the yard. Then the sound of his feet as he came back again. His parents' voices. They were communicating. The opening and closing of the front door. His father's voice, from outside. 'No, Lil, you stay here, duck.'

"Miss Robertson", the enclosed letter said. "Ask your father to bring you back when you are 17. Learn a bone every day and you can't go wrong.

Yours…"

She couldn't read the signature. Underneath it, the name was printed: "Mr Charles de Bono, FRCS". And underneath that a number: "206" with and exclamation mark "(!)" in the same writing.

From somewhere in the distance, she could hear the sounds of demolition. The shattering of glass, one window after another, the crack when the wood gave, the insistent hammering on a faraway door. They had come, too soon, to destroy Barratt's Place. She would have to go to see who needed help. But not just yet. The second letter lay on the bed. More than a letter, a small parcel with the word "Fragile" inscribed on it.

Lola opened it and took out the letter.

"Dear Miss Lola Robertson", it said. "My wife would like to give you a thimble for your work box as a token of our heartfelt appreciation for mending a stranger's sock, most patiently and exquisitely, if I may say so. Please remember me with love and gratitude to your fine parents.

Yours affectionately,

Paul Czerniak"

For a brief moment in time, her parents were illuminated and transformed by a single word, "Fine". What did it mean? Of course, she knew. Fine weather was when it didn't rain. One day in the summer a man called Peter Huttoft had scored a fine innings; she had seen it on the placards. Mrs Green's hair was fine, her mother always said, so thin and fair that under the sun she hardly had any. But fine parents. Were they? Certainly, her father endured the pain from his leg, if the condition called osteomyelitis was painful. She didn't know. And her mother endured her father, his shameful misdemeanour, and the smell that came from his wound.

The thimble was lovely, patterned with tiny red roses and wrapped in a handkerchief. She looked at the letter again. Czerniak. She tried to say it out loud but she didn't know how. She would never remember it.

There were voices now. Her father had come back in and was saying something to her mother. Something urgent. The door banged again. She went down. Her mother's hat had gone from the peg, and her apron was hanging there.

Lola put on her damp coat. It had stopped raining. She shivered. She opened the door and looked out.

The street was empty apart for a policeman standing near the bombed house. She could hear her father's voice. 'Corporal Cyril Robertson, sir.' Someone whom she could not see was taking down a statement.

'Yes, my daughter, officer. She alerted my wife and I to the fact that the curtains were drawn and there was an unusual aroma. My wife has gone to look for the youngster.'

'The youngster?'

'A lad, sir. Ten or eleven, mebbe twelve. Tall and well made for his age.'

'Any other family?'

'Not that we know of, officer.' Her father's voice dropped and she could no longer hear what he was saying. Then it came back. 'You may ascertain that from my wife. Five minutes earlier and the lady's life might have been saved. Who knows?'

Lola felt herself turning to ice. Five minutes. She had lost that length of time on the waste ground, and here was her father accusing her as if he knew.

'You did your best, sir. You did your best. That's all anyone can do.'

A black vehicle nosed past the policeman keeping watch at the end of the street, who waved it in the direction of Mrs Green's house. Her father and the officer to whom he had been talking emerged from the back into the street. Two officers jumped down from the van and opened the rear doors. Articles were brought out, a rolled up stretcher, and a grey army blanket. They went into the house. Curtains were being drawn in Barratt's Place. Every blackout curtain along the street. She should go in and draw their own. But she didn't. The ice still bound her to the place where she was standing. Five minutes lost.

Nor could she look away from the house of Amelia Green. She could hear the broken door grating open again. The police officers in the street removed their hats as the stretcher, bearing an impossibly small shape, was lifted into the back of the van. It drove off.

Then she was in the room at home, seated at the table with a policeman opposite. Her father had made a cup of tea and brought out the sugar basin. The sugar in it had hardened in the damp and was brown in patches where her father had dug in his teaspoon. The policeman didn't take sugar.

'No need to be frightened, miss.'

She was very frightened, but not of the policeman. She was frightened she would have to tell him in the presence of her father what had happened on the waste ground. She didn't have the words for it. No words that wouldn't sound rude. She was frightened because five minutes could have saved Mrs Green's life, and because the delay was the fault of herself, Lola Robertson.

'All we ask is for you to show us where you found the lady's ration book, miss. Your dad will look after you. If we may ask that of you, corporal.'

'Certainly, officer.'

Lola nodded. She couldn't remember the last time she had heard her own voice.

'Yer need yer coat, duck,' her father said.

She shook her head. 'It's still wet, father. I can manage as I am.'

Her father took off his own jacket and put it round her shoulders.

'You'll be cold, father,' she said.

'Not as cold as in them trenches, duck.'

The policeman raised his eyebrows.

'So to speak, officer,' her father said. 'So to speak.'

They went to the place. The officer took off his jacket and gave it to her father to hold while he plunged his hand into the puddle.

'Just to make sure there are no more artefacts, corporal.'

'Yes, officer.'

There was nothing.

'Didn't expect anything, but we have to check, corporal.'

'Of course, officer. Have to make sure.'

Lola's mother came back and went straight out to the privy.

'Yer best put kettle on, duck,' her father said.

Her mother said she didn't want any tea but her father poured her a cup all the same. She told Lola to remind her father he wasn't in the army now, but nevertheless took small sips, and her colour began to return. Lola wasn't quite sure if her parents were communicating or not.

'You'd better get your father to tell your mother what happened,' her mother said.

Lola suddenly saw again the impossibly small shape under and the policemen standing hatless under the raw grey sky.

She burst into tears. 'You can ask him yourself, mother.' She didn't know if she had said it out loud, or only thought it, or if the tears had really erupted or were merely lying in wait.

Her father said, 'Now, now, duck, yer gone all through the war.'

'And she pipes her eye over Amelia Green.' Her mother finished the sentence. So she knew Mrs Green's Christian name. 'It's all over the town,' she said presently.

Her mother had been out to look for Barry Green, but hadn't found him. She had been into the shop and asked. Mr Troop said he had been in and gone, that he had asked for sweets, and there was only one place he could have found the wherewithal for that. 'From his ma's purse,' Mr Troop had said. While her mother was in the shop, a stranger came in and said there was a sad case down in Barratt's.

The howls of Barry Green ricocheted from every building in the street.

Lola saw from her room that all the blackout curtains had been drawn back, and every door opened, and that everybody was outside. She saw Barry Green in front of his house and the policeman who had been standing at the entrance to Barratt's Place with him. She saw Barry Green hammer on the front door with his fists, which was by now not his front door but a rough and splintered board nailed across it. Then the fists flew at the boarded windows. She could see the blood guttering between his knuckles, and hear the remnants of the glass cracking under his feet. She noticed that his shoes were tied with string. And she heard his howls. She would hear his howls for as long as she lived.

She saw her father and mother and the neighbour Audrey Curran go over to the policeman. They would take Barry Green in. Then everybody else. Everybody would take Barry Green in. Her mother would do her duty by her late neighbour Amelia Green and take Barry in.

Lola went down and stood at the door. Audrey Curran was describing how she had been the first to see the lad, coming across the waste, not walking straight, but all over the place; how he had failed to notice the policeman standing guard and had found the street empty and the house boarded. For the demolition. Barry Green thought that. For the demolition.

The howls ceased. Barry Green's voice had started to break. His words came out as a croak.

'She gone and left me! She gone and left me!'

Lola saw her mother and father talking to the policeman again. They would take Barry in. They would explain to him. They would do their duty by their neighbour. It would be no trouble. No one had reason to starve under Mr Attlee. Her mother was crying into a dishrag.

She went in. She heard her parents come back. Without Barry Green. Her father was talking to her mother.

'Summat up with the ration book, duck,' he was saying. 'Between you and me and the gate post, the lass hadn't got no ready. The poor lass only had to ask. She were too proud, duck, too proud.'

'Where's Barry?' Lola could hardly say the name.

Her father didn't answer.

She asked her mother, 'Where's Barry Green?'

Her mother said, 'Never you mind, and don't you go spreading tales.'

Lola flushed. 'I don't spread tales, mother.'

'Nah, duck,' her father said. 'Yer ma knows yer don't.'

And at the end of the day, Lola Robertson had forgotten its unusual gifts: a thank you letter from a foreign gentleman with an unpronounceable name and a thimble from his wife for mending a sock; a letter in a crabbed script from the doctor with the bow tie asking her to come back when she was seventeen, and an unfathomable number, 206!

What she remembered was the encounter on the waste, the fingers as they touched her, as they found the parts of her she didn't have names for. More shameful, it seemed to her, than the war itself, which for all its destruction had not outraged her body and left her dirty forever. Yet worse by far was the sick and lingering fear that, had she not dallied on the way home, the difficult life of Amelia Green might have been saved.

Part II 1948

Chapter I

Stefan Czerniak went out of the front door and down the chequered path to the gate. It was the eighteenth day of May. He stepped over the white word on the pavement. CONSHY. It occurred to him, for the first time as he saw the toe of his shoe make landfall, that the word might not still be there if he – if everyone who passed by the house in Golen Avenue – were to step on it instead of over it. It would have faded, by a process of attrition. But they didn't and it hadn't.

The horse chestnuts were out. For a reason he didn't know they rode above him, their luminous flowers and brimming leaves following him, questioning him for his unknowing. Why? Why anything? Why the street? Why the flight of stone steps leading down to the parallel rail lines leading to the city, leading to the half-crazed premises on the edge of a bombsite? Why the desk, the ledger, the slack bonhomie of the other chaps?

'Bet your old man was in the you-know-what with a name like that, Zurnick. Resistance.'

'No, he was an objector.'

'A what?'

'An objector. He didn't engage.'

He could still see their faces, closed in bewilderment, then splitting into good-natured mirth. They didn't believe him.

'Guess you ain't permitted to talk about it. Under wraps, eh, Zurnick?'

And his parents. A continual presence.

His mother, the first to leave her footprints on the chequered path between the hydrangeas in the mornings, the first to go through the gate, the first to step over the word. The first back, stepping over the word again, entering the chilled and empty home. Standing at the kitchen sink, swallowing water until the taste of the laundry had gone. And his father following his mother down the path at a mathematical interval, taking off his long coat and shaking the dust from it before he came in, thrashing his beret against the wall. Why?

The dark unseen welcome in the hallway when his father would run his hand over his mother's hair and she would touch his face.

Nothing else, but he couldn't bear to be near them.

'I'll move into the attic, Ruth.'

She looked up, surprised.

'As you wish, dear.' Then, 'I hope it's not on account of your father and mother.'

He didn't answer.

She made a blue curtain out of a pre-war tablecloth. His father carried up a desk and two chairs. The bed wouldn't go up the narrow staircase. No matter. He would sleep on a mattress on the floor and prop it up against the wall during the day. His mother brought up a pegged rug.

'Will you be taking your meals with us, dear?'

'I suppose.'

'We don't want to forget what you look like.'

The attic room gave the impression of being far higher than the extra floor would suggest. Mr and Mrs Beaumont's garden lay far below, restored to its flowerbeds and lawn, its sundial and birdbath. And their own garden. Still the rows of vegetables. Still Bazal, nosing between the rows.

He stood in the queue for a ticket. 'We don't want to forget what you look like.' He hadn't said the obvious to his mother, that forgetting what he looked like was not within the realms of probability. He looked like his father: dark and foreign. He came to the front of the queue and saw himself reflected in the glass, creating a strange palimpsest of his features superimposed on those of the ticket clerk.

'Will that be St Paul's as usual, sir?'

'Yes, thank you.'

'I wonder some of them buildings is still standing, sir. Keeps chaps in a job I expect.'

One day, he would ask the ticket clerk which chap he was referring to being kept in a job, himself or the customer requiring a ticket.

He went down the steps.

The man was there again, bowler hatted, a coat folded over his arm, a rolled umbrella hanging in the crook of his elbow. Reading *The Times*. Waiting. The word assaulted Stefan Czerniak as he passed the man. A familiar word delivered sotto voce and intended for him. The train rattled in. He got on.

The man took the seat next to him and continued to read the newspaper. He started to talk in a language that sat ill with the measured English of *The Times*. 'Fucking conchie,' he said. 'Bastard.' Stefan listened. A line of *Ma Vlast* played in his head. The voice next to him went on, issuing its invective into the court circular and the obituaries. The music continued, increasing in volume until the voice was obliterated. It continued, a shining river meandering through the fields of a country he didn't know, every last note of it, until it came to an end and started again. Stefan saw the notes of it, black clusters climbing the staves, dipping and weaving between the parallel lines until they became the river Vlatava, travelling at walking pace, glittering under the high sun. He had the whole of it in his head.

The voice next to him had stopped. The man was standing near the door, also intending to get off at St Paul's. Stefan waited, stepping off the train after everyone else, when the doors were already closing. He would take the steps up; five dizzying minutes late. Not that it mattered. Nothing mattered particularly.

He was nearly at the top and could already see the attenuated light from the booking hall filtering down the stairwell when he slipped, lost his footing and fell backwards to the landing below.

Another chap helped him up. 'You hurt, sir? This your paper, sir?'

No, no, he wasn't hurt and it wasn't his paper. It was *The Times*, its pages fanned out between one step and the next.

'An unfortunate place to drop a paper, sir. Could have been nasty. Sure you're not hurt? If you're not hurt, sir...' The other chap carried on up the steps.

An official was waiting at the top.

'You on the Gant's Hill, sir? Remember the gentleman next to you? City type? Alleges you used bad language in a public place. I'll have to ask you to accompany me, sir. Nothing to worry about. Merely a formality. Looks like you've been in the wars, sir.'

He opened a door and stepped inside. 'Chair opposite if you would, sir. I have to be nearest the door. Just in case. Regulations, you see. Been in the wars?'

'I fell on the stairs.'

'A little too much last night, sir?'

Stefan didn't answer. He took the chair on the far side of the desk. The official sat down opposite. A parallelogram of sunlight illuminated a blotting pad and inkwell between them on the table.

'Well, well, just a few questions. Name, if you would, sir.'

'Stefan Czerniak.'

'Ah, that's different. Most chaps in your situation say Robin Hood.'

'My name's Czerniak.'

'Spelling, please, sir.'

'C-Z-E-R-N-I-A-K.'

The official looked up. 'I thought for a moment you were going to say H-O-O-D, sir. Well, Mr…' (he looked down at the name he had written)… 'Well, Mr Zurnick, were you using bad language?'

'No, sir.'

'The gentleman who reported you alleges that you were repeating foul words throughout the journey. Have you any recollection of that, Mr Zurnick?'

'No, sir.'

'Have you any recollection of your recent journey?'

'Yes, sir.'

'Tell me.'

'I was listening to music, sir.'

'Ah, music. And what piece of music would that be, Mr Zurnick?'

'*Vlatava*. Smetana.'

The official laid down his pen, got up from his chair and went to the door. Stefan heard his voice in the adjoining room. 'Miss Bradley, a travel warrant to Gant's Hill, please. As soon as you like. Thank you. Seems harmless enough but I'll send him off with a warning. A drop too much last night if you ask me.' The secretary called Miss Bradley hadn't asked. He came back.

'We're sending you home, Mr Zurnick. Sleep it off, there's a good chap.'

'I haven't been drinking, sir.'

'No, Mr Zurnick, of course you haven't. Be a good chap and come with me.' He looked at his watch. 'There's a Snaresbrook in at eleven minutes past. Another instance like this and we might have to reconsider, but not this time, Mr Zurnick. I'm a Strauss man myself. *Blue Danube*. Know it?'

'Yes, sir.' Mrs Beaumont liked it.

'Your cup of tea?'

'Yes, sir.'

'Who's the other fellow you mentioned?'

'Smetana.'

'Must give him a try. How are you spelling that, now…?'

The mirror in the hallway at 20 Golen Avenue caught him as he went past. He stopped and turned towards it. His father looked back. Half hidden in the dark space of the hall but unmistakeably Paul Czerniak. The brush of dark hair, the one eyebrow higher than the other as if engaged in a permanent dialectic with the world around him, the same eyes; and now the wound running up the forehead still black and seeping. He would wash it away. He would not wear it, as his father did the beret and the long dark coat and worn red scarf tied in a careless knot. He would obliterate it.

He didn't know when it had happened, this metamorphosis, this unsettling replacement of himself with a fellow so incredibly like his father. He took a step back, and in doing so noticed in the mirror the white rectangle of an envelope which he hadn't seen when he came in. The letter was addressed to himself, Stefan Czerniak esq, in a hand he didn't recognise. He went up to the attic.

A long way below in next door's garden, Mr Beaumont was seated on the bench, his head sunk into his chest, reading the newspaper, his spectacles lodged at an awkward angle across his forehead.

The letter began, "Dear Colleague…" and ended "Yours faithfully…" followed by the trajectory of the pen as it rolled down to the foot of the page. Between the beginning and the end of the letter were lines and half lines of haphazard script, words overwritten, scored out and trailing off into directionless wanderings. It said, as far as Stefan could make out, that the firm's contract had not been renewed. He tore the letter and envelope into pieces and, lifting a floorboard, slid them into the space at the corner of the attic room. He replaced the floorboard, scattering the splinters of wood with his foot. An image of a mouth spewing out foul language lodged itself in his mind, the drops of spittle, the words bubbling out.

The newspaper had fallen from Mr Beaumont's knee and he had lurched to one side. As Stefan watched, he slid from the bench. One hand seemed to be reaching for his spectacles, which were some distance away on the lawn. An expanse of white midriff had appeared where the shirt buttons had opened. Mr Beaumont was his employer. A chap didn't see his employer like this.

He had not seen anyone else's unclothed body since rugby at school. He didn't like flesh, even the word. He didn't like anyone else's and he didn't like his own. On rugby days, he would leave home with his shorts under his top clothes and put his top clothes on over them when the session had finished. On the bench there was an appalling patch of damp.

Mr Beaumont was struggling, trying to right himself with one arm and banging his head on the bench in the process. He made it onto one elbow, slumped down again and was sick.

Stefan ran down the stairs and out of the house. He ran down Golen Avenue, into Harrington Crescent, and to the church of St Saviour. Mrs Beaumont would be there. He didn't know whether she had caught the habit from his father or he from her; they were equally embarrassing in that respect.

He went in, through the west door and through a side door; from the green silence of Harrington Crescent to the white silence of the interior of the church. Mrs Beaumont wasn't there. Of the sparse congregation, of whom he could see only the backs of the shoulders and heads, there was not one corresponding to Mrs Beaumont with her grey gold curls. He said her name.

'Mrs Beaumont.'

And again.

'Mrs Beaumont.'

Of course, she would be wearing a scarf. He wouldn't recognise her from the back.

'Mrs Beaumont, please.' Louder.

A woman looked around. A pale woman, with a purple scarf tied under chin. She left her pew. He hadn't seen her without lipstick before.

No one appeared to be surprised that he hadn't been at work. Neither his mother, nor his father, seated at the table, nor Mrs Beaumont. Mrs Beaumont had stopped speaking.

'We must put a trunk call through to Pip,' his father said. 'We might catch him at the office.'

Mrs Beaumont shook her head. His mother and father exchanged glances.

'It's too late, darling,' his mother said. 'Pip will be home by now.' Then, to Mrs Beaumont, 'What about the neighbours, Freda? Don't they have a telephone?'

'The hospital put him down as Kenneth,' she said. 'I didn't have the heart to correct them. They were so sweet. They said if he makes it through the next twenty-four hours…' Her face crumpled into soundless misery.

Stefan could hardly bear it. He wanted to be away, under the horse chestnuts, on the underground, in the office. Anywhere but here.

'It's not Kenneth, it's Kenelm,' he said.

Mrs Beaumont looked up. 'Yes, dear, fancy you knowing that. He never did like Kenelm. He said it was the name of an Irish saint. Not that he bore any ill-will towards the Irish. Probably Stefan could go to the box and call the neighbours.' No one had considered that Mrs Beaumont could go back and use her own telephone. 'I have to have a word with you both, and poor Stefan has had enough for one day. Oh dear.' She started crying again, making a pretence of looking through her handbag. 'Here it is. The people next door run a hostel of some kind, for young working men, I expect. It's Crawford in case you can't read the writing, dear.'

A sudden phrase entered his mind. He could sense it travelling through the heights and hollows of the brain, through some cerebral maze that it was unable to leave. It was something someone had said and he couldn't place it. Then under the whispering arches of the trees, he did. It was something his father had said about…He reached the call box, the phrase still lodged in his head. He rang the operator and gave the number.

'What was that, sir?'

He said it again.

'Not connecting, sir. Please check that the numerals are correct.'

'The one and the seven look the same. They could be each other.'

He heard a sigh at the other end. 'We're really too busy for this kind of thing.'

'Please. It's urgent.'

Another sigh. 'I'll try once more…Putting you through now, sir. You have three minutes.'

'Crawford here.'

Stefan looked at Mrs Beaumont's scrap of paper. Yes, she had written the name Crawford. She had told him it was Crawford. He was expecting a different name.

'Are you there?'

'Mr Crawford?' The name was still unexpected.

'I haven't got all day. Are you there or aren't you?'

'I have a message for Mr Philip Beaumont. Would you be kind enough to pass it on, please, sir?' The other name came back to him. It was Robertson. The gifts of the spirit. Fragile. The word "fragile".

'You'll have to give me more information than that. Begging your pardon, sir, but we got scallywags calling and we can't be too careful. Begging your pardon, as I said.'

'Philip Beaumont,' Stefan said. 'They call him Pip.'

'Aye. What about him?'

'Could you ask him to ring home, please?'

'And who might you be?'

'Stefan. Next door.'

'Steven. Steven what?'

'Your time is up, caller.'

The line spluttered and died. He could hear his mother. 'I hope you said thank you to the gentleman.' He hadn't. There hadn't been time.

'I hope you remembered to thank the neighbour,' his mother said.

'Of course Stefan said thank you, Ruth dear.' Mrs Beaumont was standing, ready to leave. 'Pip will be calling from the hostel.'

His father got up to take Mrs Beaumont home. 'Anything we can do, Freda,' he said.

'If you could explain to Stefan that Ken and I will be very grateful, Paul, my dear.' She corrected herself. 'Ken would be very grateful. I'm sure Stefan will come with me.'

Mrs Beaumont had recovered her flow of words.

'I had a word with your parents while you were at the telephone, dear,' she said when they were outside. 'They will tell you. Have you ever seen the horse chestnuts like this before? I do hope Ken will see them again.' He thought she was going to cry. It was awful. There must be something to say to make things better. There wasn't anything.

'Dad will make a trunk call,' he heard himself saying. 'He probably has done already.'

Mrs Beaumont laughed unexpectedly. 'Oh, yes, you've noticed, dear. We knew your dad was a religious man, but he was, well, reticent about it before he went away. The war did unusual things to people. Don't tell him we've had this conversation. Your mum...'

'She's a Roman Catholic.'

'And your dad?'

'Orthodox or something, I don't know.'

'And yourself, Stefan, dear?'

He opened the gate for Mrs Beaumont. She stepped over the word on the pavement and he followed.

'Nothing. Existentialist.'

'My word. What's that, dear?'

'I'll let you know when I've found out.'

'I never did know what Ken believed in. I suppose he was nominally Church of England like the rest of us.' She was already speaking of him in the past. Of his – er – life, which still existed, tenuously, somewhere above the recumbent figure on a white bed in Oldchurch Hospital. His life. The pattern of the days: the green lawn and the birdbath collecting the scudding clouds; the firm, its crumbling brickwork tilting into a bombsite; the face reflected in the mirror of the Rover, the hair flicked in birds' wings over the ears. 'But you must go back to your parents, dear. They have something to discuss with you. I expect the chaps were missing Ken at the office today.'

'I don't know. I didn't go in, Mrs Beaumont.'

'Some good Samaritan came to the church and alerted me. I'll have to thank them when I remember who it was.'

His mother and father were still seated at the table, which had been laid with cutlery and napkins. The room smelt of the war. Or maybe the war smelt of a perpetual evening meal put together from rations and cabbage. He didn't know. The time before the war had somehow slid into the time of the war without any demarcation, and the war itself into the time after it. It was little different, except that his father was there, with his head bowed, silently offering thanks for the meal which Stefan could hear his mother serving. He went out on the pretext of hanging up his coat, and came back when his father had finished. The meal passed in silence. He washed the dishes; his father dried them; his mother put them away. Still in silence. Bazal was in the garden.

'Bazal's there,' he said.

'See to him, darling,' his mother said, taking the cloth from his father.

He watched from the window: his father bearing down on the little creature and scooping him up, the small face ducking into the shell, the feet paddling in mid-air and ploughing through the grass as soon as he found himself on the *terra firma* of the other side.

'Your father doesn't dry them properly,' his mother said. 'Freda was talking about the future of the firm. Just to warn you, dear. Your father will explain. You should have received a letter. We said you hadn't.'

The letter was in small pieces under the floorboard in the corner of the attic room. He said nothing.

Chapter II

Her father was in the reading room leaning over the paper, looking, she had no doubt, at the situations vacant. She had no doubt, also, that her mother did the same, but discreetly, coming to the library at a different time, saying to herself the incomprehensible words.

Lola pushed open the door and went in. The familiar odour, compounded of a festering wound and iodine, met her. Within a few seconds she would be used to it, as were all the other readers, as they were to other aromas: damp gabardine, historic meals, perspiration – all of which she carried through her life on her own person for all that she knew, but didn't notice.

Her father had seen her. He collected up the scraps of paper he had been writing on and opened the paper at a different page, beckoning her with his eyes.

'See yer later then, duck.'

She took his place in front of the newspaper, standing in his space, in the smell of an almost forgotten war he had left behind.

The photograph was of a younger man, but the face was the same: the mole at the edge of the mouth, the high cheek bones, the arch of the eyebrows, as if asking a perpetual question, "What was that last word, little girl?" He was wearing a tweed coat and a bow tie. The caption read: Charles de Bono MD 1884-1948. Instinctively she put her hand into her pocket in an absurd expectation that she might find the letter. "Tell your father to bring you back when you're seventeen." But the letter wasn't there. It hadn't been there for a long time. She had mislaid it, along with her other letter, from the gentleman with the unpronounceable name, whose wife had sent her a thimble for darning her husband's sock just after the war. She wouldn't recover the name. It had gone, as completely as the doctor with the bow tie had gone, whose obituary was before her on the lectern in the reading room. She would never recover her letters. They had almost certainly been lost when the demolition men came to Barratt's Place.

The small picture inserted at the bottom right hand corner of the page could have been Barratt's Place. But it wasn't. It was somewhere similar, with similar children standing in their ones and twos and threes, gazing plain-faced and unsmiling at the camera, in their pinafores or braces, with broken shoes or no shoes; the rain-soaked cobbles, the gutter running down the middle of the street, dog dirt, cabbage leaves…Charles de Bono had been born there. The family had been obliged to change the name to Bone for fear of giving offence and being thought of as giving themselves airs.

Lola skipped to the end of the obituary. He left a widow, Alexandra, a brother and two sisters. There had been no children.

She read backwards. He had suffered a short illness. She went back to the beginning. There must surely be more to a life, more than having been born with the burden of an odd-sounding name, more than the detritus of the street outside the home, more than the childless marriage, more than the widow grieving alone at home, having been given insufficient time to realise that her husband would leave her.

Charles Bone had two brothers and five sisters. He was the oldest, a fragile and sickly child, industrious at school, from which he was removed at the age of thirteen to help support the family. This was everybody and anybody; a vast majority, who were born, lived and died of a short illness, leaving the world as Amelia Green had done, unexpectedly, leaving with their secrets intact, their flashes of arrogance extinguished; everybody and anybody, with their brown humilities, leaving no footprints. She would be the same. She would have been born in a similar street. There might be a picture of children with string tying their shoes on, and she would be one of them. She would have been industrious at school. She would have left school to help support, not her own family, but her father's other family. She would have done nothing anyone remembered, coming home at the end of each day with the smells of the kitchen and the wash house in her hair, the grease under her nails, the leavings of the privy under her feet.

She read on. Charles Bone had enlisted: an unremarkable young man with arched eyebrows and a mole at the edge of his mouth. Unremarkable but for the fact that he was already thirty years old. And among the mud and dressing stations and the screams of the men in Flanders he had arrived at…she searched for a word and didn't find it. "Ask your father to bring you back when you're seventeen." He might have gone far. Her eyes leapt down the page. He might, having studied at night for many years, have gone to Harley Street. She didn't know where Harley Street was or what it represented. She continued reading. He didn't go to Harley Street.

He returned to a location on the border of Nottinghamshire, not the one where he had been born, but one like it, where servicemen had limped home from the Great War with…"What was that word, little girl?" The name was no longer Bone but de Bono. He returned with his arched eyebrows, and a bow tie, and his arrogance intact.

Lola Robertson stood in front of the open newspaper. The print and the pictures swam across the page. She blinked and looked at the picture. The man with the arched eyebrows and the bow tie looked back at her. "Ask your father to bring you back when you're seventeen."

She was seventeen now. More than seventeen, since her parents had added two years to her age so that she had a better opportunity of finding work. There was no one now to take her back to, and, even if there had been, she had lost the letter.

All at once, Miss O'Rourke was standing behind her.

'Oh, there you are, Miss Robertson. I thought I saw you come in.'

Lola turned the page of the newspaper.

'My father was in.'

'I wondered if you would like to try Virginia Woolf, dear. *The Years* is probably best to start with. Some of the others are rather…unusual, but *The Years* has an agreeable narrative.'

A sudden sentence edged into Lola's mind: "Learn a bone every day and you can't go wrong."

'Do you have a book on bones, please?' she said.

'Indeed, but you can't take it out. It's in the store. No one much asks for bones these days. If you step into the reference area, I'll bring it to you. Shall you take Mrs Woolf out, dear?'

Lola said she would. Her sudden tears had gone. She was unexpectedly in a different place, not terminally confined to other people's houses, their kitchens and privies with a rag or a mop in her hand and the perpetual sweat smell of the war on her. And in truth, the intervening years had become worse. During the war, she had been at school. Her father was a corporal. Then her difficult mother…she didn't know how to explain it even to herself, except that her mother on her own was a less difficult person than she had become on her father's return.

She took a seat at a table in the reference area and watched Miss O'Rourke as she went through a door into another room. The door closed behind her, and then opened of its own accord, revealing a room little different from the one in which she was seated, but smaller, with a table placed under a high window to catch the natural light. With their backs to her, seated at the table, were her mother and father, and opposite them the senior librarian, Mr Carpenter. Between them on the table were papers. A blotting pad and an ink well. An envelope.

'No!' The scattered readers in the reference room looked round. She blushed. 'I'm sorry.' Her parents were surely filling in papers for a divorce. There could be no other reason for them to be there, seeking the erudite help of Mr Carpenter. Although her mother's back was towards her, she could see her lips moving as she tried to make sense of the questions. She could see the frown between her eyebrows, like a small neat darn. She could see her father's face, enduring whatever was taking place as if it were a pain he had to carry around with him, as he did the pain from osteomyelitis in the tibia.

Miss O'Rourke returned, pulling the door closed behind her, carrying a large book and a yellow duster.

'This is *Gray's Anatomy*, Miss Robertson.' She placed the volume on the table in front of Lola and dusted the cover. 'You will find the whole anatomy, some of which I would normally consider improper reading for a young lady, but maybe I'm old-fashioned. How old are you, my dear?'

'Seventeen, I think,' Lola whispered in return. 'But my parents added two years when I had to go out to work.'

'I would prefer a young person to be at least eighteen to read this material.' Miss O'Rourke opened the book at the title page. 'But if your parents say you're older, we'll accept that. May I suggest you start with the biographical details of Henry Gray, dear. A touching story. And if you would return the book to the desk when you go, we'll keep it by for when you come again. Will that do?'

'Yes, yes thank you.'

The book had a strange smell, damp and faintly sickly, like school ink. There was a picture of the gentleman author, long-faced and mild. He had been born, lived and died at the age of thirty-four of a dreadful disease, *variola*, after tenderly nursing his young nephew. Between his birth and his death, he had been a surgeon and an anatomist. He had written a book that was to last a hundred years. His star had risen, had flared brightly but briefly, and had gone out. He looked back at her from the page, as Charles de Bono had done. The caretaker was going around the library, telling readers they had ten minutes left. She looked back at the pale picture of Henry Gray. 'You have ten years left, sir, and then you must go. Please finish the sentence you are writing and blot your work...'

'Ten minutes left, miss,' the caretaker said.

She returned the book to the desk. Miss O'Rourke put it under the counter, and handed her another book. 'Virginia Woolf, Miss Robertson, if you have your ticket. I think you'll like it.'

She went home. Margaret Drive was deserted. The new people had been in number 10 for a month. She could see the lady moving around inside, as if she were sweeping. The garden was tussocks of coarse grass and clods of clay earth and stones. A child's tricycle stood under the window.

The boy was at the upstairs window. He put his tongue out at her. She put hers out in return. He was called Albert and she wondered how that would sit with him in a classroom full of Peters and Johns and Howards. Lola had been bad enough. The lady inside waved. Lola waved back. Maybe he had a middle name. Maybe it was more old-fashioned even than Albert. The boy's face popped up again at the downstairs window. He put out his tongue and grinned. He had buck teeth like her father, but more pronounced than her father's. His hair was combed flat with Brylcreem and parted painstakingly on the right side. His head disappeared from the window and he was out in the garden. He picked up a clod of earth.

'Don't you dare,' she said, and he put it down.

'I wasn't going to anyway, missis,' he said.

'Yes, you were,' she said. 'I bet you were, Albert Baddy.'

'Me name's Goody, missis,' he said. 'Albert Goody.'

'If you throw that stone it's Baddy,' she said.

He frowned. He wasn't following. 'Oh.'

'Never mind,' she said. 'Tell your ma hello.'

'Yer ma don't like me ma,' she said.

She knew that. 'Then tell her hello from me,' she said.

Albert Goody said, 'Oh,' and continued to stand there. 'I'll tell me dad of you,' he said.

'And I'll tell him of you first,' she said.

Albert Goody wiped his nose with the back of his hand. His father wasn't there. 'Would yer like a ride on me trike? Me uncle gev it me.'

'It's nice,' Lola said.

'Me uncle gev it me,' Albert Goody said again. 'Yer ma don't like me uncle neither.'

Lola knew that as well. 'I'm sorry,' she said.

'Not your fault,' Albert Goody said. 'Yer'll have a ride on me trike another day.'

'Yes,' she said, 'when I've grown smaller. Promise.'

'Oh.'

Her parents were already home. She could hear their voices coming from the kitchen, audible through the closed door. In the prefab every sound was magnified, from the flush of the lavatory in the night to the barest whisper in the day. She hung up her coat. The kitchen door opened a crack.

'Yer age, duck,' her father was saying. 'They request yer age. Yer can put it in after. I don't need ter see it, duck.'

Lola opened the front door again and closed it loudly. Surely, they knew she was there.

'It was yer idea, duck. Yer might as well comply.'

'It's for the best,' her mother's voice said. 'We can't live like this.'

'Then we better complete them there papers, duck.' Her father's voice.

Lola started to climb the stairs. She heard the creak of the kitchen door as it opened wider.

'Lola, duck, yer ma wants yer.'

She went back down.

'What is it, father?'

'Summat yer ma's drempt up.'

'What is it, father?'

'Hankering after flitting, duck.'

'From here, father? We've only just arrived. Why?'

'Yer ma's got a bee in her bonnet, duck.' Her father made to go back into the kitchen. Lola stepped in front of him. She lowered her voice.

'I want to know, father. Is it what I think?'

'Depends on what yer think, duck. If yer think it's on account of the neighbour, yer not far out.'

'Which neighbour, father?'

'Yer ma will tell yer. Or she won't tell yer.'

'Are you and mother getting divorced, father?' She had to say it. 'Are you, father?' Divorce. It was an obscene word. She had never said it before. 'Are you, father?' He had turned away, towards the kitchen door. 'You must tell me.'

'Nah, not so far as I'm concerned. What gev yer that notion, duck? Better not tell yer ma. Might put ideas in her head.'

She could hear the tap running and her mother filling the kettle, coming back to take the teapot out to empty the dregs. She could see in her mind's eye the rectangle of sunlight spilling over the linoleum on the kitchen floor. She could smell the outside drain, see into its well of white scum to which the old tea leaves were being added. She could hear the kettle boiling, its lid clattering, its spout spluttering. Her mother was at the kitchen door. Her father stood back, and she went in. A sudden thought of Albert Goody's mother flitted through her mind and was gone.

'Come in, Lola,' her mother said. 'There's something your father and I need to tell you.'

The kettle was still boiling, spitting drops of bright fizzing water onto the hob.

'Yer'd better mash the tea,' her father said.

The papers were on the table. The habitual needlework frown puckered her mother's forehead. She was still wearing her pinafore and her hair was tied up in a scarf.

'Tek that thing off, Lil,' her father said. 'Yer still a pretty woman, duck.'

Her mother's frown deepened. She left the table and disappeared into the living room, leaving both doors open. Her father winked. The unmistakeable sound of hairpins dropping into an ashtray peppered the silence. Her mother returned.

Lola intercepted the glance that passed between her parents but was unable to interpret it. A faint colour rose in her mother's face. Her father was right. She was still a pretty woman.

'I'll let yer ma explain,' her father said.

Lola looked at her mother. Her mother slid the papers across to her. Nowhere was the word "divorce" visible. She went back to the beginning. Everything written there dissolved into a mist in front of her eyes.

'What are these? Mother, what are these?'

'Your father will tell you.'

She looked from one to the other of her parents, and then down at the papers on the table.

'Read them, duck,' her father said. 'Yer the scholar. Virginia Woolf, my word.' He picked up the library book and opened it. 'We never saw yer in the library, duck.'

'I was in the reference room. I saw you when Miss O'Rourke went through to find a book.' Her parents didn't ask what the book was. 'You were with Mr Carpenter.'

'Aye, duck.'

'What are these?' She still couldn't understand the print on the pages. 'You haven't filled in all the questions. Why are you having to answer questions?'

'We're looking to flit,' her father said.

'Why?'

'Never you mind.'

'If yer won't tell the lass, Lil, I'll tell her,' her father said.

Her mother said nothing.

'Yer ma…' her father continued, looking not at her but across at her mother. 'Yer ma…you tell the lass, Lil.'

'There's a vacancy for a married couple coming up at Salisbury House,' her mother said.

But you're not married, not really, not now. The words clamoured in Lola's head, trying to find a way out.

'Couple?' she said uselessly. 'Why couple?' Suddenly, the meaning of the pages in front of her became clear. Wardens to sixteen older boys. Oh. She had all at once become like Albert Goody. The mirror on the opposite wall threw her epiphany back at her. She was like Albert Goody. Just a little.

'Mr Carpenter kindly wrote your father a testimonial.' The expression tripped off her mother's tongue.

'It's them other questions,' her father said. 'Personal. I were asking yer ma her age and she weren't inclined to tell me.' Her father wrote in his own age and the date of his birth.

'Mother can write in hers last of all and put it in the envelope without us seeing,' Lola said. The envelope was already there, addressed to the Guildhall.

A pale smile lit her mother's face and went out immediately.

'Religion,' her father said. 'What religion are we, Lil? Any idea?'

Her mother hadn't any idea. 'Well, I suppose…' She didn't finish the sentence.

'"Salisbury House has a strong Christian ethos",' her father read. 'How would yer put that in English, duck?' He slid the paper across to Lola.

She didn't know. 'You could have asked Mr Carpenter,' she said. And then, 'Why not put Methodist?' She thought of the married people coming out of the chapel on VJ Day. Jean and Pip. How they noticed the string tying her shoes and probably also that she wasn't wearing a brassiere. She blushed.

'We'll go and look at it, Lil,' her father said. 'No harm done.'

Neither her mother nor her father had said what would happen to their daughter were they to take up the position, and she couldn't ask. Not in so many words.

'I'll look after the garden when you go, mother,' she said. Her mother had planted marigolds and Michaelmas daisies in the square patch of scrub under the front window.

'Yer coming with us, duck,' her father said. 'Tell the lass, Lil.'

'The accommodation comprises…' (again the complicated words tripped off her mother's tongue) 'spacious married couple's quarters and small yet adequate quarters for the domestic assistant.'

The difficult words returned to her. But you're not married. Why else did her father sleep on a camp bed downstairs? Oh. She was Albert Goody again.

Her father said, 'Yer say yer Methodist, Lil.'

'Yes, it's not as if anybody's going to test us on it, Cyril.' There was no end to her words, as if somehow the resolve to leave Margaret Drive had set her free, yet from what kind of confinement, Lola couldn't tell.

'Nevertheless, Lil, yer best know what yer talking about.'

So they were going to the Methodist chapel across the Market Square, where Lola had watched on VJ Day as the people called Jean and Pip emerged into a world at peace.

'You will look nice, won't you, dear?' her mother said. 'I'll find you a hat.'

'No you won't, mother.' The words had flown around the room before she could call them back. She watched the colour flare in her mother's face.

'So a hat of mine isn't good enough for you.' Her mother rose from her chair.

Her father stepped between them. 'Yer'll tek the lass down to yon bazaar and she'll find her own hat, Lil. Yer don't have to part with yer own.' He winked at Lola.

'As long as she looks nice for once and not her usual bossups. She'll need to let a button out of that coat and all.'

*

Lola looked at herself in the hall mirror as they went out. The young woman who looked back was someone other. Another who wore a felt hat with the brim turned down at the front. A young woman. Oh. She would never stop being like Albert Goody now she had started.

She hadn't heard her parents singing before. She blushed. Her mother's voice was high, higher than anyone else's. Someone in front turned to look. Her father addressed the minister as "padre" on the way out, introducing her mother as his "dear wife", herself as his "lovely daughter" and himself as "Corporal Robertson".

The war's over, father. But she didn't say it. She just blushed.

'We might try that again, Lil,' her father said. 'A good chap, that padre.'

Her mother didn't answer.

Chapter III

'Yes, yes, I hear you.'

His father sat opposite him at the kitchen table. Stefan couldn't remember what he had said for his father to say so earnestly that he had heard him. He looked out of the window to the garden, where the sprouts were clustered on the stems and the feather-leaved carrots were ready for lifting.

'But the question is…' His father was beginning again, predictably, and about to approach the question, whatever it had been, from a different angle.

'We can give some of them to Mrs Beaumont,' Stefan said.

His father followed his gaze, past the pre-war curtains and as far as the rows of vegetables.

'Indeed, that is laudable,' he said. '*Caritas*, love of one's fellow pilgrims. There can be no higher calling. But it is not addressing the question.'

'Would you remind me of the question, please, father?'

His father laid down the pen. 'The question of the rest of your life, Stefan. Not a big question.'

What was it about his – er – life that his father, and Mr Beaumont before him, wished to know?

'You don't want to be a drifter,' his father said.

But probably he did. Probably he wanted just that.

'Having achieved nothing,' his father continued.

No one knew. Not his father, not his mother, not Mrs Beaumont, who must have known for a cipher of time that he had seen, and summoned her from the church on the morning of her husband's illness, but had now forgotten. No one knew. No one would ever know and he wouldn't tell them. His father, who would never know, would consider such reticence in anyone else to be humility. But Stefan knew differently. It was pride. Why should he tell them? Why should he tell anyone? Why should he tell? He hadn't told anyone anything in his twenty years. Except, possibly Bazal, who had no ears as far as he knew.

His father had picked up the pen again. Not that he was expecting anything. It remained poised, in his hand, just in case anything in the way of comprehension passed between them.

'The best pen I ever had,' his father said. 'Do you remember?'

Stefan did. One day, after the war ended, he took a small packet marked "fragile" to the post office and sent it to a girl who lived on the border of Nottinghamshire, who had mended a stranger's sock, whose father had saved that same stranger from abuse for being an objector. A stranger.

'Good.'

'Don't, Paul.' His mother had come into the room. 'This is your own son, darling, not a student who won't do his sums.'

'Forgive me, Stefan.' His father laid down the pen again.

'If you would remind me of the question again, please, father.' But he remembered the question well enough.

His father had dipped the pen into the ink and written the figure "1", with a perfect circle around it. He wrote "2" underneath it, and circled that.

'We've done this before, father.'

'Forgive me, Stefan.' His father put a line through the two numerals and laid down the pen.

'Darling, he's a grown man,' his mother said. 'He's not a wayward child.'

His father wrote down "not a wayward child" and underlined it.

'What did you value in your employment with Mr Beaumont, dear?' his mother said.

'Value?'

'Your mother means something like cherish, don't you, sweetheart?' his father said.

Stefan shrugged. 'They're not the same thing,' he said. 'Value? Cherish? They're not the same thing, father.'

'The nature of the work, the society of the other chaps, a sense of fulfilment?' His father persisted. 'None of the aforesaid,' he added, then, 'what is happening with the other chaps?'

'I don't know. I presume they're in the same boat. I'll find something, father.'

'Sure you will,' his father said.

His mother frowned. 'Darling, not that expression. Stefan doesn't know what's happening with the others. The firm is closed. What your father is trying to say to you, dear, is that you might not find the work of your choice.'

His father hadn't said any such thing and he himself hadn't expressed an opinion as to his choice of work because he didn't have a choice.

'Your father and I,' his mother continued, 'have had to compromise. Our name, and by extension your name, Stefan, is regarded with suspicion because we were objectors. We are both doing work no one else would willingly do. You might have to do the same, merely because your name is Czerniak. Are you listening? You give every appearance of looking out of the window.'

'I am listening and looking out of the window at the same time, mother.'

Pip had appeared in the garden next door, then Jean. Pip lit a cigarette for Jean, and, giving her his to hold, reached over the fence to catch Bazal, who was making another bid for the vegetables. He could see Pip giving Bazal a talking to. He could see the wind ruffling the leaves of the trees. He could see Jean's laugh. He could see all the silent sounds outside, the gramophone as Mrs Beaumont put on *The Blue Danube* for her husband, the *Vlatava* of Bedrich Smetana, from its first note in the city of Prague to its long journey out into the peaceful fields of the foreign land. He could hear his mother, her reasonable counterpoint continuing somewhere below the melody.

'I don't know if you realise how…' she hesitated, searching for words…'how kind, how courageous Mr Beaumont was in giving you employment, dear, and how sensitive he was in placing you on the civilian side of the business.'

Stefan did realise. And he hadn't said thank you. It was too late now. How could he say such a word, in all its complexity, to Mr Beaumont as he was now, with only the half of him present, and that half forever weeping salt tears. The *Vlatava* of Smetana came to an end.

'I didn't say thank you.'

His parents exchanged glances. By some strange alchemy, the surface of the kitchen table was all at once covered with the newspaper, open at the situations vacant.

'You offered your gratitude every time you got on the train at Gant's Hill and set off for work.' His father was showing signs of becoming embarrassing.

'I'll look at the paper upstairs,' Stefan said.

His parents exchanged glances again. Outside, and next door, Pip and Jean were walking round the garden, smoking. Jean was wearing a pinafore. Pip's left arm hung awkwardly by his side. They stopped walking. Pip appeared to be talking, his cigarette still between his lips. Jean shook her head. A gust of wind showered them with a handful of dry leaves.

'The alternative, of course, is to look at the paper right now and here in the kitchen. But your parents will leave you to it if you prefer,' his father said.

'Don't darling, please,' his mother said. 'Your father and I have been looking as well, Stefan, dear. We are always looking. Don't think I like your father breathing in that dust every day.'

'Nor that I like your beautiful mother to be in the laundry,' his father said, then, casually, 'ever heard of this chap Aveling?' He slid the paper across to Stefan.

On the page facing the situations vacant there was a small paragraph. "Public Order Offence. Bound over to keep the peace". He slid the paper back to his father.

'Gets on at Gant's Hill,' his father said. 'City type.'

Stefan looked at the paragraph again, upside down and read the date of the offence. Aveling.

'Aveling,' he said out loud. 'Do you know him, dad?'

'Stefan doesn't need to know, darling,' his mother said.

But he did. He needed to know. 'Where is he now? Aveling?'

'At large,' his father said.

'What's a public order offence?'

'He doesn't need to know, darling,' his mother said again, then, unexpectedly, 'your father is a good man, Stefan, and doesn't speak ill of anyone. He's only warning you. Mr Aveling is well known to travellers on the underground. He likes to get people into trouble. Cast your eye over the situations vacant we have considered for ourselves and give us your opinion, then we will see what there is that you might apply for.

'What kind of trouble?'

There was no end to the glances passing between his parents. He knew well what kind of trouble, the kind of trouble their innate tact wouldn't allow them to speak of. And, for himself, he hadn't the words, not even after three years working with the other chaps in the office, where every ribald comment snapped into silence the moment he walked in. What had they thought of him? The answer to the question, which he hadn't asked himself before, suddenly presented itself. A strange chap. What else with a name like that and an old man who had like as not blown up railway lines in France during the war?

'Implicating people in acts of impropriety of one kind or another,' his father said.

Stefan felt himself blushing. His father looked away. Another glance passed between his parents.

'You are going for an instructor in liberal studies then, dad.'

'How did you know that?'

'I can read it upside down.'

'And since you can read upside down...' His father passed him a pencil, and he drew an ellipse around one of the many advertisements beginning "Clerk Wanted". He didn't read further. Anything to divert his parents from the meaning of implications of impropriety. The river Vlatava once more came to the end of its journey. He tried to play it backwards, but it foundered and stumbled, climbing over stones and slipping back. A mortifying thought was jostling with the retrograde trajectory of the notes: his parents knew about the encounter on the train, and a natural kindness prevented their mentioning it.

His mother had gone to the sideboard drawer for the writing paper. His father was straightening the nib of his pen. They were going to write letters of application for jobs they knew nothing about. But it didn't matter. The name Czerniak would take care of that. "Clerk Wanted"...there were no details, only a box number to apply to.

Pip and Jean were at the door. He could see their shapes on the frosted glass, equal in height, Jean with a hat over her frizz of hair, Pip's hair laid flat and punishingly parted at the side. Then they were inside, Pip in his gabardine belted in the middle and Jean in her brown coat.

'We've come to say good-bye, Stefan,' she said. 'We're going on the one fifteen from King's Cross. May we have a word with you before we go?'

'You'll want mum and dad.'

'No, you Stefan, but of course we've come to say good-bye to your dear parents as well.'

Pip was grappling with an object wrapped clumsily in a blanket.

Stefan took them to the kitchen. 'It's warmer in here,' he said. 'I'll get mum and dad.' They were in the garden talking to Mrs Beaumont over the fence. 'I'm sorry you're going.'

'We'll be back,' said Pip. 'Dad's got a soft spot for Jean. He snaps out of it when she's there. I reckon he could try a bit harder for mum, but he doesn't, and there you are. It's a crying shame.'

'He can't help it,' said Jean. 'It's part of the illness.'

The object slipped out of the blanket and fell to the floor. Pip said damn. Then, 'But how are matters with you, old chap? Any sign of you know what on the horizon?'

'He means a situation,' said Jean.

Stefan indicated to the newspaper, folded and lying on the dresser.

'Hopeful? May we see, old chap?' Pip reached behind him for the newspaper. 'Which one?'

'Office clerk or something. Doesn't say much.'

Pip laid the paper on the table. 'So far so good. But a chap needs to know a bit more. What does the firm deal in, for instance?'

'How can I find out?'

'Answer is, you can't,' Pip said. 'Just tread carefully, old chap. Don't know who runs the joint either.'

'Would the newspaper know?'

'Doubt it, old chap. As long as the fellow's paid for the notice to go in, they don't ask questions. Anyway, the best of British.'

'Take no notice, Stefan,' Jean said. 'Pip's upset about Ken. So are we all. We wish you the best of luck. Tell him, Pip.'

'The best of luck, old chap,' said Pip.'

'You've said that already,' said Jean. 'I meant the other.'

'Oh that.' Pip disappeared under the table and came up with the fallen object, wrapped again in the army blanket.

'Any guesses?'

Stefan hadn't. 'Too big for Bazal,' he said. He suddenly felt cold. He didn't want to be given anything. Ever. Not in his whole life.

Jean had noticed. 'We're asking a very big favour. You can say no if you like.' She undid the blanket and laid the violin case on the table.

'Can't play it now, old chap,' Pip said. 'Never could. It was mum's idea.' Suddenly, he and Jean were convulsed with helpless laughter, which stopped as soon as it started. 'Hated the thing. Off the hook now, of course, with this confounded shoulder.' Pip made a show of lifting his left arm. 'Only get it half way, you see. Not even that.'

'You'd be looking after it,' Jean said. 'We know it's a big thing to ask. It's been in the loft how long, Pip? Since 1939?' She ran her finger through the grey blush of damp on the lid.

'You seen one of these fellows before, old chap?' Pip flicked the latch and lifted the violin out, laying it by the side of the case on the table. 'Doesn't like changes of temperature. You seen one before?'

Your parents took us to a promenade concert once. But he didn't say it. It was the time Jean and Pip went back early because Jean wasn't getting on with Mrs Beaumont.

'Not at close quarters,' he said.

Pip detached a bow from the ceiling of the case and tightened it. He lifted the violin and swept the bow across an outside string. 'That's G, old chap, right down in your boots. D, A and E the squeaky one. You look bemused, old chap.'

'You can lift your arm, Pip.'

'Ah, yes, old chap, but excruciating to do it. Broke the old acromion, you see. Tricky one to mend.'

'Would you play something?'

Pip shrugged off his coat, stood up and played the beginning of *The Blue Danube*.

'He could never have been a concert violinist because he sticks his tongue out when he plays,' said Jean. Suddenly, she was helpless with laughter again, until the laughter turned to tears and she was searching in her bag for a handkerchief.

'Now your turn, old chap,' Pip said. Then, to Jean, 'Shall we dance?'

Jean stood up and took off her coat, arranging it on the back of a chair.

'I can't. I've never played one before.'

'Simple, old chap. Violin on the left. Bow on the right. Can't go wrong.'

'The A's flat, Pip.'

'Is it? Don't usually bother over much about things like that, old chap. Here.' Pip adjusted the A string. 'Try that. Suit you?'

Stefan plucked the string. 'More or less.'

'Want to try the others?'

'They're all right.'

'Know where the notes are?'

'I think so.'

'Know how to do a sharp?'

'Probably.'

'Good chap. Off you go.'

'Which note do I start on, Pip?'

Pip and Jean were already poised to begin the dance.

'Any one you like, old chap. Lower rather than higher. Take it steady at first.'

The Blue Danube played to the end and began again. And again. And again. Pip and Jean continued to go round, circling the table, faltering when the music faltered, stopping at the end of the tune and going round the other way when it started again. At the edge of his field of vision, Stefan saw that other dancers had joined them, people he hadn't seen before, an elegant man in worn out clothes and a beautiful woman wearing an apron. He closed his eyes and continued playing, the same tune, over and over again. When he opened his eyes, they would have gone, these unsettling others with their own lives and their own dance. Still he heard them, not one couple but two; he could hear the thinness of the soles of Pip's shoes, and the thickness of the other dancer's, who was a working man. He could hear the difficult breath of the working man, becoming more so with each successive circle of the room. He stopped playing and opened his eyes.

They hadn't gone. They had merely turned to stone, Jean and Pip and his mother and father, poised, ready to take the next step.

He put the violin back in its case. The dancers came back to themselves, gradually, releasing one another, standing in a line, facing him. Then Jean started to clap, followed by Pip and then his parents, undemonstratively, like the sound of raindrops falling on Bazal's shell.

He had to get away. His eyes darted around the suddenly unfamiliar room, looking for the door, but Pip had placed himself in front of it, and was saying something, 'Hey, not so fast, old chap. You're a maestro.' His mother was filling the kettle and his father was straightening the mat. Jean was laughing and crying. He flew up to the attic room, taking the stairs two at a time.

A long way below, in words he couldn't hear, Pip was saying, 'Now look what we've done.'

Chapter IV

Lola Robertson looked over the fence and found herself face to face with someone else's garden. It was a rectangular garden with a rectangular lawn and a rectangular border of flowerbeds. At the far end was a rockery: stones placed at mathematical intervals interlaced sparsely with embarrassed spikes of withered plants. A washing line went down the middle of the garden, tethered to a clothes post at one end and the back of the house at the other. Underneath the washing line there was a path, so directly underneath it that it would have been difficult to hang out the washing without leaning back.

There were late marigolds, shining ellipses of orange on the dark rain-soaked earth. Maybe they were accidental. Maybe they weren't. Maybe there was some purpose in them, to suggest to the people who lived next door to Salisbury House, with their colourless geometries, that life could be random and dazzling. Lola asked herself the amazing question. Could it? But she had forgotten the question before she had time for an answer.

The people were out. Or maybe they weren't out. The back door was fastened; all the windows were closed, and the curtains tidily and equally arranged.

Her parents were still inside, looking round, her father still nodding from time to time and making small agreeable comments, her mother looking straight ahead, tight-lipped and straight-backed.

'Lola, come in please.' Her mother's voice was at the back door. 'What do you think you're doing, making an exhibition of yourself, a great girl like you.'

Lola didn't answer. She would always be a great girl, being told by her mother to let out the buttons of her coat, even when she was thirty, and old. Her mind went back to the people she had seen coming out of the Methodist chapel on VJ Day, who were undoubtedly old but nevertheless getting married and emerging into a cheering crowd and hats dancing in the air like snowflakes.

'We didn't know where you'd gone,' her mother said.

'I was in the garden. I thought you were talking privately.' She thought her parents had mislaid the fact that she existed.

'Mrs Crawford is asking for you.'

'Me? Why?' Lola knew why. She was to be the domestic assistant.

She followed Mrs Crawford up the stairs to the second floor and along the landing to the last door. Mrs Crawford put the key in the lock, turning it this way and that without success.

'Mr Robertson, if you please,' she shouted down over the bannister railing.

Her father appeared out of nowhere and said, 'Allow me,' and then, 'Graphite, works wonders with a tricky lock. Pencil sharpenings to you and me, Mrs Crawford.' He stood back to let her into the room. Lola followed.

The room, oddly, faced the front. She could see, far below, the street and its traffic. The neighbour came home, a man in a gabardine belted in the middle. He went inside and came out with a black and white spaniel on a lead, and vanished round the corner.

Mrs Crawford was talking to her. 'Do you like the room, dear?'

'Oh yes.' She hadn't looked at it.

'You can make it your own, dear,' Mrs Crawford said. 'Your father will build a nice fire in the grate. Maybe you can run up some curtains yourself.'

The room was empty except for a bed, a dressing table, a hard chair and an armchair. The blackout curtains were still there, pulled back and hooked onto a nail. Dead flies had congregated on the windowsill. A thick grey tide mark circled the basin. It smelt strange. There would be bed bugs.

'It's lovely.'

'Of course, we'll strip the bed, dear. The lav's at the end if you don't mind sharing with the boys. Otherwise you can use your parents' bathroom.'

So it was all settled. Lola was aware of her parents conversing in low tones on the landing. She couldn't ask her question. They would hear. But she would have to ask. She would have to ask the question that had been hammering at the back of her mind since she first saw the application form. Would the domestic help be paid? Or would she be in the same situation as she had been at school, and dependent on her mother's excursions to jumble sales?

Mrs Crawford had closed the door. 'Remuneration is at the discretion of your parents, dear,' she said. 'We didn't keep a domestic help, but that's what I believe would be the case.'

'Thank you.'

'Any more questions, dear?'

She hadn't asked any. Only thought them.

'No, I don't think so. Thank you.'

'Don't let the boys tease you, dear. They're harmless for the most part, but they're all in here for a reason.'

'Thank you.' Lola hadn't seen any boys. She hadn't seen anyone but Mr and Mrs Crawford. All at once, there was another question, one she couldn't ask Mrs Crawford. She could hardly ask herself, although there hadn't been a day recently that she hadn't considered it. Does Barry Green live here?

She looked at the other doors as on the way down. Which one?

As they went out, the next-door neighbour was returning with the black and white spaniel. Her father touched the hat he wasn't wearing, as if he were making a salute. She wanted to tell him, the war's over, father. But the neighbour was doing the same, touching an absent hat. Her father extended his hand. She waited for him to say Corporal Robertson, but he didn't.

'Cyril Robertson. My dear wife Lilian. My lovely daughter Lola. Shortly to be resident next to you.'

'Pip Beaumont. This fellow's called Watson.' Then, to Lola, 'Haven't we met before?'

Lola nodded. Her eyes swam. Suddenly, she was on the other side of the Market Square on a remarkable day in 1945 when everyone was hopeful. There had never been a day like that since. The celebrations had stopped and the peace had settled into a grey and uneventful road stretching endlessly ahead.

Her mother said, 'I don't think so. We're new to the area.'

'RAF?' her father said.

'Yes, old chap,' the neighbour said. 'Not now, of course. In civvy street now. And you?'

'Corporal, engineers.'

Lola felt herself blushing. The dog licked her hand. She'd forgotten its name already.

'The best of British, old chap. Need it, looking after the fellows next door, I reckon. Must scoot back to the grindstone and all that. Mrs Robertson. Miss Robertson.' The neighbour touched his absent hat again.

She would go to the library. A long grey silence stretching endlessly ahead punctuated from time to time by an exquisite new bone. Tibia, fibula, femur, radius, ulna, humerus.

'What did you say, Lola?' Her mother's voice was hot on her face, smelling of the lipstick and powder she had put on for the occasion. Lola looked round. Her father was right: her mother was pretty, prettier than she herself would ever be.

'I didn't say anything, mother'

'You thought something then.'

'That isn't the same as saying it.'

'What did you think?'

'That the war's over and father still says he's a corporal.'

Her mother stepped into her path, turned towards her and slapped her face. 'Don't you dare, do you hear me, don't you dare ever again ridicule your father or anyone else who fought in the war. Do you hear me? Your father will never walk properly again. There were thousands who didn't come back. Do you hear me?' Hectic red flares had appeared on her mother's forehead, chin and cheeks, and white flecks of spittle had gathered at the corners of her mouth. 'Do you hear me?'

She watched her mother go on ahead and slip her arm through her father's, until they were lost in the crowd of people going along Church Street back to work. She started to cry. A woman stopped and looked. 'What's up, duck?'

'Nothing. I'm all right. Thank you.' The woman went on. Watson. The name of the dog came back to her. The regimented garden next door. The empty room with bed bugs. Barry Green. A sense of shame.

Yer killt me ma, Lola Robertson. She didn't know where the words had come from. Only that they fell from the racing clouds like scuds of rain, that they rose up from every footstep on the wet flag stones, that they were written on the face of the world. Yer killt me ma. The encounter with her on the waste and the death of his mother would be indissolubly linked in Barry Green's mind. Without realising, she had been looking for him ever since she knew of Salisbury House, looking for a face she could hardly remember, adding height to him, deepening the voice she was sure to hear again. Yer killt me ma, Lola Robertson. She reached the library. Suddenly, it wasn't the same.

Miss O'Rourke was different as she disappeared behind the counter and came up with *Gray's Anatomy,* saying little and not meeting her eye. Everyone knew. Yer killt me ma.

Lola sat at a table on her own and took her notebook and pencil out of her pocket. She drew the femur, starting at the head, going down to the neck, the trochanters, the shaft, widening it at the lower end and drawing in the articular surfaces of the…but she couldn't remember what it was called, the expanded part of the bone. Her pencil rolled onto the floor and under another table. A young man with bad acne picked it up and gave it to her. Her mother's words came back to her. At least you don't have spots. She started to cry.

'At least you don't have spots,' the young man whispered. She didn't know if she had imagined it or not. He was now back at his own table, a set square and a protractor in front of him.

Not long today? Miss O'Rourke said nothing, but her forehead puckered into a question.

'I forgot what the lower end of the femur is called,' Lola said. 'I can't move on until I have remembered.'

'Try a word starting with C.' Miss O'Rourke had all at once come back to herself. 'No? Try a word beginning with CO. Still no? With an N and a D and a Y and an L and an E.'

'Thank you, Miss O'Rourke.' Thank you for helping me, she wanted to say. I'm sorry for your loss. But she didn't know what the loss was or if, indeed, Miss O'Rourke had suffered one. Condyle. She would remember the word now, its appearance on the page, even if she didn't know how to pronounce it.

The young man with acne stood back to let her go out first. He was taller than she was, but younger. The acne covered his face and the back of his neck, accentuated by the blush that had suddenly run through the pathways between the spots. She said, 'Thank you.' She hoped he wouldn't follow her, and was immediately ashamed of the thought, as if something inside her had shrivelled away. The words, as yet unheard, again assaulted her. Yer killt me ma. And the other words. I'm not really very nice.

'It's Miss Robertson, isn't it?'

She had almost bumped into the speaker, coming in as she was going out.

'Lola Robertson? Haunting the public library. That's what I like to see.'

The young man with acne was half way down Beal Street.

Mr Brumby hovered outside the library door, his hair lifted by the breeze, his hat in his hand. 'Have you time for a word, Miss Robertson?' Then, answering his own question, 'No, my dear. I can see you haven't. Well, perhaps another time, Miss Robertson.' He had one foot inside the revolving door, which was already beginning to turn as another reader went out.

'No, I mean yes.'

'You have two minutes?'

'Yes, sir.' She was the lumpy girl with shoes tied on with string, and he was the headmaster to whom she would have to divulge the fate of his letter, that it had been neatly cut up by her mother and turned into shopping lists, which were on the third shelf down in the kitchen cupboard alongside similar rectangles of bread paper for use in the privy.

'I do not wish to intrude on your present circumstances, Miss Robertson. You are a young lady and it is some time since you were a student at school.'

'Three years, sir.'

'Ah, yes. I had calculated about that.'

'I'm sorry about your letter, sir.'

'Letter?'

'After I had left school.'

'A formality only, Miss Robertson. Most parents' circumstances did not permit of students pursuing their studies. The war, you know.'

'Yes, sir.'

The young man was out of sight.

'I understand you are...well...a person who wishes their identity to remain confidential...told me...suffice to say that if at any time in the future you require a testimonial, you will ask me, my dear. Is that a promise?'

Lola said, 'Yes, sir,' and immediately wondered what she had promised. 'Thank you, Mr Brumby.'

But he had gone, caught up in the revolving door and set down in the high hushed library vestibule, aromatic with floor polish and the unwashed smell of the war her father thought wasn't over.

And suddenly they were moving, before Lola Robertson had asked the question; not that she ever would, she admitted to herself, because she hadn't the words to ask properly if she was going to be a person who worked for her parents in exchange for board and keep, wearing brassieres and knickers from the jumble sale; reliant upon her mother for such items because she was too embarrassed to attend herself.

Albert Goody stood by the fence watching. Lola could see him clearly from her window as she gathered her belongings. He stood with his mouth ajar, shamelessly..."gawping", her mother said. 'That child's gawping. His father needs to tell him.' Albert Goody wiped the back of his hand across his nose. Lola waved. He didn't wave back. She went down.

'What's them things, Lola Robertson?'

'What things?'

'Them things out yonder. Yer house on fire?'

'We're moving, Albert Goody.'

'Yer flitting?'

'Yes.'

'Oh.'

'May I say good-bye to your mother?'

'Depends.'

'On what?'

'Dunno.'

'I'll miss you, Albert Goody.'

'Oh.'

'May I say good-bye to your mam?'

'Sez she's not in, that's what she sez.'

'Then you can say goodbye for me. Will you do that, Albert?' Lola could see Alison Goody moving around inside the room. At the same time, she could hear her mother's voice calling her. Alison Goody was closing her curtains.

She went back home. 'I've finished, mother,' she said. And she had. Her possessions, the ones she wasn't wearing, lay on the bed: her summer skirt, her blouse, her dress and her nightie, two pairs of stockings, two pairs of knickers and her spare brassiere. Her other vest. Her workbox and her pencil case. Her notebook. Her comb and face flannel and toothbrush. A hair slide. A packet of sanitary towels. A bar of green soap. A tin of dentifrice. Her worldly possessions. She rolled the knickers and brassiere inside the summer skirt and put them in the bottom of one of the brown carrier bags, then the sanitary towels wrapped in her dress. Then the workbox, pushing it down so that all her intimacies were trapped underneath. The rest of her world went into the other bag and she was ready.

Her father had on his army beret and was helping another man to lift a tea chest onto the back of a lorry, hoisting it over the tailgate and lowering it down the other side. Hadn't he been required to hand his beret in at the end of the war? He saluted the other man and indicated to the furniture standing in front of the house: a utility wardrobe, a utility dressing table with the mirror removed, a private shape covered with a dustsheet which would be the utility bed. Upright chairs. A table.

Lola carried her two bags down the stairs.

'My beautiful daughter,' her father said, without introducing the other man to her. She shook hands.

112

'Bob Gray,' he said. 'Pleased to meet you, Miss Robertson.'

Gray like Henry? That's my other profession. But she didn't say it and neither did he. His shirt sleeves were rolled up to the elbows, displaying a tattoo of a woman. She looked away, to where the chairs stood stacked in twos. Her father was tying them, seat to seat, with string. Bob Gray had rolled his sleeves down and the cuffs were flapping at the wrists.

Her mother came out with her arms full of bed linen, thinning and tired. Then the pillows, with stained ticking. Army blankets. Blackout curtains. All this in broad daylight with the neighbours looking on. Except that no one was, only Albert Goody with his mouth open and his nose running. They were all the same, worn out and dirty, turning sides into middles, scrubbing to no effect. Two burnt saucepans, one inside the other. Cutlery. Crockery.

Her father slid threepence into her hand while her mother was occupied with her own bag of possessions. 'Give it to the lad,' he said.

But Albert Goody didn't want it. He shook his head. 'Me ma gonna swipe me for tekking it.' Her father wasn't looking. She released the bright coin into the gutter of Margaret Drive.

And at the end of the afternoon, Lola Robertson hung her coat and her dress on the peg behind the door of her new room, set out her brush and comb on the dressing table, and stowed her folded knickers and spare brassiere in the drawer. She shook out her nightie and laid it on the bed. She hung her bag on the back of the chair.

She looked out of the window into the street below, to where men were cycling home from work. To where the neighbour with the regimented garden was arriving at his gate with a woman, whose frizz of hair escaped from under her hat like a halo. Lola waved. They waved back. They were called Pip and Jean, and the dog was called Watson.

At the same time, a young man with bad acne turned in at the driveway of Salisbury House, and went around the back. Presently, she heard his footsteps coming up the wooden stairs, entering the long landing and going into a room nearby.

Chapter V

'Oh, but you must tell Ken, dear. He'll be so pleased.' Mrs Beaumont was in his mother's place, her hands folded on the table.

Stefan Czerniak hadn't told Ken Beaumont anything for a long time. Nothing more than what was happening on the duck pond in Congreve Park. As if Ken were a child.

'He'll understand you, dear,' Mrs Beaumont went on. 'Would you like me to tell him? I think he ought to know.' Her face crumpled. 'Even if he doesn't quite take it all in, he'll know it's good news. I'll prepare him, dear. When the speech lady's finished, you know. I'm not convinced that's doing him much good either, but it seems to amuse him.'

'You'll have a cup of tea, Freda?' His father laid a hand over Mrs Beaumont's. It was awful. Embarrassing. How could his father, who was otherwise, and more or less, straightforward, be so embarrassing?

'I'll go round now.'

'Sure,' his father said. Then, to Mrs Beaumont, 'It's a good job Ruth isn't here. She doesn't take kindly to derelictions of the English language.'

Mrs Beaumont smiled a wan smile. 'Dear Ruth. Let yourself in Stefan, dear. Did I mention that the lady might still be there?' She would extract her hands as soon as he had gone and tuck them firmly in her pocket.

Mr Beaumont was seated in his bath chair at the table, gazing at a card bearing a line drawing of a tree, looking perplexed. A slate by the side of it was covered in hieroglyphics.

'You don't have to say what kind it is, only what it is in general.'

He looked up as Stefan went in and shrugged the shoulder that would still shrug.

'Maybe we should call it a day as your visitor has arrived, Mr Beaumont. We'll come back to that picture next time, shall we?'

Couldn't he write it down? Stefan looked at the slate. He didn't say anything.

'Of course, he could try to write something with his good hand, but that's not the point.' The speech lady, who was called Veronica, had read his mind. 'I need him to say it.'

Maybe Mr Beaumont thinks it's a trick question. There must be more to it than just a tree. Stefan didn't say that either. He helped Veronica on with her coat. He said thank you. He was becoming embarrassing, like his father. It was probably infectious.

'It looks easy, but it isn't.' The speech lady had read his mind again.

'I'm sorry,' he said. 'I'm sorry I said that.'

'You didn't say anything.'

No, he supposed not. 'Is it all right to…'

'Of course it is.' And she was gone, without knowing what it was he was going to tell Mr Beaumont.

'I've been asked for an interview, Mr Beaumont,' he said. 'It's a clerical post.' He unfolded the letter and placed it on the table, where the drawing of the tree had been. He put Mr Beaumont's spectacles straight. Mr Beaumont pitched forwards so that his eyes were inches from the script. 'Gish us a clue,' he said.

'Tree,' Stefan said. 'She didn't need the kind of tree or the Latin name for it.'

Mr Beaumont chuckled.

'I've been asked for an interview,' Stefan said again. 'For a clerical position.'

'Mayshorthaypayu, s'all.'

'He's saying make sure they pay you, that's all. Has Veronica gone?'

'Yes.'

'Any progress?' Mrs Beaumont was standing behind her husband's chair, mouthing the words.

'I think so.'

'Of course, he can talk perfectly well,' (out loud now). 'It's just that no one else understands him. Isn't that so, Ken?'

'Yesh.' Mr Beaumont chuckled. 'Gishabray.'

'And to have someone here gives me a break. We're not under any illusions that there will be a dramatic improvement. We're not auditioning for the Old Vic, are we, Ken? Now, Stefan, dear, tell us more about your job interview. Where is it?'

'Wickham Place.'

Mr Beaumont's eyebrow shot up. 'Nerdavit.'

'Ken says he's never heard of it, but don't let that put you off, dear. Do you know what the firm deals in?'

'No, it doesn't say.'

A small explosive sound came from the region of Mr Beaumont's larynx.

'Then that's all the more reason for your attending, to find out,' Mrs Beaumont said. 'We wish you the best, dear. What does your father say?'

Not much, only that the name Czerniak in itself would be an inhibition. A cold wind threw gusts of rain into his face like handfuls of gravel, sent his tie flying over his shoulder and plastered his trouser legs to his shins. He caught sight of himself in a shop window, his father in all but the beret. And the red scarf and the long black coat from which he shook fibres of white dust onto the chequered path before entering the house.

The same, also, in a minor detail which he had all but forgotten. A hole had opened in the heel of his left sock. He stopped, took off his shoe and turned the sock round so that the heel of it was at the front, pulling up the tongue of the shoe to cover it.

Still reflected in the glass of the window was an earlier incarnation of Stefan Czerniak, going to the post with a packet in his hand. A thimble from his mother for an unknown girl who lived on the border of Nottinghamshire, who had mended his father's sock, whose family lived – he tried to remember his father's expression – "in the most reduced circumstances". The lingering smell of the war: green soap and sweat and boiled cabbage. Did they all smell like that? 'Probably,' his father had said.

Inside the shop, someone pulled up the blind and his likeness melted into a display of hardware. Somewhere the sun came out, not in the east end of the city, where he had been searching for Wickham Place for some time, but on a day three years earlier where he had stood waiting with a packet marked "fragile" destined for a girl called Lola Robertson, who lived her difficult life blessed with the gifts of the spirit, whatever they might be, and didn't realise.

He went into the hardware shop and asked at the counter. 'Could you direct me to…'

'Wholesale only, sorry sir. What was that you said?'

'Could you direct me to Wickham Place, please?'

The shopkeeper went through a curtain behind the counter and shouted upstairs. 'Beryl? Wickham Place? Do we know it?' He came back. 'Don't know it, sir. Sorry.'

'Thank you. Do you know where I might ask, please?'

The shopkeeper placed his hands on the counter. 'Truth is, sir, we get a lot of young fellows like yourself dropping by. We don't know what's what at Wickham Place, and the less we know, the better, if you take my meaning. I would advise you likewise, sir.' He leaned forwards. 'You one of them, by any chance?'

And before Stefan Czerniak could ask the meaning of "them" the answer came to him, suddenly and in writing: CONSHY, the luminous word, undimmed with the passing of the years; having lost none of its opprobrium, and obscene to the extent that everyone stepped over it on their journey up Golen Avenue, or crossed to the other side.

He looked the shopkeeper in the eye.

'Yes, I'm one of them, sir.'

The words hung on the grey air between them.

'One of them, are you?'

'Yes, I am.'

'Then you'll need first right and third left, sir. Beryl,' (calling through the curtain) 'take the gentleman off the premises, would you?'

'I can let myself out, thank you, sir.'

'Very well. Make sure you're off my premises, sir. First right, third left you want. No business of mine.'

Stefan encountered himself once again in the window of 6 Wickham Place, as if he were an unpleasant acquaintance he was trying to avoid. The blackout curtains were drawn. He was ten minutes early: a foreign looking chap with the heel of his sock at the front and his tie askew. He straightened his tie in the glass.

Someone passing said, 'Beauty parlour now, is it? Could be you've come to the right place. You never know your luck.'

The door had no plaque to designate what the business might be, or by whom it was managed. He rang the bell. He heard footsteps on the stairs and a key being fitted into the lock on the other side.

The door opened and closed again. He could hear the key turning and the footsteps going back upstairs. He rang again. And again. The curtain opened a crack and closed.

The final chords of *Vlatava* were crushed under a passing wheel. He tried to recover them, starting from the end of the piece and travelling backwards, but they had gone, utterly. He went back to the beginning. Which note shall I start on? His own words came back to him. Any note. You can start wherever you like. Lower rather than higher. But there were no notes. Something seemed to have vanished. Something for which he didn't have a word, unless it was time.

He tried to recover the time, from leaving the underground at Mile End station. Looking at street names. Asking people. Being met with incomprehension. A foreign looking chap with his tie over his shoulder, hatless, asking for an address no one had heard of. No, sir, sorry. They had lived here all their lives. They delivered milk, letters, coal. They would have known if there was such a place, but there wasn't.

'Sure you're in the right London, sir?'

'You know what they say, ask a policeman. Ha.'

Until he found himself back again at Mile End station and could hear the branches of a tree rattling in the wind, inland gulls screaming, and the latest being shouted from the news stand. Fragments came back, inconsequentially: a hole in the heel of his sock, a girl who lived on the borders of Nottinghamshire, who was called Lola Robertson and was labelled fragile, who came from a family blessed with the gifts of the spirit, though they didn't know it. A hardware shop.

Wholesale only sir, sorry. One of them, are you?

Yes, I am.

'You didn't know what the chap was asking,' his father said.

'Don't, Paul,' his mother said. 'The question was put to Stefan in an intimidating way, presupposing the answer yes.'

'Sweetheart, I'm only trying to clarify the situation,' his father said.

'No, you're trying to confuse him, darling. The event has taken place and it can't be changed now. It isn't helpful to go back and think what might have been done. Stefan answered yes because he thought the shopkeeper was referring to conscientious objection, which has been his main experience and for which he has been vilified in the past. His answer was rational and courageous. He could certainly have asked at that point what was meant, but the shopkeeper's hostile attitude wasn't conducive to such a question.'

'OK, you win,' his father said. His face was suddenly grey.

'I do wish you wouldn't use that expression, darling. Fetch your father a glass of water, Stefan, dear. He isn't well.'

'I'll fetch it myself, sweetheart.' His father tried to stand and slumped back into his chair.

'What's the matter with him?' Stefan mouthed the words to his mother as he came back with the water.

'Your father can't get his breath. I don't know what the matter is, but I suspect that working in all that dust doesn't help. You might not have noticed too much but we're awake most nights with it.'

Stefan blushed. He had no wish to hear about his parents' nights. It was awful. Embarrassing.

'Everyone breathed in dust during the war, mother,'

'This is different dust. It's asbestos. It reduces to tiny particles which infiltrate the air passages.'

'Has father applied for that other…?' They were talking about his father as if he wasn't there.

'That wasn't real, dear. Your father only mentioned it to encourage you to apply for something.'

'Could it be tuberculosis?' He mouthed the words.

His mother shook her head. 'No,' she said. 'He hasn't applied yet, so he won't have heard anything.'

'OK…' his father began.

'I'll forgive you this once,' his mother said.

'…so we left you in the wholesale hardware establishment, with the shopkeeper asking you if you were "one of them" to which you answered in the affirmative, and your mother has explained why.' The colour had returned to his father's face. And the irony to his voice. Stefan supposed it was irony.

'I've never had the privilege, father.'

'What did you say?'

'Nothing.' Of being a student of mathematics of Professor Czerniak. It would have been awful.

'What were you thinking?'

'Then the keeper of the wholesale hardware business called upstairs for a lady called Beryl to show me off the premises, but I said I would let myself out. Something like that.'

'Then?'

'I was standing in front of a door in Wickham Place ringing the bell. Someone came down and opened the door, then went back upstairs. The person came down several more times and went back, and then the curtain opened.' It was all so stupid. He couldn't say to his parents that the whole episode was accompanied by a desolating sense of loss, of the *Vlatava* of Smetana, which had gone completely from him, and of something else, for which he couldn't find the word. Something more than just time.

'Did you sign anything?' His father was leaning back in his chair.

I had a hole in my sock. No, he wouldn't say that.

'Did you sign anything?'

'I wasn't admitted to the building, father. I couldn't sign anything.'

IIis father said nothing.

'I considered going back to the hardware shop, but thought better of it…' as if he had rehearsed what he was going to say to his father at the inevitable interrogation; which he had, word by word, on the underground journey back to Gant's Hill.

The *Vlatava* of Bedrich Smetana did not return. Or *The Blue Danube* of Johann Strauss. Or anything else that might have passed as life in the world, which itself was like nothing so much as the long grey stretch of Golen Avenue, with the word CONSHY at one end and Congreve Park at the other, windswept and covered with the blackened leaves of a brooding winter.

Then two letters came, one a notice of national service, the other addressed to Mr Gurniak. Stefan turned it over. There was an invisible smudge of scent as if the envelope hadn't sealed and the sender had tried again, leaving a vestige of lipstick there. The "a" of the addressee was faint, and the capital "G" wavered above the line.

He opened it. He read the contents, tore the letter into pieces and consigned it to the space under the floorboard.

Chapter VI

Lola Robertson sat in the second pew of the Methodist chapel, wedged between her parents, so tightly that her upper arms were pinned against her mother's on her left and her father's on her right; her mother's spare and indefinite under her coat, her father's radiating an unsettling heat under an army surplus jacket. She blushed. The words had not gone away, "The war's over, father". But not for him. He insisted on addressing the Methodist minister as padre. He had – and the thought lingered like distant lightning at the dark periphery of her mind – fallen into a second regimental life similar to his first. When the service was finished and when they were back at Salisbury House, he would conduct the same in the dining room. He was even now leaning forwards, concentrating on the sermon, and, she had no doubt, memorising sentences of it, masticating them, for delivery in a simpler form to the residents of Salisbury House.

She wished he wouldn't.

She wished that she wasn't seated so near the front, that she wasn't suffocated by the close proximity of her parents on either side.

She wished that her head felt less uncomfortable, surmounted as it was by a round felt hat of the choosing of her mother, with her lank premenstrual hair flattened underneath and her bad thoughts so crowded together that she had a simmering headache. Her bad thoughts multiplied throughout the service, hammering at the frontal bone with redoubled ferocity.

She wished, when the service came to an end, that she would not still be between her parents, walking back to Salisbury House, feeling the sharp elbow and hearing the *sotto voce* of her mother. How many times do I have to tell you to take your hands out of your pockets, Lola? She wished away the forthcoming Sunday dinner with its boiled cabbage and its thin etiquettes as the residents took their places at the table, her father carving, saying the grace. For what we are about to receive may the Lord make us truly thankful; her mother passing down the plates; and she herself, with the bib of her apron so tight across her chest that she could feel the sideways glances of the young men even before she entered the room with the tureens of vegetables.

She wished away Salisbury House itself, which had scraped steadily at her independence, as placidly and routinely as she scraped the leavings of gristle and greens from the Sunday plates into the bin for the weekly pig farmer to collect.

She felt a sudden hot flood in a part of her she now knew by its proper name but would not repeat, even in the vexed secrecy of her mind. For the shame of it, for the fact that it came from the mild and scholarly writings of Henry Gray, who nursed his brother (or was it his nephew or his godson?) to the detriment of his own health. For the fact that Miss O'Rourke might conceivably know, when she returned the Anatomy to the counter, which pages had been recently visited...

Her mother was nudging her, 'Stand up, Lola.'

"What a friend we have in Jesus". She wished her father would sing less...obtrusively, that he wouldn't stand to attention, that he wouldn't linger over the final line so that his voice was the only one still alive. "Take it to the Lord in prayer". Her mother and father either side of her sat down, occupying more room than they had before the hymn, and she squeezed between them, aware of the too intimate warmth of their bodies, their legs and arms on either side. She was as she had always been, between them, separating them from each other, saving her father from her mother's judgement, saving her mother from her father's...she hadn't a word for it.

Nor did she have a word for what it was like as she went each day into the rooms of the residents, into the stale cubes of air recently vacated, opening windows, emptying bins, changing sheets top to bottom every two weeks, replacing whatever magazines she found under the pillows. Folding inwards the odours of sheets and pillowcases and carrying them down to the copper in the scullery. Take it to the Lord in prayer.

Nigel Chadwick, Humphrey Bates, John Foottitt, Sidney Turner, Bernard Peacewick, Bob Fieldson, Leon Hasky, Alfred White.

'Lola Robertson?' She heard her own name clearly, spoken in a voice half way between male and female, half way between childhood and age. She looked around. Her father, for all that he was among the first to arrive at the chapel and had a habit of marching up to the front, was among the last to leave. There was no one else there, only Mr Parnell, moving the page markers to another part of the Bible.

'Lola Robertson!' Her name assaulted her from another part of the chapel. She looked behind her, meeting Mr Parnell's eyes as he glanced up from the book. He raised his eyebrows. Lola blushed. A burst of merriment followed her into the porch. The minister was shaking hands with her mother, and her father was offering his usual compliments on the sermon, calling the minister padre.

'And how is life at Salisbury House, Corporal Robertson?'

'Nothing to complain of, padre.'

'All quiet on the western front?'

'Wrong war, padre.'

'Yes, indeed, corporal. Any nearer to persuading the young chaps to attend Sunday service, sir?'

'Working on it, padre, working on it.'

'Lola Robertson!' The same indeterminate voice, followed by a snort of laughter.

'Any trouble, let me know, my dear.' The minister offered his hand. 'Remember now? Let me know.' She could see her parents going down the steps, her father putting on his hat, helping her mother. The minister was still talking to her. 'It's often easier to talk to someone outside the family.'

The laughter came again, from somewhere between her parents walking away from the chapel and herself still standing at the top of the steps. She wondered if the minister had heard it.

'If you have any trouble, remember, you know where we are.'

But she didn't. Apart from seeing the minister in the chapel, standing at the front, delivering a sermon she couldn't remember; or standing at the door.

'Good-bye, Miss Robertson.'

'Good-bye, sir.' She didn't know what else to call him. Not padre.

Not padre. I used to tell my father that the war was over until my mother became...furious. But Lola didn't say that. She followed her parents, walking too slowly to catch up with them; looking down at her hands, which were red and chapped, with half-moons of grime lodged under the nails. She probably smelt as well, of the sweat which the bar of green soap was powerless to eradicate, of the privy, of the daily grease swimming in the sink in the scullery, of the monthly. Most of all, of the monthly.

The next-door neighbours, whom she knew to be called Pip and Jean but whom she addressed as Mr and Mrs Beaumont, were at their gate talking to her mother and father. Lola hung back, pretending to tie her shoelace. To her, they were still the married people she had seen on the remarkable day when the war ended, still extraordinary, still, absurdly, inquisitive. She tied her shoelace again and again until she was aware of another person's shadow falling over her.

'Oh, Mrs Beaumont.'

'Do call me Jean, dear.'

Lola stood up. The spaniel Watson trundled towards her. 'He's beautiful.' She still couldn't call Mrs Beaumont Jean.

'He's too fat, Miss Robertson.'

'Oh!' The whisper of dismay escaped before Lola could call it back.

'You see, it's awful, isn't it?'

Lola blushed.

'You're Lola and I'm Jean. OK? You'll never guess where I picked up that dreadful expression. From Pip's parents' neighbour. He was a pacifist in the war and wears a long black coat and a beret. Quite gorgeous in a foreign kind of way. I never could pronounce his name properly.'

A sudden impression of golden rod and Michaelmas daisies overwhelmed Lola, and vanished as soon as it arrived, to be replaced by a sensation of a conversation in which she had had no part, until she handed back the sock she had been darning and found herself face to face with the recipient. "Quite gorgeous in a foreign kind of way". She had been too young to form that kind of opinion. He had worked some kind of alchemy on her parents which she had not understood either.

'I'm talking too much,' Jean said. 'You don't want to hear all that.'

But I do. Lola didn't say it.

Jean was still talking, filling her silence. 'Have you been to chapel?'

Lola glanced across to the front of Salisbury House, where her father was showing the garden to Mr Beaumont, whom she supposed she would now have to call Pip.

'Father calls the minister padre,' she said. 'He was in the army in the war.'

Jean Beaumont didn't laugh. She merely nodded. 'And what rank are you, Lola?'

'I haven't got one. I was at school when the war was on.' Her father and Mr Beaumont were still going round the garden, her father pointing out various plants with his walking stick.

'I mean now,' Jean said. 'Surely you're on the payroll?'

Lola didn't know what a payroll was. 'No, yes. I don't know. What's a payroll?'

'It means that you get paid for the work you do. Forgive me, Lola. I shouldn't have said that.' So Mr and Mrs Beaumont had realised. 'Don't misunderstand me, dear. Pip and I have the greatest respect for your dear parents. Mr and Mrs Crawford were getting too old and the young men were running them ragged.'

'I receive pocket money.' She still hadn't called Mrs Beaumont by her Christian name.

'Yes? What about…' Jean Beaumont's voice had sunk to a whisper.

'My mother buys me things like that.'

'Does she?'

Lola felt her face reddening. There was no end to her blushes. She had given away too much. Suddenly, a truth came to her, dazzlingly and undeniably. She was again bent over a complicated darning task on a day shortly after the end of the war while her parents chatted equably and peacefully with the stranger under their roof, a foreigner in a long dark coat, who addressed them respectfully, with admiration even, who had come to offer his gratitude. She felt hot tears gathering somewhere behind her eyelids. For a day that had gone. Just that. A day of golden rod and Michaelmas daisies that, all at once, she understood. Did she, she asked herself, regard her parents in that light, with respect and admiration? The answer came resoundingly back. No. She received back what she gave, a perfunctory and fragile coexistence. Jean had stopped talking.

'Lola, I'm sorry. What's the matter?'

'I'm not very nice to my mother and father.'

'Since when?'

'Always.'

'Well, you could have fooled me.'

Her father and Mr Beaumont showed signs of coming to an end of their tour of the front garden of Salisbury House.

'I'll have to go in,' Lola said.

'Yes, I suppose it's that time.' Jean looked at a watch she wasn't wearing and lowered her voice. 'Look, Lola, it's not our business but if you have any problems you can confide in us.' Then, louder,

'Of course, Watson would be most grateful for a walk. At least, I suppose he would. He hasn't expressed an opinion one way or the other, but he needs the exercise. Isn't that so, Pip?'

'Yes,' Mr Beaumont said. 'I agree. Without knowing what I'm agreeing to.'

'A walk, of course,' Jean said. 'You're agreeing on Watson's behalf. Do you take sugar, Lola?'

'Yes. No. Should I?'

'It's just that when we know you're coming we'll get some in. It's a shame to have a ration and not use it.'

Her mother had been inside for some time. She didn't look round when Lola came in.

'What was Mrs Beaumont saying?'

'Nothing much.'

Her mother turned round to face her. 'What was Mrs Beaumont saying, Lola?'

'That Watson might like a walk, that's all.' It wasn't all, of course, and her mother knew that as well as she did. She waited for the inevitable barbed comments, but none came.

'Lay the table, then. You're late enough as it is.'

Her mother had already placed the cloth, still folded, on the table and had set out handfuls of cutlery on the sideboard. Two forks had been separated from the rest.

Lola shook open the cloth and spread it on the table, trying to smooth away the diamond crease in the centre of it. The crease wouldn't go away. She would have to cover it with the cruet stand before her mother saw it.

'You'll take that cloth off for a start.' Her mother was in the room again.

'I was going to put the cruet over it, mother.'

'You'll take it off. How many times do I have to tell you to iron properly? There's another in the drawer. Get it out, will you, and let me see it. Put that one back in the wash. And those two forks. They're not properly done. There's a word for girls like you and it's bossops.'

How are you spelling that, mother? But Lola didn't say it. She didn't say anything. She could hear her mother outside the door talking to her father, talking about the diamond crease in the centre of the tablecloth. 'You know what that means.' Not addressing him by name.

The residents would presently arrive to take their places, filing in, heads down. All except Nigel Chadwick.

'Mr Chadwick's not here. Anyone seen him?' her father said. No one answered.

'Go up and knock on the door, please, Lola,' her mother said. But her father was already out of the room, taking the stairs as rapidly as his bad leg would allow.

He came back. 'Just resting,' he said. 'Be seated, gentlemen.' Because the young men were still standing.

Lola went into the scullery to dish up the vegetables. She could hear her father's sonorous prayer voice intoning the grace. 'For what we are about to receive, may the Lord make us truly thankful,' and the ragged "Amen" that followed. Then her father again. 'Now say it as if you mean it, gentlemen. 'Ah-men.' Her father again. 'What does the word mean?' No one answered.

Her father was carving, passing the plates one by one to her mother for a ladle of gravy. Her mother still wore her chapel hat, round and felt and dark green, with the brim turned down at the front. You haven't taken your hat off, mother. The war's over, father. You don't have to use the word padre.

Lola had her meal in the scullery. She could hear her father's voice, making stabs at conversation with the young men, and the high voice of Bernard Peacewick responding. She couldn't make out the words.

When the sound of cutlery fell silent, she went in again, collecting the plates. She let a knife clatter to the floor. She brought in the bread and butter pudding. While her mother served it she collected the cruet stand and refilled the jug of water. Bernard Peacewick continued to talk with her father, asking him about the previous day's match, which her father hadn't attended, but of which he gave a credible account. She had seen Bernard Peacewick soon after she arrived at Salisbury House, standing in the back yard, looking at the washing on the line.

'Where's Chadwick?'

'As I told you, resting,' her father said.

'Not when I last saw him,' said Bernard Peacewick.

'Is that so?'

Lola took what remained of the bread and butter pudding back into the scullery, the thin milky residue in the bottom of the bowl, the orphaned currants, the burnt edges of it. She finished it, despising herself, and sank the bowl in the rancid washing-up water. She could see in her mind's eye every inch of her body, white and rude, escaping from her brassiere, bulging over the top of her knickers, the hot menstrual smell rising from below. She heard the residents leave the dining room, the sound of their feet on the stairs, the doors of the rooms opening and closing. She heard her father talking to her mother in a low voice, a sharp interjection from her mother, her father's voice again; their footsteps on the stairs.

She followed them up, waiting on the landing. The door of Nigel Chadwick's room stood ajar, as did her own, oddly, because she was sure she had closed it.

She was still waiting, leaning on the bannister rail, when her parents came. They hadn't noticed her and were talking. Her father locked the door.

'She'll have to know, sooner or later.'

'What will I have to know?'

'That Mr Chadwick is unwell and is resting,' he mother said.

'Yer might as well tell the lass the truth, Lil,' her father said. 'The lad's gone awol.'

'Do you know anything about it, Lola?' her mother said. 'Did you have words?'

'Now, Lil, don't yer go blaming the lass,' her father said.

Lola went to her room. There was nothing out of place, nothing missing, no aroma to suggest that anyone other than herself had been in. From the window, she could see her father finish talking to Mr Beaumont, and then come in. She went down.

'Not much to be done about it on the Sabbath,' her father said.

Her mother sat at the dining table, still with her hat on. 'I told Lola not to leave diamonds,' she said.

'Fetch yer ma a cup of tea,' her father said. From the kitchen, Lola could hear her father. 'What are yer saying, Lil?'

'You know what a diamond in the centre of a cloth means. She left one today.'

'Try telling that to the perlice, Lil.'

'Police?'

'Yes, the perlice. If the chap isn't back by termorrer, it's the perlice. Beaumont says so. Chaps go awol from time ter time and it's the perlice.'

The next morning, Lola sat in the dining room opposite a policeman. His hat stood between them on the table, giving off a hair cream smell. He was writing down what she said in a notebook. She had a sudden wish to touch the hat, pick it up and see if it was heavy, what there was inside the tall crown.

'You can examine it later, miss,' the policeman said. 'It's always the same with young ladies, fascinated by it.'

'I'm sorry, sir.'

'Description, miss?'

'Pardon, sir?'

'Of the absent party, miss. What does the party look like? Any distinguishing features? For example, miss, if I were to state the distinguishing features of your pa I would say he walks with a limp.'

'It was a war wound, sir. It turned to osteomyelitis.' The word fell out of some forgotten heaven. She took a breath. Mr Chadwick has bad acne, sir. I'm sorry.'

'Not your fault, miss. Height and build?'

'Taller than me. Thin.'

'Hair?'

'Gingerish.'

The policeman laid down his pencil. 'Anything untoward in his room, miss?'

'I…I don't know, sir. Such as?'

'Anything the chap was reading? Anything he was trying to hide?'

'I don't know, sir.'

'Have your ma and pa told you anything about the chaps in here, miss?'

They hadn't. The only place she hadn't been asked to clean was the office, behind a door painted in the ubiquitous dark brown, always locked. There would be something in the office, always locked, a cupboard or a drawer, where records were kept.

'I don't know, sir,' she said to the policeman.

'Fair enough, miss,' he said, and nudged the hat in her direction. 'Thank you, miss.' The hat was heavier than she had thought, carefully brushed and the badge polished.

She imagined her father's entry for the 14th of November 1948 on Nigel Chadwick's record, his painstaking handwriting, the line he would draw underneath the entry. Because she knew this much that the nicely mannered sandy-haired young man with bad acne wasn't coming back. Whatever had happened to him, an absence without leave had disqualified him.

Chapter VII

Another letter came. Stefan was at home, having nothing to do except tend random saddened gardens and visit Mr Beaumont; sit gazing into his unequal watery face while Mrs Beaumont was at church.

Mr Beaumont's intelligent eye gazed back at him, scrutinising his face, going to the letter he held in his hand; returning to his face. One eyebrow quivered.

'Whsht?'

'A letter, Mr Beaumont.'

'Sshee.'

'It came yesterday.'

'Sshee?'

Stefan removed the letter from the envelope and spread it out on Mr Beaumont's knee. He watched as Mr Beaumont's good hand moved slowly back and forth across the lines. The letter slipped from his knee onto the floor. Stefan picked it up.

'Had you finished it, sir?'

'Anos?'

'I had another but I tore it up.'

'Shdntdn. Crimoffas. Donthng?'

'No, I wasn't let into the premises.'

Mr Beaumont's eyebrow shot up.

Stefan felt suddenly cold. 'I signed the letter of application.'

Mr Beaumont thumped the arm of his chair.

There the scenario ended, disappearing as completely as *Ma Vlast* had disappeared. Stefan tried to bring it back, revisiting it, going through it scene by scene, as far as his admission of the signing of the letter of application, at which point Mr Beaumont thumped the arm of the chair and the story came to a sudden end.

It wouldn't come back. It was as if he had awoken from a dream and tried to go back to sleep in order to see what happened later on.

The letter lay open on the table in front of him with the envelope beside it; the same typeface, the same slightly sickly lipstick scent which had transferred itself to his fingers, and which his parents would have noticed and no doubt discussed during one of their long sleepless nights. The lipstick smell wouldn't go away. It was like the blood on Lady Macbeth's hands. It was worse. His crime was worse. It was unspeakable. He had admitted to it in the presence of the keeper of the hardware shop. He had signed his name. A photostat of his signature, lifted from the letter of application, was enclosed with the letter in front of him, beneath a grainy image.

"Dear Mr Stefan Czerniak", the letter said,

"May we respectfully ask that you respond to this communication at your earliest convenience.

"As we pointed out in our previous, dated 9th inst, a failure to contact us may well amount to a serious breach of contract, in the event of which we will be obliged to seek legal redress.

"I remain,

"Yours faithfully,

"(pp A Kaulk, Director)"

Stefan looked closely at the picture – his picture. Then he tore the letter into pieces, lifted the floorboard and let them slip from his hand. He smelt his fingers and felt sick.

He took his place at a table again, this time seated opposite Mrs Beaumont. Somewhere, probably in the next room, *The Blue Danube* was playing on the gramophone, but he couldn't hear it.

Mrs Beaumont picked up the envelope and held it to her face.

'I can't smell anything, dear. Look, Stefan, do you observe how the centre spaces of the e and a are filled in? May I?' She unfolded the letter and opened it out on the table in front of her, turned it over, and finding nothing written on the back, placed it typed face upwards. Do your dear parents know anything about the content of these letters, Stefan?'

'No.'

'Would you like me to tell them?'

'No. Thank you, Mrs Beaumont. I'll tell them myself.'

'Will you promise me that, dear?'

'No, Mrs Beaumont, I don't think I can. My father would be…professorial…about it. He'd make it into a…matter of consequence.'

'It is a matter of consequence, Stefan. Even I can see that and I'm only a silly woman. A man with your father's intellect would see straight away what it is.'

'What is it?'

'You must have realised, dear. These people are trying to blackmail you. Do you know what that it?'

Stefan didn't, not really. He'd heard of it, of course, but he didn't know how it worked.

'Not really.'

'Well...' Mrs Beaumont picked up the letter again. 'These people are doing their best to put you in the wrong. A breach of contract is a serious misdemeanour. They'll be asking you for money soon, to prevent the matter going to court. I don't know that for a fact, Stefan. Maybe I read too many books. You are blameless, dear, and I would strongly advise you to confide in your father.'

The Blue Danube, which had been playing somewhere out of his hearing, stopped. He had never confided in his father about anything and the likelihood of it happening was diminishing as the years passed.

But that wasn't strictly true. His parents knew everything about his visit to Wickham Place. There had been, he vaguely remembered, a difference of opinion between his father and mother. A phrase flickered somewhere at the edge of his consciousness, and emerged slowly, the words unformed and grey at first, then blackening into clarity. "One of those". The keeper of the hardware shop had asked him something like that. Are you one of those? And he had answered yes, he was, one of those.

Then his mother had explained the inexplicable, that he had agreed to being "one of those" because his only experience of vilification had been as an objector. Therefore, any overt or implied criticism (he was filling the interstices between her words) would necessarily be on that account, being the one defining characteristic that made him Stefan Czerniak.

But there might be other meanings attached to "one of those". He would ask, in this other place, where he could think the unthinkable and say the unsayable.

'Mrs Beaumont, what would you understand by the expression "one of those"?'

She was still seated in front of the letter, apparently learning its contents. She looked up, unsurprised. 'Why do you ask, dear?'

'I was just interested. I heard it said, that's all. What would you understand by it? Was it used in the war for conscientious objectors?'

'It could have been, Stefan, dear.' She might have asked why he wanted to know, but she didn't. 'Nowadays it is more likely to be used in a different way.'

'Different?'

'Yes, dear. For anyone who doesn't…march to the same drum beat as most other people, forgive the military analogy.'

Then he knew. A hot flood of shame for an ill-defined and unwarranted existential guilt overwhelmed him, carried away the already absent music of Smetana on its tide and stole everything in him that might have passed for innocence.

Mrs Beaumont was still talking, somewhere far away and out of his hearing, glancing from time to time at the letter in front of her.

Of course, he couldn't show the letter to anyone now. It was somewhere under the floorboards, somewhere in the ceiling space of the room below, reposing, silently and unknown for all he knew, above the table where he was habitually seated with his mother and father, discussing a future that didn't exist.

'I am nothing.' The words came to him from somewhere, the location of which he had forgotten.

Although it was still early in the morning his father had an end of day appearance about him. Stefan looked away. Any moment now, and his parents would begin to discuss their fractured night's sleep, and he couldn't bear it. It was awful, embarrassing.

His mother was there as a shadowy presence he hadn't fully registered. He lifted the lid of the teapot and stirred the tea. No milk. The war was long over but they still didn't take milk or sugar, in their own house, or in anyone else's for fear, he supposed, of depleting their rations.

'Thank you.' His father's voice was cracked, breathless, end of day in the early morning. He hadn't shaved.

The intimacy of the thought appalled Stefan. 'You're welcome,' he said.

'Stefan dear,' his mother said, 'please don't use that expression. You'll be saying OK next.'

Stefan considered saying OK but didn't. Instead, 'I've had a letter.'

His mother said, 'That's nice, dear.' Without asking the contents of the letter. Which, he realised, was typical of his parents. The fewer questions they asked, the more likely he was to confide in them. 'That's nice, dear.' His mother said it again.

'It wasn't nice,' he said. Still his parents said nothing. He looked out of the window. 'I'll go and take Bazal back,' he said. Bazal may or may not have been there.

His father said, 'Bazal can wait. So you've received a letter. And it wasn't a nice letter.'

What do you understand by the word blackmail, father? But he didn't say it. His father took a sip of tea, and then another, and another, until his end of day face was more or less replaced by his morning face.

'Good cup of tea.'

'You're welcome.'

'Stefan dear, please.'

His father looked up. 'One thing, sir.' His father had taken to calling him sir of late. It was a bad sign. 'You've been talking of the letter you received in the past tense. Where is it now?'

Under the floorboard in my room. But he didn't say it. Along with the first one, written in a similar vein.

'So you have destroyed it?' his father said. His colour had returned and he was suddenly animated.

'Darling, don't,' his mother said. 'If it's important, he'll be sent another. No doubt, it was to do with National Service. His mother and father were again talking as if he wasn't there. 'If so, he may go through the procedure if he wishes. It's a blessing this hasn't happened before.'

All at once, the other matter, that of conscientious objection, of the luminous word drawn outside the gate which had failed to dim with time, was of little consequence compared with this new and existential aberration, the nature of which he was unsure. Unsolicited, unknown and shameful.

'There is a procedure, Stefan dear, his mother continues. If you have received a letter relating to National Service, you may go to the tribunal. If another such letter comes, we will deal with it. Everything is better for being confronted, even difficult things. I have said the same to your father, who is of the opinion that the best way to deal with his breathlessness is to ignore it. That is wrong. It is better confronted.'

And his mother might have continued, saying the same thing many times over in slightly different ways, variations on a theme. Were it not for a flake of distemper falling from the ceiling onto the table in front of her.

Another flake of distemper would flutter down, on another day, on the following day, falling slowly through the vacuum of the kitchen as a feather might fall, or a parachute, drifting, its destination uncertain. There would be writing on it. To be specific, type-print…"legal redress…I remain…Yours faithfully". He waited until the remainder of the letter had fallen into the space below the floorboards and reassembled itself in his memory.

"Dear Mr Stefan Czerniak,

"May we respectfully ask that you respond to this communication at your earliest convenience.

"As we pointed out in our previous, dated 9th inst, a failure to contact us may well result in a serious breach of contract, in the event of which we will be obliged to seek legal redress.

"I remain,

"Yours faithfully…"

He went down to the kitchen. His parents were seated at the table, as usual, a pot of tea between them and an empty cup for himself. They had been talking, until they heard his steps on the stairs. He was certain of that. He knew by the fragments of words lingering in the kitchen, floating on the curls of steam that rose from their cups of tea, crowding together under the ceiling.

He looked up, to the place above the table where he had lately seen a vision of curls of distemper loosening and falling. There was nothing, neither the fragments of the letter nor the remnants of his parents' conversation as they discussed him. Which surely they had been doing. Either that or their sleepless night.

'We have something to say to you, Stefan,' his mother said, then, following his glance past the window pane and out into the garden, 'Bazal can wait, dear. We are sometimes under the impression that you would rather communicate with Bazal than with your parents. Did you know that there's another letter for you?'

'Not particularly.'

'What kind of an answer is that?' His father's voice emerged as a jagged rasp. 'I might at a stretch accept your casual manners to me, but not to your mother, sir.' Sir again.

'Sorry, mother.'

'Thank you. Now be so good as to answer your mother's question.'

'Darling, please,' his mother said. 'The letter's behind the clock, Stefan. Your father is not asking you about the contents of the letter, only that you respond to it as you see fit since it's the third or fourth time they've contacted you.'

'Fifth, mother.' He hadn't opened the fourth. It was still intact, under the floorboard in the corner of his room. 'I'll see to Bazal.'

'Bazal should be hibernating,' his mother said. 'You may bring the letter in here and read it in the presence of your parents if you wish.' His father said nothing. 'Will you let us know, dear?'

'Yes, mother.' Know what?

'Sweetheart, leave him be,' his father said. 'We've done enough damage already. The poor guy didn't ask to be born to us.'

'Yes, of course, darling, if you say so. But I thought we were concerned about the frequency and secrecy of these letters.'

'I guess we've made our point, sweetheart.'

Guy and guess. His mother had permitted the words to pass by. Will you let us know? He had agreed to something, the nature of which he was ignorant. And there wasn't a specified time. He would let his mother know…some indeterminate fact…at some indeterminate time.

'I'll be in my room, mother.'

He opened the letter. The same typeface. The same cloying lipstick smell attached to the envelope.

"For the attention of Mr Stefan Czerniak,

"Sir,

"As a consequence of your failure to respond to our previous, we are obliged to inform you that you have become liable for a sum of £200.0s.0d sterling, payable by the 27th inst. May we assure you that upon receipt of the aforesaid sum, all communications from this address will cease.

"Yours faithfully,

"(pp A Kaulk, Director)"

"Whither, as to the bed's feet, life is shrunk." The line re-entered his mind, the last part of it first, "life is shrunk". It was from a long time ago, the last year at school, where the other chaps would leaf through the volume of John Donne, looking for the rude passages. "Die is not die in the accepted sense." A few of the chaps sniggered. Someone asked the master for an explanation, and was told that the explanation had just been given; they must examine the text. The book became common property, falling open at certain pages. The *Nocturnal* was on a facing page. He read it, rather than incur the ribaldry of the other chaps by letting the book go past him. "Life is shrunk."

His life was shrunk to this, a demand for what appeared to be an obscene amount. He didn't know anything about – and the words were abhorrent to him – sums sterling. The subject of "sums sterling" was never mentioned by his parents, the only reference being delivered obliquely. Have you enough to post the parcel? A parcel containing his mother's thimble addressed to a girl who lived on the border of Nottinghamshire, and marked "fragile". Have you enough for your train journey from Gant's Hill? Have you enough? Have you enough? Three years after the end of the war and it was still the same. Have you enough?

Clearly, the sum mentioned in the letter was more than enough. For anyone. No one had that much. Stefan couldn't imagine what it would look like. It was too much. For anyone.

He lifted the floorboard in the corner of the room and retrieved the previous letter, the one he hadn't opened. The bottle of ink was downstairs and his parents would ask him why he needed it. A lead pencil would suffice. It was enough. Enough to score through the addresses, his own, and write in large capitals, in someone else's hand: NOT AT THIS ADDRESS.

Kneeling on the floor, he looked down into the space under the floorboard. A familiar smell rose up to meet him, of damp and smoke, of boiled cabbage and green soap. That was where the war had gone. Not far. Under the floorboards. There was no sign of the fragments of the letters he had torn up previously.

He went downstairs, passing the door of the kitchen where his parents were no doubt still seated at the table, discussing him wordlessly.

He said farewell. Wordlessly. To his mother. To his father. He let himself out of the front door, walked down the chequered path and stepped over the luminous word: CONSHY. Under the red fire of the sun, he walked up Golen Avenue. He carried on walking, threading the streets until he came to Gant's Hill station, where he dropped the two letters into the open mouth of a pillar-box.

He carried on walking.

Chapter VIII

Lola Robertson knew the origin of the smell immediately. It was from a long time ago, from the day the war in Japan ended, when she had gone home carrying marigolds and carnations for her mother, cradling their tired flower heads in the bend of her elbow. The smell had met her as soon as she went into the front room in Barratt's Place. Later there would be a word for it: osteomyelitis.

Leon Haskey had requested seconds. She took the saucepan into the dining room, and observed that the noses of Humphry Peacewick, Alfred White and Bob Field were wrinkled in displeasure. Glances were passing between them.

'Another helping, Mr Haskey?'

'Yes please, miss.' He stood up to allow her to deliver a ladle of porridge to the bowl in front of him.

'Any more?'

'Just Mr Haskey, Lola, as I told you,' her mother said. 'Take the saucepan away now, please, and scrape the rest into the bucket outside. You don't need another helping yourself, I'm sure.' One or two of the young men sniggered.

Leon Haskey pushed the bowl away from him. 'I've changed my mind, Miss Robertson,' he said. 'I might if you were but you're not so I'm not.'

'How many words is that, Mr Haskey?' her father said. 'Nearly twenty? Why, yer've beaten yer own record.'

More sniggers. Leon Haskey fell silent.

Lola scraped the saucepan into bucket outside, then put it into the cold greasy water in the sink. She watched grey fragments of porridge detach themselves and float slowly to the surface of the water, drifting idly, congregating into clumps. She would have to go up and clean the empty room. But not yet.

It's my fault. The words swam into her mind as slowly and greyly as the remnants of porridge swam to the edges of the sink.

The dining room door opened and she could hear the footsteps of the young men, thundering upstairs and hobnailing along the linoleum on the top corridor. The door of the dining room remained open. She could hear her father moving the chairs back to the wall, her mother replacing the cruet on top of the sideboard, collecting up the serviettes and threading them into their rings.

Presently, an atmosphere compounded of strong tea and osteomyelitis arrived in the scullery, followed by the presence of her mother, who dropped two serviettes onto the draining board.

'For the wash,' she said.

'Mother?' Lola wiped her hands on the dishcloth.

'What now, Lola? I haven't got all day.'

'Father's leg.'

'What about your father's leg?'

'It's gone bad again.'

Her mother said nothing.

'Mother, it's unpleasant. Probably father hasn't noticed.'

Her mother turned round to face her. 'And you think I haven't either? I expect it's the upheaval of Mr Chadwick and all that. It puts your father in a bad light, you know.'

Lola didn't know. It came to her, standing by the sink with the dishcloth still in her hands that she considered that she knew more than her mother in all respects, and had done for many years, her entire life. 'I expect so, mother,' she said.

'It's called shock, Lola. We saw a lot of it in the war, but of course you've forgotten that there was a war and how we all suffered privations.' Lola didn't know that her mother had such a word in her vocabulary. 'Since you know the fancy name for it, you can take your father to the hospital, dear. No doubt it won't cost him. That's what folks tell me.' And so her mother went on until her words rose and burst in the scullery like the bubbles rising to the surface of the water in the copper.

But Lola had stopped taking notice, not long after the word "dear". Dear. Her mother didn't call her dear, and she never had, not for a long time. Her father called her duck, but that was something different.

'Yes, mother,' she said. 'I'll take him.'

'Leave Mr Chadwick's room for the time being, dear.' The word again. So she had heard properly. 'In all likelihood, the police will be back.'

'Yes, mother. I'll take father. Does he know?'

'He will when I tell him,' her mother said. She had now put on her apron and tied a rag round her head, tucking the ends of it in at the front and the wisps of hair in at the back.

Lola wanted to say something nice. But she couldn't. She would take her father. He would call her duck. He would call himself Corporal Robertson. The nurses would like him.

The x-ray pictures dripped rhythmically into the gulley beneath them, losing their shine as they dried and sticking to the light box behind them. The doctor was seated at the desk writing something. He hadn't looked up since she and her father were shown in by the nurse and asked to sit down. Outside, starlings gathered on the telegraph wires, shuffling and preening, their feather gleaming ink blue in the sunlight. The doctor put down his pen. The starlings lifted from the wire and vanished above the window frame.

'Mr Robertson.'

'Corporal, sir.'

'Ah.' The doctor looked up. 'And this is?'

'My daughter, sir.'

'Indeed, your daughter.'

'Is it serious, doctor?'

'This ailment is never good, Mr Robertson. I won't tax your mind by naming it. But never good, Mr Robertson. Difficult to treat. Doesn't quite go away. Always hanging around somewhere waiting to strike again. That sort of thing. As I say, I won't trouble you with the name of it.'

Lola blushed. Any moment now, her father would tell the doctor what the disease of the tibia was, and tell him that his daughter knew the names of all the bones in the body. But he didn't. 'Very good, sir,' he said.

'Occupation?'

'Sir?'

'What is your occupation, Mr Robertson? I presume you're no longer on active service.'

'Warden of Salisbury House, sir.'

'Ah, Mr Crawford's successor. That going well, Mr Robertson?'

The starlings settled on the telegraph wire again, flapping their wings, regaining their balance. Lola waited for her father to say that everything was going well. The doctor looked at him and waited, one eyebrow raised. She didn't know what he was called. There may have been a name on the door, she couldn't remember. She looked at the right hand, the signet ring on the small finger, the pen beating a tattoo on the page of notes.

'In general, yes, sir,' her father said presently.

'And in particular?'

The doctor laid down the pen and leaned back in his chair.

'A minor problem recently,' her father said.

'A minor problem?'

'A young chap went awol, sir.'

'As I believe is the habit of young men at Salisbury House, Mr Robertson. Anything else? Family life satisfactory'

'Yes, sir. Beautiful wife, lovely daughter as you see. Knows the names of all the bones in the body.'

'All the bones in the body. Indeed. Well, well.'

Lola blushed.

'You might remind me of the name of the affected bone, Miss Robertson.' The doctor started writing again, not looking at her.

'Left tibia, sir.'

'Correct, Miss Robertson. And the name of the thin bone next to it?'

'Left fibula, sir.'

'You're sure it's not the fibia?'

'It's the fibula, sir.'

The doctor got up and went to the door. He walked with a limp. 'Miss Taylor, please?' His voice echoed down the corridor, bouncing off the cream painted walls, slithering through the pipes, hitting the ceiling. 'Miss Taylor, are you there?'

He came back and rolled up his trouser leg.

'Osteomyelitis, Mr Robertson,' he said. 'Never get rid of it. Has a nasty habit of rearing its ugly head at times of – er – difficulty. You and I, Mr Robertson, have to knock it on its ugly head. Ah, come in, Miss Taylor. I told you I would find you a young lady, and I have. From the looks of her hands, she's no stranger to hard work. Look after her.'

Lola went into the empty room in spite of what her mother had said. The window was still open, letting in the breath of traffic and the fret of rain.

She moved the bed and armchair over to one side, swept underneath and moved them back. She moved the upright chair and dresser and did the same. She rolled up the rug. She placed the coat stand on the bed, taking from one if its arms a navy tie, still knotted and carrying the lingering neck smell of its late owner. She undid the knot, folded the tie and placed it on the dresser. She went down to the scullery for a pail of water and vinegar and mopped the floorboards; the skirting boards with a damp rag, the window frames and sills. The upright chair and table, inside the drawers, the light switch. The glass lampshade.

'I told you not to do that, Lola.' Her mother was in the room, running her finger over surfaces, adjusting curtains. 'The least you could have done was tell your mother about your father.'

You could have asked him yourself, mother. She didn't say it.

'It's just as well as it happens,' her mother went on. 'He's moving in today.'

'He? Who?'

Her mother had already gone, leaving behind in the cleaned room a fragment of herself: green soap, female perspiration. Lola went to the window and looked down. Mr Beaumont was coming home, his gabardine undone and his tie flying over his shoulder. He went down the side passage and into the back door, coming out with Watson. Pip. Lola waved. Mr Beaumont didn't see her, but she waved all the same. She waved again when he came back and let Watson into the house.

Enclosed within the cream walls of the hospital was Miss Taylor, peeling her father's x-rays from the lighted box in the doctor's room and walking back to the x-ray department with them, their frames clanking together. Miss Taylor: who needed help from a girl who knew the bone was called a fibula and not a fibia; Miss Taylor, who was stowing her father's illness into the drying cabinet, knocking it on its ugly head. That's what we have to do, you and I, Mr Robertson.

Lola watched Mr Beaumont going back to work until he turned the corner into Holme Road. She still watched him, though she could not see him, going past the gas works, joining the other men returning after dinner, climbing the wooden stairs, going to a desk, where, having taken off his gabardine and hung it on a peg, he seated himself in front of a ledger. She watched as he unscrewed the top of his fountain pen, loosened his tie and skeltered down the rows of figures and specifications of locomotives and turbines. So much she knew from Jean. What was a turbine? Jean didn't rightly know what it did, but it had a part called a stator and a part called a rotor. It was…a kind of engine, she supposed. When they had their next gala, Jean would take her to look at the turbines.

The floor of the empty room was dry. Lola replaced the furniture, the bed and the armchair on one side and the dresser, the table and upright chair on the other. She replaced the coat stand. The navy tie she put in her apron pocket. She removed a sliver of paper lodged between the floorboards. She took the rug downstairs, threw

142

it over the washing line and belaboured it with the stiff brush. Then she took it back up and laid it on the floorboards. She looked around for the sliver of paper she had found, but it had gone.

She saw it once more, when she emptied the pail into the outside drain, washed clean of whatever might have been written on it, resting on the stagnant surface of the water a long way down.

Late in the night, she heard the newcomer arrive in the corridor, accompanied by her father, one set of unequal steps, the other heavy and hobnailed, the drag of a suitcase. Her father was talking, pleasantly.

'A pleasure to welcome yer, sir. We'll find summat else for yer feet, lad. Yer can't go clomping in them things on the polished floor.'

Lola heard her father wink. She was sure she did. A conspiracy, man to man, Corporal Robertson, warden of Salisbury House and another in hobnailed boots, bringing a suitcase.

'Thank you, sir.' A voice both familiar and unfamiliar. She was waiting for him to say more, but he didn't.

The door of the empty room opened and closed, and the two sets of steps, one unequal and the other hobnailed, were silenced. Then her father came out. She heard him going down the stairs, clattering about in the scullery, and returning slowly, carrying a cup of something. Horlicks. He set it down outside the door, knocked and said, 'Nightcap, young man.' He went down.

The door of the room opened presently and a voice came out. 'C***!' She heard a glob of spittle hit the linoleum. She would have to clean it up in the morning. She would have to serve porridge to its owner. She would have to see him, face to face.

But before that, unexpectedly, she heard the voices of her parents, slipping through the gap under the door of the scullery where she was feeding sheets into the mangle. Her own sheets. She had come on during the night, for a reason, and on account of a person she knew only too well, who was even then being discussed in her hearing. She stopped turning the mangle to smooth out the following edge of the sheet, and then began turning the handle again, thinking, she told herself, that the squeak and clank of it might alert her parents to her presence. But no.

'We had to.' Her mother's voice rose shrilly above its customary volume. 'We had to do our duty by Amelia. Take your hands off me, Cyril, for heavens' sake!'

'Calm down, duck. I merely made mention of the fact that the young feller is a rightun. And with respect, Lil, it won't be yer own tits he'll be after, it'll be yon lass's.'

A gasp of outrage followed her father's footsteps up the stairs. The scullery door was open and her mother stood there, white faced and trembling.

'You might have waited for the rest of the sheets, Lola. We're not made of money, you know.'

'I came on in the night, mother. I had to do mine separately.'

'Very well.' Her mother went over to the sink and retched.

'Are you all right, mother?'

'You'll find out sooner or later, Lola. We always intended to do our duty by Amelia and now the time has come. It's a cross we have to bear.'

'Barry Green has moved into Mr Chadwick's room. I know, mother.'

'Have you seen him?'

'I had to clean up something on the landing this morning. Only sputum. I heard his voice when father brought up the Horlicks.'

'What do you mean, spootum?'

'Spit, mother. It's the smoke from the factory, I expect.' She was defending Barry Green already.

'Your father will have a word with you.'

But her father didn't. Not that day or the next, or the next. Her mother carried the dishes in from the scullery. Leon Hasky wanted to know why. Why didn't Miss Robertson carry them in anymore? Lola could hear his voice from the scullery, oddly well bred. She wondered, suddenly, if his people had been objectors in the war. It was an odd name, like the name of the visitor whose sock she had once mended, whose wife had sent her a thimble. Maybe the name would come back to her. One day.

Barry Green was there, at the table, somehow visible through the closed door of the scullery, and round the corner at the bottom of the stairs. But she hadn't seen him. To her, he was the same as he had been when she last saw him, on the waste going to Barratt's Place, on the day his mother closed the blackout curtains at the back and lay down by the gas oven.

*

One night soon after Barry Green's arrival at Salisbury House, she was woken up by the sound of her name being called. A pencil of light entered her room, as if the door had been opened. She got out of bed and pushed at the door, rattling it to test the lock.

The next morning, her father told her that there had been a complaint about noise coming from the direction of her room.

'Not ter worry yerself, duck.' Her father still didn't say anything about the new resident, nothing to warn her.

'Father.'

'Yes, duck.'

'Someone called my name in the night.'

'Happen yer mind were still on young Samuel in the temple, duck.'

'I meant it, Father.'

'I know yer did, duck.'

Lola waited, expecting her father to say more. But he didn't. She wanted, childishly, to remind him of the times she had accompanied him to the hospital. But then, she thought, as probably her father did as well, those outings were as much for her benefit as his.

Somewhere in the hospital down a dreary corridor smelling of disinfectant there was Miss Taylor, who had too much to do and who needed help. And her name had been suggested, because she knew to call the slender bone of the lower leg the fibula and not the fibia. But she would never get there. She would never get there, because she was Lola Robertson from Barratt's Place.

Chapter IX

Into Eastern Avenue, then to Cambridge Park. He began to count his steps. One. Two. Three. Four. Five. Six. Are you one of those then? His right foot came down heavily on the word "those". There was nothing he could do to make it otherwise. Are you one of those, sir?

The High Road in Leytonstone. He might look odd, he thought: to the passengers riding on the trolley bus, to the drivers of motor cars, to the women with prams…to the chaps back from the war, still seated on benches as if they had been there for three years, unable to move because of their wounds. His father had met a chap like that once, Stefan was sure of it, a chap with a bad leg. He tried to remember, but it was no use. Are you one of those, sir? Are you one of those? Those, sir? Those?

A sharp red pain had developed on the back of the heel of his right foot. He sat down on a bench and peeled off his sock. He remembered now. A chap who lived on the border of Nottinghamshire, who had intervened in some unpleasantness on a train, a girl who had mended his father's sock, an embittered wife…Michaelmas daisies and golden rod. There had been some trouble in the family, the nature of which his father was unsure, an infidelity perhaps. All were blessed with the gifts of the spirit, although they didn't know it. That's what his father had said. Yesterday. Three years ago. A millennium away.

The blister had broken leaving an oozing sore surrounded by jags of white skin. The shadow of another head approached his own on the pavement, both of them inspecting the foot. He felt suddenly faint. He leaned back. The nearness of the other man offended him. There was an intimacy in it that he couldn't quite place.

'It's a bad'un, young feller. Here, help yerself. If yer go and faint, yer'll be in fer drunk and disorderly. Here, tek it.'

A bottle was pushed into his hand. He tried to shake his head.

'Tek it.' The bottle was held to his lips. Fire spread through his throat and lungs and to every extremity of his body, to his hand trying to resist the thrust of the bottle, to the heel with the broken blister. 'Here, drink it down, young feller. I dunna want it. Drink it down.'

Across the road, there was a letterbox, a line of railings behind it, and behind the railings laurel bushes, above the laurels the glaring sky. Someone was trying to post a letter in the box, someone not tall enough to reach the slot. In some other life, Stefan heard the drop of letters into a box, outside an underground station. He wondered what the letters were, to whom they were addressed, why they were being posted. Over the road, someone was still trying to reach the mouth of the letterbox and couldn't. He would have to go and help, take the letters from the person who couldn't reach the slot and post them, as the other letters had been posted, in another life.

He fixed his eyes on the letterbox, the railings, the dark laurels. The sky battered his eyes. He would have to go across the road and help. The letter might be important. It might be marked fragile. It might be travelling to the border of Nottinghamshire. He stood up. The pavement he stood on, the kerb, the road beyond the kerb, dissolved and darkened. He would reach the other side of the road before the world dissolved. A line of music played in his head. It must have been coming from the bandstand, in some park behind the letterbox, beyond the railings, a park with a pond. He would recover the first eight notes of *The Blue Danube* if it was the last thing he did.

'Jesus Christ, he stinks of it.' The voice had an oddly familiar ring to it. The toe of a shoe nudged him below the ribs, rolled him over, like a caterpillar. The shoe, he noticed, was a polished black brogue, the turn-ups of the trousers of a dark grey pinstriped fabric. Stefan Czerniak hadn't realised previously that he possessed this sartorial knowledge. A hand came down and wiped the toe of the shoe with a folded handkerchief. Someone had been sick. He could see the rank fluid spreading across the pavement. The owner of the shoe, of the folded handkerchief, of the oddly familiar voice, took a step backwards. The ferrule of a rolled umbrella stood by the shoes, balancing on the kerb, almost in the gutter. Across the road, behind the railings, behind the laurels, the music ran to its end.

He lifted his head. The man wearing the black brogues had gone away, as had the child trying to reach the mouth of the letterbox, as had the railings and the laurels. Only the music remained, whose title he now couldn't remember, playing itself over and over again. And the smell.

He must have been walking for some time, leaving, as he saw, a horseshoe of blood from the broken blister. It didn't hurt any more. Nothing hurt any more. He tried again to remember the title of the music but it had gone utterly. His name, but it had gone.

'I seem to have partaken of the waters of Lethe, sir,' he heard himself saying.

The man, seated opposite, raised an eyebrow. 'Come again?'

'The waters of Lethe,' he said. 'I seem to have mislaid my name.'

'Wouldn't be Robertson of Barratt's Place, by any chance?' the man said. 'Found this in your pocket.'

He caught sight of himself taking the scrap of paper. 'No, not Robertson.'

'Any idea who this Robertson is? Might be able to help us get you back to your folks. Familiar?' The man raised an eyebrow.

'Yes, yes it could be. Where am I?'

The man pushed a peaked cap across the table. 'Give you clue?'

'Thank you, sir. I don't know how I got here.'

'A chap dropped by and told us there was a young fellow in a bad way.'

'I ought to thank the chap.'

'You can try. Chap called Aveling. City type.'

'Do I know him?'

'You mean do we know him, and the answer to that is yes. We don't encourage him, Mr Robertson.'

'It isn't Robertson, sir. It's Czerniak.'

'How are you spelling that?'

'C Z E R N I A K.'

'Christian name?'

'Stefan.' His mind had suddenly cleared. He was in a basement room. Through a high window, he could see the area railings, the feet of people passing by, bicycle wheels, a cart and a brown dog.

'Steven.'

'Stefan, sir. S T E F A N.'

'Address?'

'I'm not going back.'

The man laid down his pen. 'That's fair enough, Mr...' (he consulted the page in front of him) 'Churnick,' but we have a duty to inform your people that you are safe and well. Trouble at home,' (he looked down at the page again) 'Stefan?'

'Yes, sir. No. Not at home. I don't want them to know.'

'Then we fit you out with another pair of socks and let you go? I'm Captain,' (the name was lost in a door slamming closed elsewhere in the building) 'by the way.'

'Captain?'

'Salvation Army.'

'My people were objectors.'

The captain glanced down at the page. 'How do you say that name again?'

'Churnick.'

The captain made a bracket and wrote down "CHURNICK" inside it. 'Not that kind of army, Mr Churnick.'

'I know, sir.' All at once, he knew everything. Nearly everything. 'I was being blackmailed. Shall I go on?'

'As you wish, Mr Churnick.'

'Sir?'

'If it would help, Mr Churnick. If you might regret it later, no.'

'I'm taking your time, sir.'

'Time is a relatively recent concept, Mr Churnick. It is an elastic commodity and expands or contracts in an inverse ratio according to the demands made upon it. You say that you were being blackmailed and that you don't wish to return home, yes?'

'No, sir. I've just realised what was troubling me.' There was no end to his knowledge.

'Indeed, Mr Churnick?'

'You have solved the conundrum, sir.' The captain peeled off a pair of wire-framed spectacles and laid them on the desk in front of him, where they continued to peer, round-eyed and impartial. He could hear the voices, the captain's and his own, continuing their conversation from a far distance. 'Do you know what is meant by expression...' He wrote it down underneath the name CZERNIAK.

'It depends very much on the circumstances, Mr Churnick.'

'Yes, sir.' A family of objectors...a page of John Donne passed round at school...other things at school? No, probably not. The thrust of fire into his mouth.

'Police know about the blackmail?'

'No, sir.'

'Under normal circumstances, as I have said, Mr Churnick, we would wish to convey a message to the loved ones to the effect that the chap is safe and well, without giving any other information. Shall we do that?'

'No, sir, thank you...'

'Mr Churnick?' The voice returned from some distant place. 'I thought we'd lost you for a moment. We were talking about the elastic nature of time and your decision not to go home. You were apparently elsewhere. We advise you not to accept refreshment of that kind again, but we hardly need to tell you that. Where are you bound for?'

'I don't know. I'll think of something. Get a job...'

'May I make a suggestion, Mr Churnick? You don't have to agree. That you stay here. That is if you don't mind mucking in with the other chaps. As I say, you don't have to agree.'

'No, sir. Yes, sir. Thank you, sir.'

'Good, good.' The captain put on his spectacles. 'I do have to warn chaps that thanks are offered before meals.'

'All of them?'

'All of them.'

The footsteps continued to walk by on the pavement above the basement area, the horns of motor vehicles, a cart of milk crates rattling past.'

'Thank you, sir. I'll think about it.'

'Your people are unbelievers?'

'No, sir.'

For some reason, he was lying on the pavement again but had been moved under the bench. Above his head were the sparse wooden slats of the seat and the glint of a glass bottle balanced between them. One shoe, the one he had removed to inspect the broken blister, had been placed on his middle, the sock rolled up and tucked into it.

Feet were going past, stepping over a luminous thread of vomit. A threepenny bit rolled towards him, awkwardly on its small angles, meant for a chap lying under a bench who wasn't him. He seemed to have mislaid his name. He tried to lift his head, but it was too heavy. He would close his eyes. If he did so, he might return to some previous option, which for the moment was opaque.

The sun pushed under the bench, warm and malodorous. He felt himself being rolled onto it and pulled out. The cuffs of the hands, he noticed, had been pushed back above the wrists.

'This yours, sir?' The threepenny bit was placed on his middle next to the shoe. The ferrule of a rolled umbrella alongside polished black shoes swept into view and was gone.

'What have you been drinking, sir?'

Stefan didn't know.

'Name, sir?'

He didn't know that either, not at the precise moment in time, which was, he suddenly remembered being told, an elastic concept with the property of expanding or contracting according to the demands made or not made upon it. There was something else. In an inverse ratio. He couldn't get his mind round it.

Presently, parallel pipes were travelling along the wall, a little below the ceiling, elastic in concept, diverging and converging according to the necessities made upon them, leaping up to clear a door space, falling down again to enter an open door.

'He still with us?'

'Just about.'

'Not the usual kind of chap, eh?'

'Looks pretty routine to me.'

'No, not this one. Always tell by the fingernails. Clean, you see. From a good home, I'll bet…Coming through! Chap found under a bench, sister. We reckon you'll need the old you-know-what.'

'You can have a go at these if you like, pal.' The orderly was through the curtains, putting a handful of coloured paper strips on the counterpane. 'Here, I'll start you off. All got sticky on, see? Make a loop and thread the next one through and you've got a chain, hey presto! Good, eh? You'll soon get the hang. Any advance on the other matter yet, John?'

'No, sir. But I don't think it's John.' The pieces of coloured paper danced in front of his eyes.

'Had to call you something. We work down the alphabet, see, when we have chaps who don't know their names.'

'You pronounce it…' but he had forgotten. 'I could try and write it down. It's a foreign name.'

'Ah.'

'My father was an objector.'

'Ah, one of those, eh? No disrespect, John. Anything else you can tell us?'

'I'm not going back.'

'See that, John? It's a device for keeping the foot elevated – up in the air in other words. That foot won't permit you to go anywhere at present. Ever heard of septicaemia? When you can see the carotid artery jumping in the neck, the chap's got septicaemia. Never fails. Don't want that, do you?'

'No, sir.'

'Lucky to be here, John, though you might dispute that.'

'No, sir. I'm lucky. It's Czerniak.'

But the orderly had gone, and was talking to the man in the next bed. 'You can have a go at these if you like, Ken. All got sticky on. Make a loop and put the next one through and, hey presto, you've got a chain. Good, eh? Any idea who thought of it? I'll let you into a secret, Ken. A chap called Einstein. Remember that for future reference. Einstein. Albert Einstein.'

The orderly passed on. 'Larry, fancy a bit of scientific endeavour, eh? You can have a go at these if you like, pal.'

'Ken?'

The man in the next bed put his head through the curtains. 'Not Ken any more than you're John. Jeez, you look rough, old chap.' The head went back, but the voice went on, arriving in bursts, attenuated by the rippling breath of patterned curtains.

'Know what these are, old chap? Paper chains, that's what they are. What are they for? Christmas, that's what they're for. Know when Christmas is? No, thought you wouldn't. Tell you when it is, when you see them bloody paper chains hanging off ceilings and things. Drop down in the night. Give you the willies, they do. But I'll tell you one thing, old chap, them nurses singing with them there cloaks red side out, reduces a chap to smithereens. Away in a manger, know that one? Jeez, reduces a chap, that's what it does. Then the old padre comes marching in, jeez.'

'Then the King hisself.' A voice chimed in from elsewhere.

'Then the King, yeah. No, old chap, not the King as I knows of. And you get when Christmas is over? When all them paper chains come down. Collect germs, see, old chap. Germs. Got to get rid of them germs. I don't speak for yourself since you've been badly, but a chap can do worse than stop in one of these here places for the festive whatsits. As I say, old chap, I don't speak for yourself since you've been badly.'

The paper chains went overnight and no one saw them go. The next day was white and plain with a bite of cold. The orderly was standing at the foot of the bed.

'It's Czerniak, pronounced Churnick.'

'How are you spelling that, pal?'

'C Z E R N I A K.'

'Come again.'

'C Z E R N I A K.'

'That so? And how do you say it again?'

'Churnick. I'm not going back, sir.'

'So you keep telling us, John.'

'I don't think it's John, sir.'

'He doesn't think it's John, sister.' The orderly was talking somewhere out of sight. 'He's said a foreign name and it sounds like that one.'

A suitcase fastened with a strap was lying on the floor of the office. Stefan was seated in front of it. Outside the window, he could see the clatter of the top branches of the trees and taste the cold of the wind.

Sister Davenport was seated at the desk. A faint scent rose from the case, of mines, of trains, of polish. Of home.

'I don't want to go back.' He reached down and touched the case.

'Read the label, please, John,' the sister said. 'Is the person identified on the label yourself?'

'I believe so, sister.'

'Say that name, please.'

'Czerniak.'

'Christian name, please.'

'Stefan.'

'Whose writing do you think that is?'

'Paul Czerniak's.'

'He being?'

'My father. I don't wish to return home, sister.'

'How may we contact your father, John?'

'I'm not going back...'

'Would you be so kind as to try again to open the case, Mr Connolly? We haven't been successful so far, John.'

'With respect, sir, you won't do it that way. It's...different. May I help?'

The sister nodded to the orderly.

'All yours, pal.'

The case opened. The room was filled with silence. Presently someone spoke, soundlessly.

'Are these items of clothing yours, John?'

'Some of them. Some are my father's. Some are new.' A howl of grief rose from somewhere nearby and settled under the ceiling.

'Give John a handkerchief, if you would, Mr Connolly.'

'They can't afford it, sister. My father cleans in a factory and mother's in a laundry. They were objectors.'

'That explains a lot. You do not wish to be a financial burden to your parents, therefore you left home.' Not a question, a statement. 'You're not the first and you won't be the last.'

'The firm closed.'

'The firm closed?'

'Yes.'

'The firm closed, Mr Connolly. There's also a letter, John. Would you prefer to read it in privacy?'

'No, sister. Thank you.' But it wasn't a letter. It was an envelope, addressed to him in his father's writing, containing two bank notes. 'They can't afford it, sister. What shall I do?'

'And there is also a violin, John. Would you be so kind as to bring it, Mr Connolly?'

'It's Pip's. He gave it to me because of his war injuries. It was an excuse. How can you prove it's me?' The room spun round his head. The sister and orderly were still speaking, but to someone else.

'It's you?'

'You don't know who I am.'

'Mr Connolly, how do we know that John is Stefan Czerniak?'

'I would hazard a guess that it's something to do with his dexterity in opening the case, sister.'

'Unless he's a professional case-breaker, Mr Connolly. Would you be so kind as to open the violin? We need to establish that it belongs to him.'

'He'll have to be asked to play something, don't you think?'

The room stopped spinning.

'But I can't, sister.'

'You can't what?'

'Play anything.'

'God bless you, we wouldn't dream of asking you, dear. There's a letter in the case.'

'It'll be from Pip.'

'How nice.'

'Do we tell him, Mr Connolly? What do you think?'

'You know best, sister.'

'Mr Connolly was asked to go to the entrance of the hospital to receive belongings for a young man who was possibly an in-patient. The gentleman who brought the belongings, Mr Connolly thought, was remarkably like you in appearance, a phenomenon which was confirmed by the duty nurse. We established the gentleman's name, but we didn't say that you were here. We merely said we would make enquiries. Your father accepted that. We none of us see eye to eye with our parents all the time, but he is a good man, Stefan. There will be other formalities, of course…'

Chapter X

One day, someone reported that they had seen a young man hanging over the town bridge.

Lola heard it from strangers standing outside the gates of Salisbury House as she emptied a pail of floor water down the drain. The water splashed over, turning to ice as it hit the tiles of the yard.

Hanging from the town bridge. Her mother was all at once at the scullery door. The voices at the gate continued, loud on the thick cold air.

'Yes, hanging ovver town bridge. Leastways, it could have been to say hanging from town bridge, but what I heard was hanging ovver. What d'yer mek of it?'

'Bless his soul. Only a young'un, did yer say?'

'Only a young'un. Yer'd have seen him about town.'

The scullery door slammed shut and opened again.

'Come in, Lola. Leave that. You've got a lot to answer for, my girl.'

'Let go of me, mother. Lola tried to shake her arm free, but her mother held her fast, just above the elbow, pulling her into the scullery.

'Fetch me the cloths, Lola.'

'Cloths?'

'You know what I'm talking about. Fetch me the cloths.'

'I don't know what you mean, mother. What cloths?'

'The table cloths. How many times do I have to tell you?'

Lola reddened. 'As you please, mother.' She went into the dining room, opened the sideboard drawer and pulled out the cloths: the checked for every day and the white damask for Sunday.

'Open them out.'

Please wouldn't go amiss, mother. She didn't say it. The telephone was ringing in the hall.

'Answer that, Lola. Say Mrs Robertson's out. I knew it.' Her mother was unfolding the cloths on the scullery table, shaking them out and peering into the creases. The telephone was still ringing.

'Hello. Salisbury House.' She reached around and closed the scullery door on her mother's noise. 'Hello. Salisbury House.' She didn't know very well how to continue with a telephone conversation after the initial greeting. She was frightened of its distant crackly voice. 'Hello.'

'Is that Mrs Robertson?'

'No.'

'Oh, I am speaking to Salisbury House, am I?'

'Yes, yes.'

'Who are you then, dear?'

'Lola Robertson.'

'This is Freda Beaumont, Pip's mother. Do you think you could give Pip a message, dear?'

'Yes. Yes, I can. I'm sorry.'

'Could you say we think we've found him. Pip will know what you mean. Could you do that for me, dear?'

'Yes, yes, I can.' Lola was aware of her mother standing behind her. "We think we've found him". Through the open scullery, she could see the cloths spread out on the table, the weekday checked and the Sunday damask. The damask cloth had a diamond crease in the centre fold.

'Thank you, dear, and if Pip should wish to call us might he use your telephone, please dear?'

'Yes, I'll tell my parents.'

'Thank you, dear. Are you by any chance the young lady who does the marvellous needlework? Mr Czerniak was telling us…' But the phone had gone dead.

What was that name? Lola had forgotten it the moment it was spoken, but an impression of an evening not long after the end of the war came back to her; golden rod and Michaelmas daisies in an armful on the table in Barratt's Place; a stranger under their roof.

'They've found him? Is he alive?' Tears ran down her mother's face, gathering under her chin and falling onto the bib of her pinafore.

'It was Pip's mother. She was talking about a neighbour. They think they've found him.'

'Not Mr Chadwick then?'

'No, mother. We have to give Pip the message. He may need to use the telephone.'

But her mother's face had closed. 'You know what I'm going to say, Lola. Look at that table cloth.'

'I've seen it.'

'Well, what have you got to say for yourself?'

'The cloth's too heavy for the mangle and doesn't go in straight. One side of it catches and it comes out creased.'

'You know what it means? It means a death.'

'That's silly, mother.'

'You're saying your mother's superstitious. Is that it?' Her mother's face was inches from her own, bleached and ironed out. Her mouth continued working after the words had finished.

Another voice intervened, high pitched, insinuating, half way between child and adult. 'Yer ma's saying yer killt un, Lola Robertson.'

'Answer me, Lola.'

'I didn't say that, mother.'

'You implied as much.'

'I thought I heard Barry Green just now. Is he in?'

'He's supposed to have gone to that place he goes to. Where did you think you heard him?'

'I thought I heard his voice, mother, that's all. I must have been mistaken.'

'Barry Green's much to be pitied, Lola. I suppose even you know that.'

'Yes, mother.'

'And you'd best give the message next door before you forget.'

Lola had forgotten about the message already. She had forgotten the foreign sounding name. The other voices were still in her head. You're saying your mother's superstitious, is that it? Yer killt un, Lola Robertson.

'Move, Lola. The men are out for dinner. Didn't you hear the buzzer?'

She hadn't.

She waited at the gate until Pip returned with Watson.

'Your mother's been on the telephone to say they think they've found him.'

'Your young chap. He's found, is he? Good show...' Pip's voice trailed off.

'No, Pip, it was your mother. Someone else.'

'Oh, not young Chadwick.'

'People who live next door to your mother. I can't remember the name.'

'Czerniak. Not unlike Chadwick. The young chap's a bit...unusual. Walked out one day a few weeks ago and didn't come back. Very nice people. Objectors.'

'They think he's been found.'

'Where?'

'Your mother didn't say. I think she wants you to telephone her.'

'Telephone. Got it. And what about young Chadwick?'

'I overheard people at the gate talking about someone being seen on the bridge.'

Pip Beaumont took off his glasses. 'Cheese cutters. Can't fathom why they make these fellows out of wire. Get you behind the ears.' His undressed eyes were round, grey and innocent. He'd never killed anyone, even in the RAF, even in the war. 'It's all over the town. All over the town, Lola, I'm afraid. They're out dragging the river. There's a crowd on the bridge watching. Your dad's gone to help.'

'I'd better go.'

'No, don't.' Pip put his hand out as if to stop her. 'Promise me. I tell you what. Find Jean a library book. I'll tell Lilian where you've gone. Anything'll do. A bit of romance in it. It'll save me going on the way back.' The grey eyes widened. Watson whimpered. 'Don't go to the river, Lola. Promise me. I'll just put this little chap inside while you're getting your coat and walk with you. Here, Jean's library ticket.'

Lola wandered round the shelves. She had a feeling that Jean would like something with doctors and nurses, with a happy ending. But she chose *Hilda Lessways*.

'It's for our neighbour,' she told Miss O'Rourke.

Miss O'Rourke's voice said, 'She'll like Mr Bennett.' Her face said, 'No bones?'

'I haven't had time to come in,' Lola heard her own voice saying. She wondered what her face was saying, if it was describing her work at Salisbury House, if it reflected her preoccupation with the boat going out on the river and the men in oilskins, the poles and the nets, the silence of the line of watchers on the bridge.

'You haven't had time for Mr Gray, of course.' Miss O'Rourke stamped the book and handed it back to her. 'I hear there's a vacancy at the hospital for a darkroom assistant. Please give it a thought, Miss Robertson.'

'I can't...'

'But maybe you can, Miss Robertson. Let us know what you decide. And let me know how your neighbour gets on with *Hilda Lessways*. We don't have much call for the works of Arnold Bennett these days, which is a pity. A man of his time, no doubt, but none the worse for that.'

'Thank you, Miss O'Rourke.'

'Maybe you can. Please think about it.'

But Lola knew that she couldn't. She went out, approaching the revolving door, reading the first page of *Hilda Lessways* as she did so. Another reader was also making for the door, and stepped aside to let her go first. She said thank you, absently, half turning to acknowledge the gallantry, half registering the slight frame of the young man, and the facial disfigurement. She turned round and went back in, letting the empty door swivel.

He had gone. Probably he hadn't been there. She walked up and down between the shelves. She would ask Miss O'Rourke. But she couldn't. Or could she? She couldn't, in the end, because Miss O'Rourke had also vanished, as completely as the vision of a young man afflicted with acne.

Then, outside, she saw him. Or she thought she did. In the company of a woman, a lame woman who was leaning on his arm; down at heel with her auburn hair out of curl and hanging lank below the back of her hat.

It wasn't a crowd so much as a tide of people outside, moving as the river did, slowly and with purpose, yet with its own ripple and eddies. Lola Robertson was carried along, still trying to recover the sudden glimpse she had had of someone who must surely have been Nigel Chadwick, and the woman with him. His mother, she told herself, infirm and needing immediate help, too immediate to wait for what she imagined would be the sluggish process of release from Salisbury House. It wouldn't be anyone but his mother, not even with the unnatural auburn hair, the red polish showing on the finger nails of the hand that held her bag, and the worn down heels that carried her uncertain weight. Lola realised that she was blushing. Blushing, when the whole of the town, the whole of the tide of people, wore its collective pallor on its face and made its way to the East Wharf and the town bridge.

Pip had warned her not to go there. But she had arrived, unknowingly, and was jostled to the front, where the press of people behind caused the stone parapet to dig into her ribs. She should leave and go home, but she couldn't move. Yet she needn't look. She would make herself not look.

And her resolve might have held, had it not been for her father's voice carried on the north wind.

'On the count of three, gentlemen.'

Her eyes were suddenly open, taking in the whole scene: the men on the bank, the nets and ropes and life belts, the hooks; the waiting ambulance, a doctor in a white coat, nurses, policemen, the Methodist minister Mr Jardine; something caught and turning on the brown surface of the river. The object rolled over and over, evading its capture.

'Ready, gentlemen?' Her father had taken off his coat. He was wearing his corporal's hat. The war's over, father.

'One...two...'

When she opened her eyes she was in a room she recognised. Not because she had been there before, but because of the smell, old-fashioned yet comfortable. Safe. Methodist.

'Are you with us, Lola? Does she take sugar, corporal?'

'No, thank you, padre.'

'Put a spoonful in nevertheless, dear. It'll bring her round a little. The poor dear's frozen. Drink up, darling. The sugar will do you good.' Mrs Jardine nudged a cup and saucer towards her.

'Thank you.' Lola didn't know if she had said it or not, so she said it again.

'It's the shock, corporal.'

'I didn't know she were there, padre.'

'Pip told me not to go.' Lola could hear her own voice clearly, but the words seemed to have gone unnoticed.

'Jean Beaumont's husband, dear.'

'My daughter takes their dog out from time ter time.'

'Ah. A good girl.'

'She's a good lass, padre.'

'Someone said I'd killed him.' Her words again seemed to have fallen on deaf ears.

'Does she...?'

'Not that I know of, padre.'

'Of course she doesn't.' Mrs Jardine again. 'She's a sensible, good living girl. We could do with her in the Sunday School, Mr Robertson. I'll discuss it with you another day, Lola darling.' Mrs Jardine picked up *Hilda Lessways*, which had somehow migrated to the table. 'Nice, dear. I'm pleased young people still read Arnold Bennett.'

Yer killt en, Lola Robertson. The voice skeltered down the staircase and met her as she went into Salisbury House. There was a smell of Pond's peach powder.

'Best not ter tell yer ma,' her father said. He hadn't heard the incriminating voice.

But her mother was already in the hallway, wiping chapped hands on her apron, her pale mouth working silently.

'Where have you been, Lola?'

'I took the message to Pip and he asked if I wouldn't mind bringing a library book for Jean.'

Pip must have forgotten to tell her mother.

'It's all very well Mr Beaumont asking if you could take time off to go gallivanting around the town, but didn't you think it might be manners to ask your mother yourself? Did you ask?'

'No, mother.'

'And why not?'

'It's not your business, mother. I don't receive a wage. You don't pay national insurance for me.'

'What's she talking about, Cyril?'

'I told yer, Lil. Yer'd best inform the lass of developments.'

'You tell her, Cyril. I didn't understand. What's got into her, talking to her mother like that?'

Her father didn't answer.

'What's got into you, Lola?' Tears glistened on her mother's cheeks.

I'm sorry, mother. Lola didn't say it. She wanted to wipe the tears away and kiss her mother's soft bewildered face. But she didn't do that either.

'Tell her, Cyril.'

'Presently, Lil, presently. They've been out on the river. Chaps went down to lend a hand, yer know.'

'Oh.' Her mother didn't want to know.

'I'll set the table for tea, mother.'

Lola went into the dining room, took a cloth from the drawer and shook it out. She checked the centre fold for a diamond crease. There wasn't one. The cloth, she realised, was being tugged and straightened from the other end.

'It's all right, mother. I can manage.'

'It's not yer ma, Lola Robertson.' It was Barry Green. 'If yer give me them cutleries, I'll set 'em out for yer.'

'Thank you, Barry Green.'

Barry Green was distributing the knives and forks and spoons as if he were playing darts.

'You have to put them straight, Barry Green.'

'Straighten 'em up after, Lola Robertson. Ant seen much of yer. How are yer?'

Lola looked up.

'Very well, thank you, Barry Green.' The young man looked back at her. Washed. Combed. The tie was tidily knotted and the collar was straight. He wore a dark green pullover. His hands, setting the cutlery at idiosyncratic angles, were clean, and the nails neatly cut. He'd found another mother.

'I wanted ter say summat to yer, Lola Robertson.'

'What was that, Barry Green?'

'That I'm sorry, Lola Robertson. And I'm vexed if yer leaving on my account, Lola Robertson.'

Outside the window, the rooks were going home to Thorold Woods in the mauve twilight.

'I'm not leaving, Barry Green.' She stopped. There had been "developments" of which she was ignorant. 'Not that I know of.' But she did know. There was already someone else in the house, someone who used Pond's peach.

'Didn't yer?'

Lola shut the dining room door. 'Tell me, Barry Green.'

'It's up to yer ma and pa to tell yer, Lola Robertson.'

'They haven't done. You've got to, Barry Green.'

'What'll yer do if I refuse, Lola Robertson? Will yer tell?'

'No, Barry Green. You know I won't. I didn't then and I won't now.'

The door of the dining room was opening. Her mother was coming in, followed by another woman. The scent of peach powder came in with them.

'My daughter will make you a cup of tea, Alison. Mr Green, if you would leave us, please. We have business to attend to. Lola, if you would kindly make Mrs Goody a cup of tea. And bring the sugar basin.'

Lola Robertson caught sight of herself in the hall mirror. Except that it wasn't her. The Lola Robertson reflected there with the striped burgundy wallpaper at her back was, surprisingly, not a child. The years had been added to her without her knowledge. Her face, she realised, was an entity she rarely thought of except in its only photographic representation as part of her class at school, a round face with a slightly downturned mouth and the kind of skin that would erupt into spots every month for the rest of her life.

There were no spots. Her face had thinned, and might well have been rouged, except that she knew the blush was one of shame and betrayal. Not her own. It was that of her mother, who for some reason had invited under her roof as an employee the very woman, and she was suddenly certain beyond the shadow of a doubt of the fact, who had been her father's...she couldn't find the word.

Lola Robertson watched in the mirror as her eyes filled with the intelligence of it all. The visit from the police had frightened her mother and father. They were doing something wrong. They were employing her and not paying her. She knew nothing about national insurance and who had to pay how much, but she had seen Mr Beveridge's picture many times in the reading room, and the words had come to her from nowhere, "You don't pay national insurance for me". And they were true words.

And from nowhere also came the knowledge of the reason for her mother's martyrdom, for martyrdom it was. She would be kind to Alison Goody. She would talk to her as a friend. She would take Albert, who had the looks of the Father, Cyril Robertson, under her wing and see that he did his lessons every day. And by her goodness, she would heap coals of retribution on her husband's head.

Suddenly, there was no end to Lola's knowing. She could, if she had been asked, have listed every bone in the human body, named their prominences and notches, their relationships to each other. She could draw them, each one. She could bear witness to their wonder and beauty and elegance.

She ran up the stairs and along the corridor to her room. The case which had replaced the bags in which she had brought her belongings from Margaret Drive was still under the bed, wrapped in blackout material. She opened it, dusted the inside and pulled out some envelopes lodged in the pocket, which she had found accidentally one day, folded together on the floor of her workbox.

She emptied her dresser, laying the items side by side on the bed: a summer dress, a cardigan, a skirt, two blouses; two pairs of knickers, a spare brassiere, handkerchiefs, stockings, sanitary pads, a belt and pins. Her face flannel and soap. Her pen and pencil. She started to pack the case.

Two floors below the dining room door opened and her mother's voice came out. Lola couldn't hear what she was saying. Presently her father's unequal footsteps made their way to the scullery. The kettle was being filled. Her father was making a cup of tea for Alison Goody.

The envelopes she put in last without reading them. Her other shoes were still on the floor, half way under the bed. Lola opened the case again and made room. And she saw then her mother's writing on one of the envelopes. There was something hot and stinging at the back of her eyes. She pushed the envelope in the pocket at the back of the case where she had found it, together with the others. She mustn't read them. Not yet. Not for a long time.

Not until she had left Salisbury House and her mother and father. Not until she had found somewhere else to live. Not until she had asked if she might assist Miss Taylor in the darkroom. Maybe not even then.

She opened the window and straightened the curtains. She wiped around the sink. She stripped the bed, folding the sheets, pillow slips and blankets, smoothing the ticking. She would take *Hilda Lessways* in a string bag and hang it on the handle of Jean's door.

She would go before the colour left her face and she paled into the other Lola Robertson. She would go before she had time to work out how long three pounds and two shillings and sixpence would last. She would go before she knew the extent of her loss, and before she had worked out if the opposite of innocence was experience, or guilt.

Part III – 1951

Chapter I

From the darkroom, Lola Robertson could hear her father's voice. She heard Miss Taylor call him into the x-ray room and ask him to take off his shoe and sock.

'I'll look after your stick for you, if you like, Corporal Robertson. How is your osteomyelitis these days?'

Her father's response was lost in the separate clunks of the plate as Miss Taylor positioned it under her father's leg and of the x-ray machine as she swung it into place.

'Keep still now, please, sir.' The safelights in the darkroom flickered.

Lola was listening, her right hand holding a frame, half immersed in the wash tank. She let the frame she was holding sink into the tank. She was waiting for the usual question.

'How is she, Miss Taylor?'

'Do you know, Corporal Robertson, we've been so busy I've hardly had the chance to pass the time of day with her.'

'If yer see her, Miss Taylor, say her ma and pa send their best regards. Only if yer see her. Much obliged to yer.'

But her father didn't ask how she was. He merely thanked Miss Taylor for her attention. Lola could hear him, pulling up the chair to sit down while he put on his shoe and sock. She heard the creak of the lead door as Miss Taylor opened it for him, and her father's unequal footsteps going away. Good-bye. Good-bye. The creak of the door as it closed. The turn of the key in the lock.

She heard the sound of the hatch door as Miss Taylor put the plate inside, and she heard the thud of the hatch being closed from the other side.

She opened the darkroom side of the hatch and took out the plates. Miss Taylor had tucked a scrap of paper under the clip with the name "Robertson" pencilled on it. She needn't have done.

Her father's x-rays glimmered in the red glow of the safelights; the tibia and fibula, from the front and from the side, rising out of the dark alkaline bath. The bones emerging from the void, as remarkable as they had been on the first day of the creation of the world.

For a second time, they were no longer Cyril Robertson's. They were the pattern, and Lola could never get over the magic of it all, of the whole order of human beings, who, although they looked every one different from every other one, had this in common, that they lived and walked in the identical temple of the body.

She hadn't discussed these thoughts with anyone, of course. She lifted the film out of the developing bath, rinsed it and plunged it into the acid. They might regard the statement as something quite obvious, but Lola Robertson didn't. She imagined the Lord God sketching out the structure as Henry Gray had done, testing it for durability, distributing the weight through the spine and the pelvis, then equally through the identical femora and the identical tibiae, down to the splayed multiple hinges of the feet.

Miss Taylor was coming through the light trap.

'That was your father, Lola.'

'I know.'

'I could always give him a message, dear.'

'Yes.'

'Would you like me to?'

'I don't know. I'll think about it. Thank you, Miss Taylor.'

'How do they look?'

Lola lifted the first x-ray out of the acid and dunked it in the water. She blinked as Miss Taylor switched on the white light. Cold water ran down her wrist and under her cuff.

'Do you see what I see, Lola?'

'I think so.' There was a faint black crack running through the infected part of the bone.'

'I'll tell HRH.'

But he was already there.

'Mind yourself, corporal. Three right angles to negotiate, sir.' The voice of the doctor, whose name she knew to be Mr Hatchard. He was talking loudly as if the darkness impaired hearing as well as eyesight. Everyone did that. Even Miss Taylor.

'Are the corporal's x-rays cooked, young lady?'

'Yes, sir.' Lola held up the first, the view from the front of the leg.

'Now the other one, young lady. Ah, as I suspected. Do you see what I see? Don't answer for her, Miss Taylor. These ladies are magicians with closely guarded secrets, corporal. You can't get a word out of them.'

'Not in front of the patient, Mr Hatchard. Now, if you'll excuse us, please. I'll bring the pictures to your office in a few minutes.'

Her father hadn't shown any sign of recognition. Maybe he hadn't noticed her. But he had. She saw him look at her and look away. Something must have happened. Something terrible, and it must be her fault.

'I'll kill him!' Miss Taylor drew furiously on her cigarette. 'Who does he think he is, bringing patients into the darkroom! No doubt he thought he was doing the patient a favour. Is that Bovril?'

'It's Oxo. Did my father say anything, Miss Taylor?'

'Lola, I can't remember. I'm so cross everything else has gone out of my mind.'

Lola took that to be a no. Her father hadn't said anything; no message, no enquiry after her health. Something had surely happened.

'I tell you what, you can do a chest this afternoon. It's time you did.'

This was the consolation prize.

'Thank you, Miss Taylor. Will you set the exposure for me?'

Lola knew well how to do a chest x-ray. She had seen Miss Taylor many times, placing her hand lightly on the patient's back if they were female, to make sure they had taken their brassiere off, walking them to the plate and positioning the arms forwards.

'I'd rather it be a lady, Miss Taylor, and not someone I know.' People still looked her up and down and recognised her as the girl from Barratt's Place, who had worn string for shoelaces and whose father had gone to war and come back with a fancy woman in tow. Except that Alison Goody was in no way fancy. She was a woman with quiet frizzy hair and a humble oval face, who when out early every day with a scarf over her head to do the cleaning at the Catholic church.

'Male patients are easier, Lola. You can see where you are with them.'

Lola blushed. She didn't want to x-ray a man. Ever. She couldn't quite work out why. Maybe every male patient would become her father.

He hadn't asked after her. He hadn't left a message, or acknowledged her when he saw her in the darkroom. He surely must have seen her.

'It is possible that your father didn't notice you in the darkroom.' Miss Taylor lit another cigarette but stubbed it out immediately. 'Heaven knows what these things do to the lungs. Tell me what you're going to say to the patient, Lola.'

'I'll call the patient in by their name.'

'Mr Smith, for example. What if there are two Mr Smiths? Or even if Mr Jones stands up. He's so anxious to get this over with he'll answer to anything.'

'I must make sure this is the right Mr Smith. I'll have to ask him his Christian name.'

'Try not to use the term Christian though, Lola.'

'No, his first name. And another identifying detail like his date of birth.'

'Good girl.'

'Then I'll explain that we're going to x-ray his chest, and tell him that he will be asked to breathe in and hold his breath.'

'How?'

'Loudly enough for him to hear, Miss Taylor.'

'Good girl. And when you're satisfied that he can go home?'

'I'll tell him how to find out his results.'

'He will want to ask you if you've found anything. You are the woman with the x-ray eyes. What will you say? Will you say you don't know and leave it at that?'

'No, Miss Taylor. I'll explain that a doctor reads the x-ray, not the person who takes it.'

'Will he believe you?'

'Probably not.'

'Why not?'

'Because he thinks I'm a know-all. I give people that impression,' Lola said, to the empty room.

Miss Taylor had gone out. She returned presently, bringing in a request form. 'Not this one, Lola. We'll see what the next one is. Would you be so kind as to go to the dispensary for the hibitane? It might not be ready for collection, but just wait for it, if you would.'

At the end of the day, Lola was writing the names on the x-rays, holding them under the light to decipher the pencil in the top left corner, writing the patients' details in white ink. She laid one aside, one without a name pencilled on. It must have been the patient Miss Taylor x-rayed while she was in the dispensary.

She cleaned the pen and the rim of the inkbottle. Then she matched the x-rays with the request forms. All except the one without a name. She held it up to the light. She could see that it was a female patient, a thin female patient with a narrow chest. At the bottom of the x-ray, she saw the hands on the hips, a ring on the left hand, the beginning of a row of hooks and eyes fastening the skirt on the left side. The spine wasn't quite straight. Many women were like that. They were women who worked, women who had got by on rations for many years.

But it was the lung on the right side that was wrong. Lola knew that lungs appeared black because they contained air. This patient's lung was white, nearly up to the middle. It was almost certainly the patient Miss Taylor had seen while she was waiting for hibitane in the dispensary.

Lola's mind raced on. She had been sent away because she knew the patient. She was sure of it. And she knew the patient so well that Miss Taylor hadn't pencilled the name on the undeveloped film, nor had she left the request form with the others.

It was ten minutes to six. If she hurried, she would catch Jean Beaumont coming out of work. Jean would know. Lola wasn't sure of what she was expecting Jean to know, but all the same she would say something helpful.

But Jean didn't appear. Lola stood gazing into the window of Fortesque's, looking at her own everyday frame reflected back at her in front of the still models with their narrow skirts, loose coats and high heels. Someone passed behind her, another woman, going home. Familiar, yet not familiar. Lola continued to gaze into the shop window, watching the woman passing by, watching her for an eternity. It couldn't be. But it was. Her mother surely would be at Salisbury House, presiding over the evening meal, moving the cruet to ensure that there wasn't a diamond crease concealed under it. Yet she wasn't at Salisbury House. She was in the Market Square as the shops were closing. She was walking past the display in Fortesque's without looking, not even so much as to notice the young woman standing there.

Lola turned and saw her mother cross to the other side. She saw that her mother's hair was out of curl and that she was in the town without gloves. The hem of her coat was down on one side. Lola Robertson's x-ray eyes looked through the brown threadbare coat, and the mauve twinset and the brassiere, through the skin pulled tightly across the ribs and the knuckles of the thoracic vertebrae, and saw the lung fields, one black and filled with air, the other white half way up and filled with...fluid, Miss Taylor would say; and when you see that there is often, not always, something nasty hiding itself away.

Her mother turned. Lola could see her profile, white and pinched, looking in the window of Carr's for something to take home for her father's tea. An Eccles cake. Something sweet, with currants.

Then all at once, there was Jean, slipping her arm through her mother's and bearing her off like a precious gift towards Salisbury House.

Lola stood in front of the shop window, looking into it until the lights went off and the models slipped back into the shadows.

In the manse at the back of the chapel, she could see the figure of Mrs Jardine moving around in the living room.

She knocked on the door. 'I hope I haven't come at an inconvenient time, Mrs Jardine.'

'Why, it's Lola. Come in, dear.' Mrs Jardine opened the door wide and stepped back. Her first name was Emma. 'My husband isn't back yet. I'm quite on my own. Do come in, Lola.' She could imagine Mrs Jardine's next words queuing up, waiting for delivery. We haven't seen you at chapel recently, Lola. But she didn't say them. 'You are troubled, my dear. Do come in. We hear you're at the hospital. How nice. Sit down now. What is it?'

'I'm worried about my mother.'

'Yes, dear.'

'Is she…ill, do you know, Mrs Jardine? Please?'

'Geoffrey could ask Corporal Robertson to get in touch with you, dear. That would be best, perhaps.'

'You can't tell me then?'

'I could tell you, dear, but I might tell you the wrong thing. My husband will speak with Corporal Robertson. May he tell your father you've been here?'

Lola nodded. She felt in her pocket for her handkerchief but couldn't find it. Mrs Jardine went to the sideboard drawer and brought back a small lace-edged square with a pink flower embroidered in the corner. 'It's from the jumble sale,' she said. 'I always keep them, just in case. Does your father know where you live?'

Lola didn't say anything.

Mrs Jardine spread her hands helplessly. A ginger cat wandered in, leaving the door ajar. The draught gathered round Lola's ankles. She folded the lace handkerchief and put it in her pocket.

She couldn't remember if she had thanked Mrs Jardine. The streets at the south end of the town were empty of everything except the diffuse light from windows spilling out onto the damp pavements. Curtains were being drawn against the night. She turned the corner into Crown Street. There was a man with a dog ahead of her, stopping by each door, peering at the numbers, taking his glasses off, wiping them, putting them back on. All at once, the dog was bounding towards her, ears flying, lead trailing.

'Watson!'

The dog pushed his soft grizzled head into her hand.

'I'm so sorry. He's quite harmless. Never grown up, that's his problem. Excuse me, but you don't happen to know a Miss Robertson who lives near here, do you?'

'I might do, sir.'

'Lola!' Pip Beaumont held out his hand to her as if she were…she searched in her mind for a comparison…the managing director's wife. Someone worthy. She started to cry. Pip said, 'Hey,' and fished a newly ironed handkerchief out of his pocket. 'Hey, Lola.'

'I would ask you in, Pip, but…'

'Chaps aren't welcome. Is there a café or something?

'There's a public house.'

'No, Lola. Jean would never forgive me.'

'I'll ask Mrs Priest if we can sit in the parlour.'

'Parlour! That sounds grand.'

'That's what she calls it. It's number twenty-three.'

Pip Beaumont carried the aroma of the factory with him: a combination of motor oil and cigarette smoke. She hadn't noticed before. Probably she herself walked around carrying the smell of the x-ray department: disinfectant and photographic acid.

'Do I smell of the hospital?' she said.

'There was a time when everyone smelt of the war,' Pip said. 'Do you remember? Probably we noticed it more in London. It was always masonry dust and smoke and boiled cabbage, and they were the better smells.' He had lost his RAF speech. There was no one to share it with.

'This is it. It isn't a palace, I'm afraid.'

'All the better for that.' Pip was making conciliatory noises preparing her for some difficult news. She wanted to tell him he needn't; he could say what he had come to say. 'It certainly is a palace, Lola. My word! Someone even does the step with that red stuff.'

175

'Cardinal polish. I'll have to ask you not to tread on it and spoil it, Pip.'

'Is she a dragon then?'

'Who?'

'The landlady.'

'No, not really. She says she likes to have people from the hospital.'

'Clean, I suppose.'

'Respectable. But on this occasion, I won't be. You can come into my room, Pip.' She blushed. 'I think she might be out anyway.' Suddenly, she saw her room through a visitor's eyes, washed in the sick light from an unshaded overhead bulb, harsh and unloving. 'Sit down, Pip. Would you like a cup of tea?' She dived into her bag and extracted a packet of Brooke Bond. 'Does Jean still collect the stamps?' She would keep him talking until he had mislaid the bad news he had come to deliver.

'Lola?'

'Yes, Pip.'

'Jean's with your mother. She took her down to the hospital this afternoon. Two o'clock. Could have been one o'clock. And she brought her back. Don't quite know the ins and outs, Lola, but Jean brought your mother back. Your mother's…much as usual, Lola. Looks much the same. Just wanted you to know. Lilian looks much the same. Just been the cough lately. And an ache in the shoulder.'

'What did they tell her?'

'A touch of pleurisy. She's got a touch of pleurisy, that's what the MO said. No point in…you know.' Pip Beaumont looked at her helplessly. 'She came back with an Eccles cake for your father's tea.'

'Are there any…tablets?' Watson heaved himself up, and settled down on her foot.

'The district nurse sees to all that. We'll do what we can, Lola.'

'I ought to go and see mother. Oughtn't I?'

Pip Beaumont didn't answer.

'Oughtn't I?' She vaguely wondered if that was a real word. "Ought". The letters of it arranged themselves in her mind. They looked odd somehow. 'How is father?'

'Much as usual, Lola. Much as usual.'

'Is Alison still there?'

'So I believe. Lola.' Pip was searching for words. 'Thing is…not right in view of the business with your mother, damned tactless in fact, but best coming from us than...you see what I mean?'

'I think I know already, Pip. It must be quite soon.'

She knew as well, that should the baby be a girl, Jean and Pip would wish her to be baptised with the name Lilian.

She knew, too, that when she came back from seeing Pip off Mrs Priest would be in the hallway, shaking DDT powder along the skirtings, and sniffing the air.

And she knew, because she was and would always be Lola Robertson from Barratt's Place, that before the end of the day the illness of the mother would have become the lasting fault of the daughter.

Chapter II

Stefan Czerniak stepped over the luminous word in front of the gate and went up the chequered path to the front door, placing his feet only on the white tiles, as if by doing so some undefined ill might be avoided.

He stood in front of the door watching the figure behind the glass: a man above average in height with a shock of dark hair, strongly marked brows and fear in his eyes. They didn't want him there. The man behind the glass ran his hand through his hair as if to subdue it into some semblance of…conformity. The hair sprang back against the heavy patterned background of the door curtain. It should have been unusual that the other man had come to the door and insinuated himself between the curtain and the glass. But it wasn't. It was always so. He would wait there with his frightened eyes and shocked hair, between the curtain and the glass, showing no signs of recognition. Until he turned to go away.

Then Stefan was going back down the chequered path, still walking on the white tiles, because the undefined ill had passed by him. He stepped over the word – CONSHY – seeing it upside down and back to front. Still luminous after so many years. The plaque by the door had been polished. Paul Czerniak, Professor of Mathematics, the owner of the accolade residing somewhere between the glass and the curtain, looking back at him but not answering the door; turning away in the same instant that he himself turned away.

A stone narrowly missed him and skittered into the gutter. He picked it up and put it in his pocket. Another. Weightier. A third, jagged, grazed the side of his face at the angle of the jaw. He picked it up, put it in his pocket and continued to walk up Golen Avenue. A fourth, glancing off his shoulder and dropping down in front of him. He put it in his pocket, the other pocket, the one holding the letter addressed to him in his mother's handwriting. He continued to walk. A fifth stone, and a warm thread of blood.

"Dear…" The letter ran on. But not the letter in his pocket, gradually collecting a covering of stones and grit. It was an earlier letter, to a girl who lived on the border of Nottinghamshire, who had mended his father's sock one day not long after the end of the war, a day filtered through pale sunshine, and a family blessed, each in their separate ways, with the gifts of the spirit though they did not know it. He had taken it to the post and queued, a letter to a girl he didn't know, a letter enclosed in a small packet with his mother's thimble and for that reason marked "fragile". The address was Barratt's Place. His father had described it: a door opening into a front room, a mother pale and downtrodden, a father seated in a chair in the corner, his leg extended on account of some terrible wound, a girl sewing in the corner. Designated fragile. All with the gifts of the spirit.

"My dear Stefan…" He sat down on a wall. He would take the letter addressed in his mother's handwriting to Congreve Park and read it. After the people had gone by. He could see their shadows approaching, heads first, a man's bowler hat, a woman's with a feather, their shoulders leaning into one another. A rolled umbrella. A newspaper.

He looked up. The man was saying something to the woman, *sotto voce*, of such interest that she turned to look at him. His eyes met hers briefly before she looked away. Oddly, the man was walking on the inside. That should not be so. He considered his father, an aloof figure trapped between the glass and the door curtain, who turned away, who would not permit his mother to walk on the outside. The man continued to talk to his companion. They were coming nearer. Stefan looked away. He opened his mother's letter and held it in his hand.

He didn't look up when he heard the sudden expletive, the scuffling of feet and the brittle voice of the woman. He didn't look up until he was shown into the room and asked to sit down on a wooden chair facing a desk. There was a faint scent of something flowery like lavender in the room.

'You'll excuse us, sir. We were obliged to ascertain your name from the letter you had in your possession. If you please, give an account of yourself, Mr Zurniak, supposing that is you, of course.'

'Czerniak, sir. Stefan Czerniak.'

'If you'll please give an account of yourself.' Somewhere a door opened and a tea trolley rattled in. 'Thank you, Ruby. The lady and gentleman, please, one sugar in each. I'll ask this young man.' The officer raised his voice. 'Would you like a cup of tea, Mr Zurniak?'

'Czerniak, sir. As in church.' A cup of tea was placed in front of him.

'Sugar?'

'No, no thank you. Thank you, sir.'

'The other gentleman, sir?'

'No thank you, Ruby, the witness has declined.'

'Give an account of yourself, if you please, Mr Czerniak. The gentleman here alleges that you put out your foot causing him to trip and fall. Is that correct, sir?'

'I have no recollection, sir.'

'Very well, sir. We will ask the gentleman in question. Mr Aveling, if you please.'

A newspaper was spread out on the kitchen table, open at the situations vacant, several of which were marked with perfect ellipses. Outside in the glancing sun, a tortoise was staggering through the runner beans. He had to intervene, to scoop up the small joyful creature and hold it in his palm, watch its legs paddling in the air and its bright inquisitive eyes. His father was saying something. Bazal can wait. But there was something else. The public abuse of objectors. Someone's name.

'Mr Aveling?'

'My wife will bear me out, sir. The defendant intended mischief; there's no question about it.'

'Darling, we're not in court. He might not be quite…well.'

'Officer, if I might intervene…' The voice of the witness was oddly familiar, coming as it did from a distant garden. What was left of a lawn at the end of the war. A roller crusted in red rust. Someone coaxing a mower into life, pushing it back and forth in short determined forays.

'If you could bear with us, witness, we will hear this gentleman out first. Mr Aveling, continue, if you would please.'

'Had dealings with the defendant in the past, officer. Comes from a family of conchies and ne'er do wells. Foreigners. Communists most likely, though no hard evidence. Not the type we want here.'

A chair crashed to the floor.

'Objection, officer.'

The chair was righted.

'Sit down, please, sir. You will be able to speak presently. Anything further, Mr Aveling?'

'No, I think not, officer.'

'The young man doesn't seem quite well.' The woman's voice again.

'You may speak now, witness. You saw the incident, I believe.'

'Yes, officer. I was coming down Golen Avenue and noticed Mr Czerniak seated on a wall, having suffered what appeared to be an injury to the face. The gentleman over there was approaching from the opposite direction, engaged in conversation with his companion. The said gentleman appeared to trip and fall. I went forwards to assist and observed uneven paving. I did not observe Mr Czerniak's foot, officer.'

'Are you acquainted with Mr Czerniak, sir?'

'My parents more than myself, officer. After the war I remained in the east. I have come back for family reasons.'

'I notice your black tie, sir. May I offer our condolences.'

'Thank you, officer.'

'In view of the present circumstances, Mr Aveling, and in view of the paucity of evidence, I will record this event as an unfortunate accident. Maybe you would be able to shed some light on the origin of the injury to Mr Czerniak's face. Did you witness the assault? No? Fair enough. May I take this opportunity of reminding you that the war is over, Mr Aveling. Probably you would see Mr Czerniak home, Mr Beaumont. Much obliged to you, sir.'

Stefan was conscious of the scent of lavender edging nearer, not unpleasant but unsettling. He was on his feet, facing the woman who had spoken, taking her extended hand, behaving like a gentleman. Behaving like his father.

'You'll forgive my husband, Mr Czerniak.' She wore a grey costume with a glittering brooch in the lapel. Her eyebrows were arched in perpetual questioning, her lipstick like a wind-blown peony on her face. A fellow traveller in an unforgiving world.

'Of course. Please don't worry.' He thought of the pond in Congreve Park, its countenance ruffled and unwelcoming, the brown mallards thrown about helplessly. 'Of course. Please don't worry. It was nothing.' I am nothing, someone once said. Sartre.

'My husband's a good man.'

Stefan didn't know if he had answered. If he had, he hadn't heard his voice, either in the chamber of his mind or in the hollow of the room, which was all at once in his sight. The cube of it, the brown of it, the plain woodenness of it, smelling, underneath the aura of lavender, faintly of disinfectant, urine and strong tea. The original officer had gone and had been replaced by someone else, standing by the door with a bunch of keys, ready to lock them out.

'They want us to go.'

'It looks like it.' She held out her hand again. 'Good-bye, Mr Czerniak.'

He didn't know if he answered.

'You would have made the appropriate response, old chap,' Lad Beaumont said. 'You were brought up that way. Good people, your mum and dad. Talking of whom, which we weren't, of course, I've been tasked with seeing you…you know.'

'I don't live there, Lad.'

'No? Well, I'll be damned. Since when?'

'Since…'

'How long haven't you lived there, Stefan old chap? Something amiss? Sorry to hear that. Not that I've heard it until you tell me, so to speak.'

'Three years or so. I was being blackmailed. It doesn't matter.'

'Blackmail, was it? But it does matter, old chap. Did you pay them anything? Hey up.' Lad Beaumont stopped short of the luminous word on the pavement. 'You'll come in, old chap, won't you? Probably not your cup of tea but you'll do Freda a power of good.'

Stefan's hand closed round the letter addressed in his mother's writing, still in his pocket, in the company of miscellaneous stones and grit. Still unread.

'Mother sent me a letter.'

'She told you, old chap?' Lad nudged at the white edge of the word with the toe of his shoe. Black shoes. Unworn black shoes. 'Hey, old chap, don't say you haven't heard?'

'I was about to read the letter when…'

'Aveling, known him for years. Used to terrorise us as boys. Funny thing is, he doesn't get any older. And that woman. God.'

'His wife?'

'So to speak.'

'She was all right.' Stefan looked past her head again, past the hat with the feather, to the paper chains looped across the windows of the room they had lately been in. He hadn't noticed them at the time.

'You didn't know about dad then, old chap?'

'It's probably in the letter. I'm so sorry…'

'You'll come in, won't you, Stef? Not every chap's cup of tea, as I say. I'll make your excuses if you prefer.'

Freda Beaumont had already seen them from the narrow window above the door, where she was closing a crack in the curtains.

'Heard our voices. Can still make your excuses, old chap. Diplomatic service, you see. Good at tact.'

Paper chains, red, white and blue, travelled across the front windows, looping from side to side in front of the curtains.

'Good Lord,' said Lad. 'What are they for? Looks as if they've been there since the war. Didn't see them before.'

'Festival of Britain. I can take them down if you like.'

'If you don't mind, old chap. If you don't mind…you know.'

Mrs Beaumont was at the front door. Running down the path. At the gate. Flustering with the sneck.

'It was sudden, you know, Stefan dear. At the end. I didn't know it had happened. Then I saw…that the light had gone out. You know. Oh dear, where's my hankie. Probably I don't need one. Stefan dear…' she lowered her voice, 'your parents are here. I'll understand if…you know. They've never told us what happened, but you had your reasons, dear.'

'Let me do the gate, mum. We'll be here all day.'

'Yes, they've been here all day, Stefan dear.'

He followed Mrs Beaumont up the path to the front door. Followed her worn down heels and the wavering seams of her stockings, her creased skirt and the disordered halo of her hair, expecting to be excused and forgiven. As she herself excused and forgave, her son for his lightness, her husband for his darkness.

'I shouldn't have said that, old chap,' Lad muttered. 'Should I?' He wanted an answer. 'Not under the circs. Should have left it behind at the white cliffs and all that.'

'She didn't hear properly.'

'She did, old chap. She heard all right. Line of defence, you see, old chap. Turns things round. Remember Munich? Surprised she even noticed…you know. Good job…a bloke was home on furlough.'

The door of the front room stood half way open. Mrs Beaumont's voice was inside.

'Talking to your dad, old chap. Never knew he was a religious gent. Kept that well hidden. Not criticising him, mind you, old chap. Very noble. Your mum's in the back. Makes a champion cup of cha.' He caught hold of Stefan's sleeve. 'Don't know what they've done. Not my business, but they're decent people. Never met better, and I've knocked around the world a fair bit. Your mum's in the kitchen, old chap. I'll leave you to it. Give me a call if…you know.'

Ruth Czerniak turned as he entered. He watched the colour drain from her face and her hands tremble as she hurried to put the kettle down on the hob. Her hair was grey, drawn back into a pleat. She had no lipstick.

'Stefan! You got my letter?'

'I rang the bell and father came to the door but he went away again.'

His mother frowned. 'Your father's been here since first thing this morning. What time did you ring the bell?'

'I don't know. I met Lad. He told me.'

'Yes, Lad's on home leave.'

'No, I haven't, mother. I must do that.'

'Stefan, what are you saying?'

'I haven't offered my condolences to Mrs Beaumont. I must do that. I could see you thinking it.'

A faint colour crept back into his mother's face. 'Did you read my letter?'

'Will you open it for me?' He handed his mother her letter.

'But it's addressed to you, dear.'

'Please, Ruth.'

She looked up. 'Very well, Stefan.'

'Did you write it?'

'Why, yes dear, of course I did. Here, it's yours.'

Mrs Beaumont's steps were in the passage. 'It's optional. Of course it's optional. No one has to do these things.'

Stefan caught his mother's eye, and finding no answer sought one from Lad, who was following Freda. Lad wrote a word in the air, long, complicated, Latinate and the wrong way round. Optional. Old chap.

'I will, Mrs Beaumont,' he said. He knew when he walked into the house that he would.

A heap of paper chains lay on the table; more paper chains. Motes of dust danced in the light coming through a tear in a curtain, danced and died in the yellow flame of a candle burning on the mantelpiece. A stack of National Geographics. The Times still open. The affairs of the world stopped in mid-sentence. A crossword unfinished.

The chairs pushed back to the wall, and in the centre of the room the mortal remains of Kenelm Beaumont. The casket lid was closed, and lying on the top of it Mr Beaumont's ring, spectacles and pocket watch. The watch had stopped. Stefan picked it up, set the hands, shook it. It suddenly became vitally important that Mr Beaumont's watch should start again.

'It won't go!' The voice was loud, outraged. 'It won't go.'

'The spring has been taken out, Stefan. Freda wished it.'

'I'm sorry, I didn't see you there, dad.'

Little by little the room filled with the rasp of Paul Czerniak's difficult breathing; little by little the figure of him emerged from the gloom. Standing, wearing his long dark coat, a shirt done up to the neck. No collar. No tie. Outside, people were arriving, dealing with the sneck on the gate, walking up the path.

'Is Bazal still here?'

The new people were in the hallway, taking off their coats. Someone was crying. Jean. And his father. He could see the lines of silver running down his father's face.

'Bazal's still here, yes.'

'I'd better be heading back, dad, when...Is there a dog?'

'That's Watson. A fine little chap.'

Everyone had moved into the middle room.

'Would you tell mother?'

'What should I tell her?' His father's question followed him out of the house and down the path and through the impossible gate.

What should I tell her? Stefan didn't know. He couldn't remember if he had answered. A question in another world.

He let himself into the front door of his lodgings. Everything was as usual: the table in the hallway with the uncollected letters; the cracked linoleum; the smell. The room was as usual, the wooden chair seated at the table, the mat placed sparsely on the floorboards, the cupboard with its open door, the utility wardrobe and the bed. The unshaded bulb. The sticks in the grate. The violin.

He sat down at the table and read his mother's letter.

Chapter III

The overhead light in the storeroom fizzled and flickered and went out. Lola made her way along the shelves of files until she came to the switch. She pushed the loose wire back into the fitting and hammered it home with the heel of her hand. The store leapt into its habitual being. A cockroach skittered away, into the files.

Rani, Emily. Roach, James. Robb, Alfred. Robert, Harry. Roberts, Maud. Robertson, Cyril. Robinson, Cecily. Rogers, Hannah. Rought, Billy. She looked again. Lilian Robertson wasn't there. She looked through a third time. Hot shame flooded her neck and washed over her face. It hadn't happened. She had imagined it all, assumed that the unnamed x-ray belonged to her mother. She had exaggerated the entire thing; invested it with a meaning it didn't have.

The storeroom light fizzed and sputtered. A dreadful thought jumped out of the darkness, caught hold of her and crushed her as she fumbled with the loose wires: the thought that her mother should be ill, that something might come out of it, something…different… for herself, in her own life. She might be asked to go back. Welcomed. Needed. She felt the shame of it running like rivers between every hair on her head.

'Lola! Lola! Are you there, dear?' The door opened a crack. 'Oh dear, don't say the light's gone again.'

'I was trying to mend it,' she said, which was true. Which was monstrously and irrevocably untrue. She had told Miss Taylor a…she couldn't think the word. Hot tears gathered behind her eyes. She slammed the door of the room, shutting Miss Taylor outside and her disgrace inside. The impromptu falsehood had, in the second it took to utter it, made the whole of her false, her whole life, the past, the present, the future. All of a sudden, she had found she had no right to feel morally superior to anyone, to her parents, to Alison Goody, to Barry Green. She started to cry.

'Lola!' Miss Taylor was knocking on the door. She was talking to someone else. 'Thank you, Jozef. I think she's suffered an electrical shock. She said she was trying to mend the light. Lola! Can you hear me, dear?'

'Lulu!' Lola hadn't heard Jozef Schmidt's voice before. He came and went silently, finding his way into the darkroom, taking the x-rays out of the tank when they were ready, draining them and clattering them round the corner to casualty. She could tell Jozef about her lie. The buried word welled up in her throat, bilious and terrible. Lie. Lie. And he wouldn't judge her. He wouldn't know her words. He wouldn't say anything. Nothing she could understand.

'Careful, Jozef. She might have fallen behind the door. *Danke schön.*'

Then she was in casualty behind curtains, wrapped in a red blanket with a sphygmomanometer cuff wrapped loosely round her arm and a thermometer in her mouth. Everyone else had gone. She took the thermometer out of her mouth, swallowed, and put it in again. She felt unbearably tired. People were talking, a long way off, their voices coming and going. Miss Taylor, the new doctor, nurse Hines. Talking about her. The blood pressure and the temperature were satisfactory. Nurse Hines would bring her a cup of strong tea. A lucky escape this time, but the wiring in the storeroom must be seen to. She was suddenly a heroine.

She took the thermometer out of her mouth again and slipped down from the trolley. She couldn't find her shoes, or her blouse and skirt or her white coat. A faint aroma of vomit, and something mortifying and intimate from under the red blanket met her. She wrapped the blanket more closely around her.

'It was my fault.'

She tried to make her way to where the voices had come from, but when she reached the place they had gone. She started to cry. 'It was my own fault.'

Jozef Schmidt was seated in the staff room opposite her. She could hear Miss Taylor banging around in the dark room. Fuming. A half-smoked cigarette occupied the ashtray sending a spiral of blue smoke up to the ceiling. She had in her hands a cup of tea. Jozef Schmidt was listening. Listening to her talking in a language he couldn't understand.

'I did something terribly wrong, Jozef. I told Miss Taylor I was mending the light switch and that was only a bit true. We weren't busy and I was looking for my mother's x-rays.'

And she went on, telling this man she hardly knew, who had no idea what she was saying, how she had found an x-ray without an accompanying pro forma, an abnormal x-ray; how Miss Taylor sent her on some errand every time the patient, whom Lola knew without doubt to be Lilian Robertson, her mother, attended; how she no longer saw her mother, how there were problems in the family. And again, how she had said to Miss Taylor that she was mending the light switch when in reality she was looking, uselessly in the event, for the x-rays of her mother.

Until she heard Miss Taylor saying good-bye to her patient, and the cigarette had fallen away into ash, and Jozef Schmidt, seated opposite her in the drab frayed staff room, with the green paint peeling from the walls and a pile of Woman's Own on the table, said, 'Lulu, it is all right. *Ich verstehe*. It will be all right.'

But it wasn't all right. Miss Taylor had taken Jozef Schmidt's place. She was lighting another Players. 'Like one, dear?' She passed the packet over to Lola. Lola looked at the picture of the sailor on the front and gave it back to Miss Taylor. She said she was sorry. Miss Taylor nodded. She said it was her own fault and she should have had the light switch seen to. She wasn't aware that there was any filing outstanding.

'There wasn't,' Lola said. She took a breath. 'I was looking for Lilian Robertson's x-rays.'

Miss Taylor got up and went to the window. The blue smoke curled against the glass trying to get out, hovering there, dissipating, until the roof of pharmacy was visible again.

'Was that wrong, Miss Taylor?'

'You have only one fault, Lola, and it is hardly a fault.'

Under the red blanket, Lola shivered.

'I told an untruth, Miss Taylor. I said I was trying to put the wires back properly inside the switch but it was only a bit true. I was trying to find mother's x-rays. Is that it? I'm sorry.'

'Is that it?'

'The fault I have.'

Miss Taylor came back to the chair and stubbed out her cigarette. 'Oh no, it isn't that. It's something much more complex than a few words said in self-defence. Hasn't anyone ever told you?'

'No.' Lola didn't know what it was that no one had ever told her. A terrible realisation came to her, that it was something to do with her body. She was fat. She smelt. She smelt of the monthly even when it wasn't that time. Miss Taylor always carried a faint scent of hibitane around with her, as if she bathed in it and cleaned her teeth with it.

'Is it…?' Tears gathered behind her eyes.

'No, no, you keep yourself nicely, Lola.' Miss Taylor lit another cigarette. 'You know too much for your own…happiness. Mrs Robertson's x-rays have been retained for the time being in the chest clinic. Let me show you something. You needn't get up.'

Miss Taylor went out and returned with two chest x-rays. She held them up to the window.

'Lola, one of these x-rays is good. The other is entirely adequate for diagnostic purposes but not perfect. You took the good picture. I took the picture which was merely adequate. They're the same patient. Now, if you put your things on, dear, Jozef will walk you home. It's for the best.'

Jozef Schmidt was waiting at the door, his hands in his pockets. He wore a long dark coat with the collar turned up. As if, she thought, he were embarking on some clandestine mission in the process of which he didn't wish to be recognised.

'I live in Crown Street,' she said. 'It isn't a very nice street. I'm sorry.'

'Lulu, it's all right,' he said. '*Ich verstehe.*'

They walked in silence, so profound a silence that she wondered if Jozef Schmidt had imparted the whole of his vocabulary. Which – and she had stepped blindly and deafly into Durne Street, neither seeing the bicycle nor hearing the bell – if they were the only words he knew would have been appropriate in the majority of hospital situations, either as a whole or in fragments. He caught her sleeve.

'I'm sorry, Jozef.'

'Lulu, it's all right.'

Then she saw her father, his unmistakable and difficult walk, in the distance and approaching.

'That's my father. I'd rather not meet him, Jozef. We are…' she searched for a word…'not friends.'

But it was all right, even before Jozef Schmidt said the words. Her father was suddenly not there. He had vanished. She glanced into the interiors of the shops, getting ready for the end of the day, pulling down their blinds. Closing their eyes to the fact that here was Lola Robertson, formerly of Barratt's Place, in the company of a man who was neither a relative nor a neighbour. An unmistakably foreign man, who reminded her vaguely of a visitor whose sock she had mended one evening not long after the end of the war. Before everything became so horribly complicated.

Her father might never have been there, walking towards them. She might have conjured up his presence in the instant that Jozef Schmidt caught hold of her sleeve.

'I live at number twenty-three,' she said. 'I'll be all right now, Jozef. Thank you. Thank you.'

Lulu, it's all right. But he didn't say it. Instead, he put his hands on her shoulders and turned her towards him. She looked up into his eyes and knew then, if she didn't know before, that she had fallen hopelessly under a spell, the nature of which she couldn't have explained, even to herself.

Mrs Priest was over the road, walking back home with a string bag.

'My landlady,' she said.

Mrs Priest had seen her but hadn't said hello.

'She hasn't forgiven me for the time my parents' neighbour brought his dog.'

Jozef Schmidt's eyes sparkled. Suddenly, there was everything she wanted to tell him, and she had squandered the walk home in silence. Tomorrow the spell would be broken.

Then she realised the nature of the spell: it was nothing more and nothing less than kindness; devastating and unbearable kindness. She would be too embarrassed even to pass the time of day with him tomorrow. His hands fell from her shoulders '*Gute nacht, Lulu.*'

'Good night.' She couldn't say his name.

Mrs Priest was waiting in the hallway.

'Your rent book, Miss Robertson. You are up to date until the end of the month.'

'I'll pay you for next month now, if you like, Mrs Priest.'

'That won't be necessary, Miss Robertson. You'll read why in the letter.' The brown corner of an envelope protruded from inside the back cover of the rent book.

Lola said nothing. She caught sight of a young woman in the mirror, her brown hair windblown and the shock of recognition still in her eyes, her face flushed. Someone other.

'You might well look at yourself, Miss Robertson. Making sure we looked our best for the fancy man, are we?'

Yes, Mrs Priest, Lola thought. That's what I was doing. She went into her room and locked the door. She cut two slices of bread and looked in the cupboard for the plum jam. It had gone.

That's what she had been doing. That's what her pretty mother had done when she first set eyes on Cyril Robertson; what even the women in the Bible had done, the Queen of Sheba, Mary Magdalene; what the first woman Eve had done when, looking into the still pool in the cool of the day she had been astonished by the life in the face looking back at her. She spread margarine on the bread, wiped her hands and opened Mrs Priest's letter.

"Miss Lola Robertson, if it will please you to vacate your room by the 30th inst my niece is expected. In the event of your requiring a reference, I regret to inform you that I am unable to supply it on account of your infringement of rule 7a as set down in rent Book namely the encouragement of pet animals and other pests and rule 13f namely the bringing of the premises into ill repute and you will know why. Evaline Priest."

Lola idly picked up a pencil and inserted two commas into the text. Then she took down the picture, the one of Jesus suffering the little children. She took her plate and knife along to the scullery and washed them up. Mrs Priest was moving around upstairs, going from one room to another, opening doors and closing them. Keeping a clean house. That's what she had said when Lola moved in. 'I keep a clean house, Miss Lola Robertson. That's why I am letting you have the room because I've had young women from the hospital before.'

She went to the bottom drawer of the dresser and counted her savings. There was enough for a month's rent somewhere else and some spare for getting by until her next pay. She made a pile of things on the chair, and pulled the suitcase out from under the bed. Then she stopped, standing in the middle of the room with the trappings of her life around her. She didn't much care. Part of her, the living part, was still outside in Crown Street in the last few seconds before she had heard the amazing words. '*Gute nacht, Lulu. Gute nacht.*'

She stripped the bed and tidied the room, drawing the curtains back, letting in the dazzling twilight. She wrapped her face flannel and soap and tooth brush in a teacloth and placed them in the bottom of the case.

There was a knock on the door. Lola sat down on the frayed stripes of the mattress holding her breath. The knock on the door came again. She could hear Mrs Priest outside, trying the knob, turning it one way and then the other.

'Yes?'

'It's Mrs Priest.' The door opened and the landlady was standing there, her hair in curlers and wearing a man's dressing gown. 'Well, Miss Robertson, am I to be invited into my own room?' Lola stood back and held the door open. Mrs Priest was just inside sniffing the air. 'Well, here's a how-do-you-do.' Then, presently, 'Did you get my letter?'

'Yes, Mrs Priest.'

'I'll take my key back then, Miss Robertson.'

Curtains were being drawn in the house across the road. A wireless was on somewhere, a thin, lonely sound in the gathering dark.

'I'm not going tonight. I'm making it clean for when your niece comes.'

'My niece?'

'When she comes. It says in the letter.'

'Oh yes, sent you that one, did I? When will you be going?'

'I'll let you know, Mrs Priest. As soon as I've found somewhere.'

Lola remade the bed. She would no doubt have to ask Mrs Priest for a rent rebate for the outstanding days until the end of the month. But she knew she wouldn't. She could hear the landlady climbing the stairs, and her footsteps walking across the ceiling. Somewhere in the distance, a dog barked. Someone outside striking a match. Someone passing the front of the house whistling *Lili Marlene*.

'You could come and stay with mother and I,' Miss Taylor said. Lola didn't know Miss Taylor had a mother. She didn't know anything about her domestic arrangements.

'Thank you, Miss Taylor, but I think I know of somewhere.'

'Well, let me know, dear.' Miss Taylor stubbed out her cigarette and lit another one. 'Did she give you a reason?'

Lola delved into her pocket for the letter, scattering a collection of pencils, a comb and a left radiological marker on the floor. 'You can read it. It's not private.' She watched Miss Taylor's eyes moving along the lines. 'I put some extra commas in.'

'If I read this correctly, I blame myself, Lola, dear. I shouldn't have asked Jozef to walk you home. Some people in the town…I don't need to tell you.'

Lola blushed. 'Yes, Miss Taylor.' Her name was Gwendoline, but no one ever called her that. Her own name was Lola and no one ever called her anything else. Unless they called her Lulu. 'He kept calling me Lulu.'

'It's a German opera,' Miss Taylor said. Lola didn't know much about operas. 'Some people say it suits Jozef Schmidt to make pretence that he doesn't understand English,' Miss Taylor went on, still scrutinising Mrs Priest's letter, 'but it isn't that.' She went to the window and opened it. Across the town, the mid-day buzzer sounded from Parkin George. Pip would be going home, his gabardine unbelted and his tie flying over his shoulder. He would take Watson down to the grass and bring him back. In Salisbury House, the residents, those who were there, would file into the dining room, for rissoles or fish cakes or anything else that could be resurrected from the day before. Her father would say the grace. Her mother…Lola's eyes opened wide…her mother, she suddenly knew beyond the shadow of a doubt, wouldn't be there. In her place would be Alison, serving, moving around the table meekly as if she would rather be invisible. Alison Goody would forego her own meal in order to take a portion upstairs to Lilian, half propped in bed because, for some inexplicable reason, and certainly she hadn't been told the reason, she couldn't breathe lying down. She could hardly breathe sitting up, but lying down she felt as if she were in the hold of the Lusitania, drowning as the black water lapped around her head.

'Where are you going, Lola?'

Without realising, she was reaching for her coat, running her fingers through her hair, straightening the seams of her stockings.

'To see mother. I won't be long. I'll run all the way.'

'My dear, you must have an extended dinner hour,' Miss Taylor was saying. 'The only reason you might reasonably say you are expected back within the hour is if…you know.'

Lola didn't know.

She rang the front door bell and went in. There was no one there. She went into the dining room and through into the scullery. It was empty. And clean. The sun, sitting on the sill and reaching down onto the draining board, burnished the stacked saucepans, the colander turned upside down to drain, the scrubbed ladle. The sink had been scoured and the cloth rinsed out.

There was the slightest sound behind her, a feather on the surface of the world. She turned round.

'Alison!'

'I've sent your father up, Miss Robertson.'

'It's Lola, not Miss Robertson.'

A pale wisp of a smile passed across Alison Goody's face.

Chapter IV

He realised that he was considering the nature of the eyes that watched him. He had been doing so for some time, since the train left Mile End Station and headed eastwards: Bow road, Bromley by Bow, West Ham, Plaistow, Upton Park.

Stefan Czerniak read the same paragraph again and again without any comprehension, leaning over the print until it was no more than a turbulent sea of letters, tightening his hold on the book until the black of it came off on his fingers. He should have changed at Mile End. Except that the thread binding him to the watcher had become unbreakable and fast, loosening only and suddenly as the train drew into East Ham Station and she disembarked.

Because the watcher, he noticed with surprise, had been female. He caught sight of her passing the window of the still stationary train, making her way towards the exit, leaving in the carriage her pastel coloured perfume. He saw himself, the part of him that had lately been held prisoner, suddenly released and slip through the ceiling of the train, the arched roof of the tunnel, through the foundations of the London Borough of East Ham and out into the scintillating air, where he lodged, like any daily sparrow in a grime-leaved tree viewing the exodus from the station.

The other part of him, distinguished by nothing except that he had so much of the appearance of his father, stepped off the train as the doors were closing. Carrying his violin and with a satchel over his shoulder, he made for the steps.

He might still be in time to come between her and the catastrophe awaiting her. He followed her as she went up the stairs, seeing in his mind's eye what she hadn't seen, the dropped newspaper in her path, lying with its pages open between the stairs. He was gaining on her, but always she was ahead of him, climbing higher and higher up a spiral staircase that wasn't there. Out of sight, so that all he knew was the tap of her heels on the stone.

The train came to a halt with a dull thud.

'Won't do that much good, sir.'

He righted the violin case and lodged it between his knees.

'End of journey, sir. Everybody change, please. End of journey, sir. Everybody change, please. End of journey. Change now, please, sir. Where have you been? Timbuktoo?'

'I must have fallen asleep.'

'This yours, sir?' The guard picked up his book.

'Yes, thank you, sir.' Something by Sartre. I am nothing. Except that he was. Someone had been watching him. Someone female who didn't know he was or wasn't or had ever been or would shortly be again, a conchie. The thread was still there in the woken world, still attached. Tenuous and frayed and terrible.

So that he was reeled in, through the unlikely streets of East Ham. Burges, Watson, Hertford, around the heel of the gasometer, over a fence and into the valley. The sun slipped behind a cloud and came out again.

He kept on walking, dragging his feet out of the sticky mud of the marsh, following the river. Until he realised the thread had broken and he was alone under the wide dome of a sky leaking sunlight.

The building leaned over him, tall and vertiginous and indifferent. A faint pastel coloured scent hung on the air. He went in through the main gate, past a lodge where the door stood open.

'Hey you. You checked in?'

'No, sir.'

The man was seated at a table, a paper spread out in front of him. A mug of steaming tea.

'You come after job then.' A statement, not a question. He looked Stefan up and down. 'We've had quainter types than you, sir, no disrespect intended. What's yer fiddle? Ha, ha, ha. Foller me. Leave yer violin here. Previous chap fell under the influence. If yer don't mind me saying, yer don't look any too good yerself.' Stefan followed. 'It's Jerome, by the way.' The man turned round and shook hands. 'After an old saint. Not many chaps named after an old saint. Yer not named after a saint yerself, are yer, sir?'

'Yes,' Stefan said. Now possessed of three attributes: nothingness, of which Jean-Paul Sartre had informed him, a significance, the nature of which he was ignorant, since he had been watched – and saintliness.

'That so?'

'Stefan. My father's religious.' He thought of the gaunt face, trapped between the door curtain and the glass.

'Religious, eh? Yer ma also?'

'She's Catholic. My father's Orthodox.'

'And yerself, sir?'

The walk through the empty yards was endless. 'I might have to sit down soon, sir. What do they make here?' The rose scent became stronger.

'Don't rightly know, sir. Yer speaking to the door wallah. Checks in, does the time and checks out, clocks a few horses in the interim.'

The buildings continued, high windowed, sightless, voiceless.

'Does anyone work here?' Stefan said. The man called Jerome should know. He was the doorkeeper in the house of the Lord. The phrase came to him from nowhere. 'My father's religious.'

'So you said, sir, and none the worse for that, though some might disagree.' The voice came from a far distance. 'Though some might disagree. Caught it badly in the East End. In here, sir. After you. I'll give the gaffer a bell. What name do I give? Needn't be yer own.'

'Czerniak.'

The man called Jerome counted out the syllables on his fingers. 'You one of them, sir?' He lowered his voice. 'Yer know, commies. No disrespect.'

'I'm nothing,' Stefan said. A half-finished cigarette rested in an ashtray on the table. A grey sandwich cut in strips. His mouth watered. He swallowed and looked away.

'Got a young chap for you, Mr Arper. Don't look quite the ticket.' The doorkeeper was back, hovering outside the room, talking in a deafening whisper. 'Don't look quite the ticket, Mr Arper, but nice enough mannered. Won't be no trouble, sir.'

'Sober?'

'Yeah. Foreigner. Got a fiddle. Don't say I don't have yer best interests at eart, sir.'

'Thank you, Jerry. You may get back to your duties. Before you go...'

'Yes, sir?'

'Any questions?'

'Asked what we make ere. Most chaps, they want ter know the remuneration, sir, but this un, what do we make. I tell him I dunno, sir. Make out ignorant, yer see. Check in, check out, clock a few horses in the interim. Don't know no more.'

'I'll see what I make of him.'

The door opened. The man called Harper came in and stubbed out the cigarette. A masked man. Stefan stood.

'Sit down, Mr Czerniak. You've come for the job.' A statement, not a question. 'It's my pleasure to inform you that you may start at your earliest convenience.'

'Thank you, sir.'

'Simon Harper.' He held out his hand. 'Questions. As to the hours. Monday to Friday half past six in the evening until eight o'clock in the morning. As to remuneration. Paid in advance, four pounds and ten shillings per week. Not princely, Mr Czerniak, but the duties are not onerous, solitude excepted. All right with solitude.' Not a question. Mr Harper tapped his pencil on the table. 'I'll tell you why I'm giving you the job, Mr Czerniak. You may have worked that one out for yourself.'

'No, sir.'

'Then I'll tell you. You can look a chap in the eye. Most fellows can't.' Simon Harper peeled back the mask. 'Still all right, Mr Czerniak.'

'Yes, sir. I'm sorry, sir.'

'Don't be. Most chaps in my place didn't come back. As to questions. What do we make here? The answer is, nothing. Nothing at all. The premises are waiting for demolition. What is your present trade, Mr Czerniak?'

'I'm sorry, sir?'

'Are you in a post at the present time?'

'Not to speak of, sir.'

'Not to speak of. But I'm inviting you to speak, Mr Czerniak.'

'Gardening.'

'Pays well?'

'No, sir.'

'Your folk help out?'

'No, sir.'

'No?'

'They would if they knew.'

'But they don't know.'

'No, sir.' He suddenly felt unbearably tired, undone by the pallid sunlight, hypnotised by words issuing from some far-away echo chamber. 'I'm sorry, sir, I might have to sit down soon.'

'You are already seated, Mr Czerniak.' He heard the words clatter around the empty pocket of the room, hitting the yellow paper on the walls, bouncing off and crowding against the sooted windowpane. Somewhere a clock ticked, becoming louder and louder, until, reaching the summit of its endeavour it fell, hurtling into nothing.

A cup of tea had been placed in front of him.

'Thank you, sir. I should be going. I've taken up a lot of your time.'

'Fifteen minutes so far. Have you ever seen anyone about your condition, Mr Czerniak?'

'No, sir.'

'We'll show you the premises then, if you feel up to it. The night watchman makes a complete round every two hours, which leaves a break of approximately fifteen minutes between rounds. It is a lonely job, Mr Czerniak, but a necessary one. You will wish to ask if anyone enters the premises at night, in which case the answer is yes. You turn a blind eye in such instances, Mr Czerniak. I don't want an employee to come to harm. There is nothing inside to take. Everything has been removed. The building is scheduled for demolition. Does the word "munitions" mean anything to you?'

'Yes, sir.'

'I take it your people were objectors. You are here, Mr Czerniak, to turn a blind eye to anything untoward you may observe in the course of your duties. As I said, I don't want my night watchman to come to harm. You are not preserving a munitions facility. You are merely fulfilling an official requirement that a disused premise is supervised until such time as it is razed to the ground and consigned to history. You will be remunerated in advance as you leave. Jerry will see to that. Naturally, you won't be expected to come in until tomorrow night. Remember your violin, Mr Czerniak.'

He looked back. The munitions factory had gone. In its place was the gasometer, rising out of the marsh, swallowing the light. A phrase came back to him. Turn a blind eye; as the sun had done, beginning its shallow fall at the back of the gasometer; as the night would do, creeping over the marsh, throwing a blackout curtain over the emptied machine shops and silencing the pigeons roosting above the piping that ran across the ceilings. Until it was one more of the difficult places he was in the habit of visiting during his absences from the common life of the world.

He went down the eight steps into the basement and knocked on the door.

'Who is it?'

'Czerniak.'

The door opened. 'The answer is no, Czerniak. You'll find your goods in the hallway. No rent, no room. That was the what-do-you-call-it. Unless you want to pawn that there fiddle.'

'No, sir.'

'Then we part company, Czerniak.'

'Very well, sir.' Stefan turned to go. The door closed and opened again.

'A fellow came looking for you today. With a fancy woman. Dolled up to the nines. Didn't like the look of them. You're not on the game are you, Czerniak?'

'No, sir.'

'Thought not. Had to ask. Chap left this.'

Stefan took the envelope. 'Thank you, sir. I'll be going. I'll be back for the things later.'

'You owe me ten bob, Czerniak. Try 15 Ludlow Gardens, but don't tell the bloke I sent you.'

A faint scent drifted up from the envelope. Stefan put it in his pocket. He sat down on a bench outside a public house, listening to the rusted swing of the sign.

'Are you a patron, sir? Patrons only, sir. This ain't a doss ouse.'

The chap next to him got up and sat down again once the barman had gone back in.

'Is that John? Well, I'll be darned, if it isn't John. Hey old fellow.' The other chap punched his arm. 'Hey, John?'

'No, I'm sorry, sir, it isn't John.'

'No?' The man's face crumpled. 'Well, I'll be darned. You have a doppelgänger. Remember old Connolly and them paper chains? Well, I'll be darned. If you aren't the chap's double. Ah you a paytrone, sah?' He hit his sides and doubled up in mirth. 'Well, I'll be darned, if it ain't old John and he don't recollect.'

The scent from the letter in Stefan's pocket was overpowering. 'Yes, of course, it's Larry, isn't it?'

But the other man had vanished into nowhere, neither up the street where passengers were disembarking from a trolley bus, nor down the street where a woman was facing a shop window, tidying her hair and putting on lipstick; walking towards him.

She took the lipstick out of her bag. 'Give it to your mother, sir.'

But he already had, one day at the end of the war when Jean Beaumont was in the garden at Golen Avenue, passing a small package over the fence. It's for your mother. I hope it's her colour.

'Like one?' The woman was offering him a cigarette, shaking the packet so that he could take one; sitting beside him.

'Patrons only,' he said.

The woman smiled. 'Who cares?' She lit a cigarette, dropping the match onto the ground. 'What about you? What's your vice?' Her eyes swept over him.

'I'm objector,' he said.

'You're no fun then. What a waste.' She got up and strolled away, her heels punctuating the twilight. Did you read the letter? But she hadn't said it. Someone else had, a long time ago; his mother. The match the woman had dropped still burned, yellow and fitful, at his feet. He took the envelope out of his pocket and held it over the flame, which sipped feebly at the corner, flared and died, leaving the text of the letter exposed. He brushed away the charred fragments.

"Mr Czerniak,

You may not be aware that an approach has been made to your father, Paul Czerniak, esq, who becomes liable for the sum of £500 sterling owing to the sustained failure on your part to contact…"

'In here, sir.' He was being manhandled into the public house, the letter still in his hand. A draught of sweet dark air fanned his face.

He was taken to a place at the back of the room and a pint pot was set in front of him, frothing over and running down the sides.

'If you would, sir, thank you.' Someone took the violin from him, opened it and whistled. 'A Guaneri, no less.'

He heard his own voice, protesting. 'No, sir, it's Pip Beaumont's. I doubt if it's a Guaneri.'

'We've tightened the bow for you, sir.'

'It needs tuning.'

'The chaps doesn't mind, sir, tuned or not tuned. All they wants is a spot of melody.'

Stefan Czerniak looked out at the audience turned expectantly towards him. Masks of faces, the gaslight hollowing them out, turning eyes and noses and mouths into formless apertures, the flesh into unfleshed bones.

A line of Smetana meandered through his mind, slowly at first, then more quickly, running, dancing, leaping from note to note. He followed it for as long as he could hear it, then the next line and the next, the length of the river Vlatava as it wound its way under the golden sky and out of the city of Prague, through the fields settling peacefully into the night. He played it again. And again. He looked up. The men were standing.

Every one of them, their hats in their hands, the tears bright on their faces.

'Drink up, sir.'

'He's an objector. He's no fun.' A woman's voice.

Somewhere outside a clock was striking midnight, its flat notes entering the room through a slit where the window fell short of the frame. On the mantelpiece, a tower of coins amounting to ten shillings owed to his previous landlord. A Guaneri in beggar's clothes propped up against the wall. A table with a loaf of bread and a quarter of margarine. Something dubious in an opened tin, left over from the war.

Seated on the sagging mattress himself, Stefan Czerniak, with no intellectual evidence to prove that his life's walk had taken him through the day just gone. Only the lingering taste of beer and two envelopes, one containing what remained of remuneration for work he had not yet done, and the other, half burned, containing a letter.

He got up and went over to the table. Undeserved gains, and a terrible demand made to a father who was eternally trapped between the glass of the door and the curtain at the back of it. He picked up the charred envelope and tried to take out the letter. But it had broken into black flakes. Gone, as effectively as if it had never been written.

Chapter V

'She needs to be sitting up, father. She can't breathe lying down.'

'Yer must rest, duck. Doctor said.' Her father was trying to resist her mother's attempts to get out of bed. One of her legs was over the edge, pitifully thin, the nails uncut and curling over. There was a bowl of custard on the bedside table.

Her father swung round. 'Yes, nurse Robertson.' His face was white with rage and impotence. 'Certainly, nurse Robertson. Yer come swanning in like lady muck and thinks yer knows what's best for yer ma.'

'Help me, dear.' Her mother's arms were now on top of the counterpane, pushing it down, struggling, so that her nightie was off one shoulder and gaping at the front. 'Your father means well.'

'Mother can't breathe lying down, father.'

Her father stepped back from the bed. 'Since yer know so much, nurse Robertson, I'll leave yer to it.'

'Will you send Alison up, father?'

'What else d'yer say, duck?'

'Please, father.'

'That's better, duck. Give yer pa a kiss.' Her father's face was bristly and unwashed, and his shirt was stained under the arms.

'Will you send Alison up, please, father.'

'Mrs Goody don't like ter touch yer ma, duck.'

'And a clean nightie from the airing cupboard, father. Please.'

'Yes, sarge, three bags full, sarge.'

'And Alison, please, father.'

'I'm here, Miss Robertson.' Alison Goody stood framed in the door wringing her hands.

'Thank you, dear.'

Lola followed her mother's eyes to where they rested on the other woman. With gratitude. And something else, she thought, but didn't know what it was.

Alison didn't notice. She was drawing the curtains, shaking out the nightdress and warming it in front of the coal fire that burned weakly in the grate.

'I'll bring some more coals, Miss Robertson.'

'It's Lola.' But Alison Goody had gone. Lola could hear her going down the stairs, along the passage and through the scullery to the back. Then coming up again, more slowly, carrying the scuttle.

'I was waiting for you, Alison.'

'I didn't want to intrude on your mother's privacy, Miss Robertson.'

'I don't mind, dear.' Her mother's gaze was again directed towards Alison Goody.

'We need to put a clean nightie on and prop you up, mother. Have you had a wash?' She knew her mother hadn't, not much of one. 'Did father help you to have a wash?'

'Yes, dear.' Her mother's face coloured slightly under her pallor. She whispered something.

'What was that mother?'

'A lick and a promise. Not…you know…down there. Not your father.' Her lips quivered.

'I'll help you, Lilian.' Alison Goody was suddenly rolling up her sleeves. 'God made us all the same. I'll fetch a bowl.'

'You know, Lola…' Miss Taylor continued filing her nails, inspecting them, as if the dainty pink shells would somehow conjure up a tide of words.

'No, Miss Taylor, it won't.'

'You didn't know what I was going to say, dear.' She looked up. 'Probably you do know.'

'You were going to say that I might move back to Salisbury House to help look after my mother, and that might…'

'Save you looking for somewhere else to live. Yes, I was going to say something like that. Probably a little more nuanced.' Miss Taylor slipped the nail file back into her pocket. 'Well? Lola?'

The staff room swam in front of Lola's eyes: the hospital cups upside down on the draining board, the blackout curtains at the windows, the light box with an x-ray of a forearm clipped in front of it, curling slightly as it dried. And Miss Taylor, a magazine on her knee.

'Lola?'

'I wasn't asked.'

Miss Taylor said nothing. She got up and took the x-ray down from the box. 'Climbing trees and fell off. Can you spot it? It's quite subtle.'

'Yes, Miss Taylor. It's a greenstick at the lower end of the radius.'

'So you weren't asked, Lola. That's a shame. More than a shame.'

'My father said I wasn't needed. He said they knew where to find me. I suppose he meant here.' She started to cry. 'Father will make her lie flat and she'll drown.'

'I'll be back, dear.'

Someone else had come in. Lola looked up. Jozef Schmidt was seated in Miss Taylor's chair, with her magazine on his knee, doing the crossword.

'Lulu.'

'Did Miss Taylor say anything?'

'*Nein.*'

'I'm being silly, Jozef.'

Jozef Schmidt put down the pencil and looked up. Lola noticed, for the first time, the dull glint of a ring on the third finger of his right hand.

'*Lulu, wie geht es?*'

'Mother's ill and father doesn't want me there. He'll make her lie flat and she'll drown. She's got fluid on her lung, Jozef. She has to be sitting up otherwise she can't breathe.'

Someone in the room was crying; the great heaving sobs shaking the chair in which she was sitting, the torrent of tears running down the windows and walls, falling onto the hand that held hers. Falling because her mother was dying, because her father didn't want her to be there, and falling, she realised with shame and mortification, because she had let herself fall in love with a married man. Headlong, desperately, secretly.

'*Danke,* Jozef.' Miss Taylor must surely have noticed but she went over to the sink and started drying the cups, still talking. 'We have done what little we can, Lola. A district nurse will go twice a day and see that your mother is comfortable. Does that put your mind at rest a little, dear?'

'Does father know?'

'Not yet, Lola. I will make a telephone call. Your father's a little frightened of me, you know.'

'Thank you, Miss Taylor. I didn't know.'

'What didn't you know?'

That Jozef is married. 'That father's frightened of you.'

'Everyone is. A stentorian voice and an overbearing manner. Radiographer's disease. Is there anything you wish to ask, Lola, dear?'

Is Jozef married? 'Is my mother suffering?'

Miss Taylor sat down and picked up the crossword.

'He's finished it, the scamp. I'll have to have words with him. In answer to your question, dear, your mother will be given whatever assistance she needs to keep her as comfortable as possible.'

Lola looked across at Miss Taylor. She must be quite old, she thought, probably forty-four. She didn't know why she suddenly knew an exact age, but there it was. Many times relatives would have drawn her aside in the dim solitude of the x-ray room while their wives were in the changing cubicle climbing back into their corsets, or their husbands fitting on their hernia truss, and asked her the same question. Is he or she suffering, Miss Taylor? And Miss Taylor would have said the same non-committal words in reply.

'Which of course isn't answering your question, Lola.'

'No, Miss Taylor.'

'Can I help you with anything else, dear?'

'Is Jozef married?' She blushed furiously. She had said it. The words were there, hovering in the synapse between them, beyond recall.

Miss Taylor laughed. 'No one knows, dear.'

'He wears a ring on his right hand. Do they do that in Germany when they are married, instead of the left?'

'I don't know, Lola. In the war there were countless pictures around of Hitler poring over maps with various officials and I never noticed which hand they wore their wedding rings on, or even if they wore wedding rings. We had other things to worry about.' Miss Taylor sounded like her mother.

'Anyway, the war's over.'

Now she sounded like herself, Lola Robertson, still covered in shame that she had asked such a question. Miss Taylor was locking cupboards and drawers in the office, getting ready to go. She came back and combed her hair in the mirror.

'Where are you going, dear?'

Lola didn't know. Or she did know but she couldn't tell Miss Taylor. She was going back to Crown Street and after tea she was going to the low streets near the river to see if she could find somewhere else to live.

'Back to Crown Street,' she said in the end.

'I'll say it this once and not bother you again, Lola, but you are welcome to stay with mother and I if you can't find anywhere else suitable. Please think about it, dear.'

Lola said she would. But she could only think about it with something that amounted to fear, a fear that lodged in the middle of her chest until she was scarcely able to breathe.

When Miss Taylor had gone she went into the office, climbed on the stool and took the manual of hospital radiography down from the shelf. She laid it on the desk and opened it at preface xi. The first ever x-ray. The most wonderful, most romantic, story in the world, Miss Taylor had said: how Anna Bertha Ludwig had offered her hand to Wilhelm Roentgen, not only in marriage, but to be immortalised in every treatise ever to be written on medical radiography for the remainder of their earthly lives and beyond. An image lacking in sharpness, but unmistakably a hand. With a ring on the third finger.

Lola pored over it. It looked like a left hand, but x-rays had an uncanny habit of turning themselves round so that left was right, and black was white. The bones in the picture were black and the background white, whereas in her experience the opposite was the case. The bones were white and the background was black. She didn't know enough about it. This left hand might well be a right hand, wearing a wedding ring.

She turned to appendix xxiii, elements of x-ray photography. She didn't understand it, but she carried on, her eyes racing along the lines of print, her mind returning to Anna Bertha's hand, trying to make left right and right left. Until the door of the office opened and Jozef stood there with the keys in his hand.

'*Lulu, noch hier*?'

'I took extra time at dinner to go home and I've stayed behind to study.' There was no end to her fabrications; white black and black white. She blushed. 'I'm going now, Jozef.'

And he would go with her. She knew that. He would be waiting at the hospital gates, having dropped the keys off at the lodge; waiting with the collar of his coat turned up and his hands in his pockets. They would walk, as they had before, in silence, but would stop at the corner of Crown Street, after which he would watch her until she reached number 23. She would turn and wave. He would then vanish from her life until the next day.

Lola took her keys from her bag and turned to wave. Jozef Schmidt was standing at the corner with his hands in his pockets. He waved back, then turned to go.

She fitted her latchkey into the lock but it wouldn't open. A curtain rippled. Someone was in the front room. Her room. Mrs Priest opened the door.

'I'm sorry, Mrs Priest, the key won't work.'

'No, I suppose it won't, Miss Robertson. The lock has been changed, just as a precaution. I keep a clean house, Miss Robertson, as I have said before. You'll find your goods in the hallway and if you'll please to see that they are removed at your earliest convenience, I should be most grateful. In the event that you haven't found somewhere else and in the event that one of your fancy men can't do with you…' Mrs Priest's mouth twitched…'I have left the News on the table. I'm not an unreasonable woman, Miss Robertson, but I can't condone goings on. If you wish to comport yourself in that manner and it's no business of mine if you do, you can try Harwich Street. Yes. That's H-A-R-W-I-C-H. I'm not an unreasonable woman, Miss Robertson, as I say. You may leave your goods until you have found a room and you may avail yourself of the kitchen to make your tea after which I should be obliged if you go and find somewhere. Under the circumstances, you'll understand that I'm unable to provide a testimonial. Is that all you wish to know, Miss Robertson?'

'Yes, Mrs Priest.'

The landlady followed her to the kitchen and stood in the doorway while she cut a slice of bread and spread margarine on it. She wrote down an address from the newspaper, the first one. 'I'll be going now, Mrs Priest.'

'I'll 'elp yer, Lola Robertson.'

Albert Goody was suddenly at the door.

For a girl of indifferent looks…Lola could see some such sentence composing itself behind the row of black curls that sat along Mrs Priest's forehead.

'This is my half-brother, Mrs Priest.' She didn't quite know in what relationship she stood to Albert Goody. Maybe Albert Goody didn't know of the relationship. His freckled nose crinkled into a grin. She bumped her suitcase out of the door. She could hear Mrs Priest dropping the latch.

'Thank you, Albert.'

'Yer pullt a fast one, Lola Robertson.'

'In what way, Albert Goody?'

'Yer said I were yer bro.'

'Half bro.'

'Ain't no different.'

'I suppose not, Albert.'

'Why yer flitting?'

Lola said nothing.

'Ain't no business of mine, Lola Robertson. Can I be yer half-bro?'

'Yes, Albert, on condition that you keep it quiet. Don't tell your mam. Do you know where we're going?'

'Yes, Lola Robertson. To bawdy house.'

'Boarding house, Albert. Don't tell your mam that you took me to a bawdy house.'

'Ain't no different, Lola Robertson.'

'The spelling's different, Albert.'

'I canna spell.'

'I'll teach you, Albert Goody. What were you doing at school?'

'Nah.'

'Didn't you go?'

'Nah.'

'What do you want to do when you're grown up, Albert Goody?' But Albert Goody was grown up. Grown up and ingenuous.

'Nah.'

'How old are you, Albert?'

'I dunno. I canna spell.'

'That's counting.'

'Canna count neither, Lola Robertson.'

'Not even the twelve disciples?' She thought of Alison, going pale-faced to the Catholic church every day.

'Don't yer mean apostles? I can count them all right. I ain't daft, Lola Robertson.'

She stood at the window of her new room looking out. Elsewhere in the luminous night her mother was propped up against pillows, a glass of water on the bedside table and a bottle of tablets, unlabelled. Her mother would be sleeping fitfully, watching the red glow from the fire flickering on the walls and ceilings of her room. Just her room. Not her husband's. Her father, she had noticed, no longer shared the bedroom.

Nearby, Alison Goody, with her door left ajar so that she could hear the slightest sound from Lilian's room. Having washed and put her clothes back on again, in readiness. The same clothes that she always wore: a brown skirt and a fawn cardigan darned neatly at the elbows.

And elsewhere in the night also a man whose name she could scarcely contemplate, who wore a ring on the third finger of his right hand.

Somewhere in the house a wireless was on, its music drifting in on the night, solitary, attenuated and aimless. And from the next room, sounds she had no words to describe.

There was no one to read her thoughts but Lola blushed. She went over to the basin and splashed her face with cold water. Then she began slowly to undress, wash herself and put on her nightdress. She needed to use the WC but she dare not. She would have to walk past the door with the nameless sounds behind it.

In the small hours she woke, still needing to use the WC. There was someone trying the door. She put the light on, and watched the handle, turning, turning again.

'Who is it?'

'Lady? Let me in.'

'Who is it?'

'Fancy a…?' She couldn't make out the last word.

'No.'

'Go on, lady, show a gentleman yer…'

A shameful heat invaded the lower part of her body. She folded the bedclothes down.

'No, I'm sorry, sir. I'm not well.'

The door handle turned again. Then the footsteps went away, unevenly, along the landing. The first light of the next day glimmered blue above the rooftops of the houses on the other side of the road.

She put on her brassiere and petticoat, her knickers and her suspender belt. Then she sat down to put on her stockings. Her lower legs, she observed, were covered in a rash. She put on her blouse, skirt and cardigan. She badly needed the WC.

The landing was silent and empty. She let the room door close behind her.

When she returned, she couldn't get back in. It was half past six by the clock in reception, and there was no one there. She went back upstairs and sat down on the floor outside her room, leaning against the locked door. She felt tired, unbearably tired, more tired than she had ever felt in her life.

In the dream, a man was leaning over her. She could smell the tobacco on his breath and the stale perspiration under his arms. He was touching her, unbuttoning her cardigan and her blouse. She tried to wake up, but she couldn't. Her eyes wouldn't open, and her voice wouldn't speak. She couldn't fight off the hands moving over her body. She couldn't get to her feet and run.

Somewhere in the building, a door slammed. The lift gates were opening and footsteps were coming along the landing. Someone said, 'Lilian?' and passed by. The footsteps became quieter, disappearing behind a swing door at the other end. Someone was going to her mother. Lola knew that. She tried to stand, but she couldn't. Yet she had to. At the other side of the swing door, her mother had slipped down the bed and was drowning. She needed help to sit up because she couldn't breathe.

The footsteps were returning, but this time they were accompanied by those of a woman. A woman who was young and light of heart. And pretty. She had always been pretty.

Chapter VI

'Stefan dear, your father left this in case you should come along while they're away.' Mrs Beaumont's voice was behind him, hovering above the chequered path.

He didn't look round. He continued to stand at the door, eye to eye with his father, who was, according to his habit, trapped between the glass and the door curtain. He registered the slight surprise on his father's face.

'Away?'

The expression turned to one of fear. He saw his father, wearing his long black coat and beret with a red scarf round his neck, setting off down the chequered path that led to the mines, a satchel over his shoulder. Father! He saw from the door how his father continued down the path and through the gate, how the car door was opened for him, and closed on him. Father! But his father had already vanished in a cloud of exhaust smoke. He hadn't looked back. And then something had snapped in Stefan's head. He could feel it, like a small explosion, sudden and eventful, and accompanied by an overpowering scent from the horse chestnut trees. Because it was May, and it was 1940.

'Father!' He rang the doorbell and tried the handle. Someone touched his arm.

'Stefan dear, it's Freda. Freda Beaumont.'

He turned round.

'Your dear parents have gone away, Stefan. Here, they left this in case you should like to go in.' Mrs Beaumont handed him a brown envelope with what felt like a key inside. 'The back door, dear. They've taken the front door key with them naturally. Say something, dear.'

'They've never gone away.'

But they had. His father had. He had walked down the black and white chequered path between the hydrangeas without looking back. 'Did father look back, Mrs Beaumont?'

A small frown gathered in the middle of her forehead. 'Well, that I don't know, Stefan dear. Your father asked me to let you know, should you call, which you have done, that they have journeyed north to attend the funeral of the wife of someone he knew at the end of the war. I think I've got that right, dear. It was rather a long sentence.'

'The war?'

'The war was a long sentence for all of us, dear, but I was referring to your father's message. You know how he is.' Mrs Beaumont tugged at his sleeve. 'Come in, Stefan, and have a cup of tea. I'll put some music on the gramophone. I haven't listened much since Ken…you know. It was Ken who liked *The Blue Danube*. Family by the name of Robertson. I've just remembered the name. Poor Mrs Robertson.' The gifts of the spirit and they didn't know it.

'Let's see what we have.' Mrs Beaumont was riffling through the gramophone records. 'I'll let you choose while I make the tea, Stefan. This is such a pleasure, dear.'

'I'll make the tea, Mrs Beaumont.'

'Do call me Freda, dear. If you like. You'll find some rich tea in the tin. I'll see if I can find something by Smetana for you. Do you remember when we went to the Albert Hall? We thought everything would be all right after the war, and look what happened to us.'

Stefan could hear Mrs Beaumont talking, somewhere far away, on a day in the late summer when he was in the garden watching a spiral of cigarette smoke rising into the sunlit air from the other side of the fence.

'I've found something, dear.' She was in the kitchen, putting rich tea biscuits out on a plate. 'Your father gave it to us, for looking after your mother while he was away, he said. It was always a little…' she searched for a word…'cerebral for Ken. He was more of a Strauss man, you know, but we might try it for a few minutes and see what you think.'

Mrs Beaumont poured out the tea. 'Still no milk? No, I suppose not. It's surprising how we got used to those privations.'

'I hadn't heard that before, Mrs Beaumont.'

'Thank goodness, Stefan dear. I thought you were never going to speak.'

'Have I been away long?'

'About half an hour, dear. It's Smetana's Quartet in E minor. Did you like it?'

'It was…' he didn't have a word. The music was still playing in his head, coming to the final harmonic and then returning to the beginning.

'The poor man lost his hearing,' Mrs Beaumont was still talking, 'and that final note represents his suffering. He could only hear a squeak. Mustn't that have been awful? Did you want to have a look over the house for your dear parents? They would appreciate that.'

Stalks of sprouts lay uncollected and beans hung black from their canes. His foot nudged something small and unresisting on the ground. He scooped up Bazal and peered into the bright eyes. 'Look what happened to us all.'

He went into the house through the scullery door. Everything was the same. Yet everything was different. More spacious. More empty. More…silent. His feet echoed on the floorboards. The clock had been removed from the mantelpiece. Only the letters, were still there, behind its absence and waiting for attention, giving off a faint but overwhelming pink scent.

Mr Stefan Czerniak. Postmarked 1948 and unopened. Still waiting for attention.

Then, behind it another, and another, and another. Mr Stefan Czerniak, c/o Mr Paul Czerniak. All unopened. And four more, tied together with mending thread. Mr Paul Czerniak. All opened. Carefully, and the flaps of the envelopes folded down. Stefan took his own letters. He went back next door and rang the bell.

'You should have walked in, dear.' He could hear Smetana's quartet playing in the middle room. 'Stefan? Talk to me, dear.'

'I'll be back to do the garden, Mrs Beaumont.'

'Thank goodness, dear. I thought…'

'The house is empty.'

'Well, yes, dear. You know how I mumble sometimes. Your parents have gone away. You probably didn't hear me. I am a scallywag, really…'

The officer was filling in a form. 'Name rings a bell.'

'I was brought in not long ago.'

'In trouble, eh?'

Stefan didn't answer.

'In trouble, eh?'

'Yes, sir. My parents' house looks empty.'

The officer glanced up.

213

'Empty.' He wrote down the word in a notebook and enclosed it in quotation marks. 'How would you define "empty"?'

'I don't know, sir. The clock had gone.'

'"The clock had gone." In quotation marks. 'Anything else, sir?'

'There were letters addressed to my father.'

'Behind the clock, eh?'

'The clock had gone, sir. They were on the mantelpiece.'

'"On the mantelpiece. Addressed to my father." In quotation marks. 'Empty.'

'I didn't look, sir. They were addressed to my father.'

'I'm telling you. They were empty. Your father did the right thing, Mr Czerniak. He brought them to me. Right thing to do. No exceptions. Any jiggery pokery, inform the law.'

The officer went over to the filing cabinet, unlocked it and drew out a folder. 'They were empty because the contents are in here. All sent from an address in Wickham Place. Wickham Place don't exist, Mr Czerniak. What we call a spurious address. Know that word?'

'Yes, sir.' Did my father pay anything? But he didn't say it. He couldn't.

'You surmised...know that word, Mr Czerniak...that your ma and pa were...you know what I'm going to say. No business of mine why the house is empty. Tried asking them? First line of enquiry, always ask the party concerned. Next thing from your point of view, sir, make enquiries of the neighbours. See what I mean?' He stood up and held out his hand. 'You did the right thing, Mr Czerniak. Came to the law. Anything untoward in future, come to the law. You'll want to know if we've found the perpetrators.'

He didn't.

Nor did he know if the conversation had taken place, or if he had gone back to instil some sense of order into his parents' garden. Or if he had heard Mrs Beaumont say that a condition of the lungs might account for the special emptiness and the audible absence of time, because his dear father was unable to work.

Or if anything had taken place.

Except for the concrete evidence of the disused factory sinking into the violet sea of the night, and the ring of the shoes on the stone, which were indisputably his own, down at heel with the laces frayed. And the quartet of Bedrich Smetana playing in his head, the whole of it, until the final harmonic.

He remembered it, every single note, every subtlety, every shift of key, as far as the end when the dance stopped and all that remained was a high-pitched cry in the darkness.

It came again, piercing the velvet cover of the night, the brick of the factory blocks with their hooded eyes. Then it went back to the beginning in E minor. Every note, as if by its wholeness it might remove all the absences in his life.

He was back at the gatehouse sitting at the table poring over the newspaper left there; open at the racing page with thick pencil crosses marking out a horse now and then, their breath smoking in the chill of the small hours, Jerome placing a bet on his grey board of a pillow. Mr Harper peeling off his mask. The quartet stopped. Simon Harper peeling off his mask.

Stefan saw the taut leathered face and the black aperture of the mouth moving in speech.

Turn a blind eye. Have you ever seen anyone about your condition, Mr Czerniak?

No, sir. What condition? Did he wear his...condition...written on his face as the other man wore on his face his own absence – of nose, lips, eyebrows, blame? Blessed with the gifts of the spirit and he doesn't know it.

The sound came again, a scream out of the void, trailing off into a thin harmonic on the sky. He went out, closing the gatehouse door, and followed the sound to its origin, as he thought, in the machine shop. He tried the door. It opened easily and he went in, leaving it ajar.

The scream came again. It was neither louder nor nearer, but neither was it less loud, nor farther away. It echoed round the shed, losing itself in the high girders and ricocheting off the walls. He shone the torch around the walls, over the vaulted ceiling, into the corners.

'Is anyone there?'

Turn a blind eye, Mr Czerniak. The figure brushed against his arm and the door slammed shut.

Then he was back in the gatehouse with the list of runners for the day's race in front of him. The horse's name was circled in dark pencil. *Turn a blind eye.*

A shadow passed in front of the window and made an exit through the locked gate to the rear of the premises. The gatekeeper, Jerome, would come in soon. Found any good ones, he would say, tapping his pencil on the newspaper.

The first wan light of day already washed the factory blocks, leeching the darkness from their faces, shining their eyes. The sun came up, and with it a cold wind, scuttling leaves into corners and kicking papers around the yard. There was still an hour of the night shift to go. A crow perched briefly on the roof ridge, flapped its wings and lifted off.

Stefan took the broom from its mooring on the back wall of the lodge, collected the shovel and bucket and went out to sweep. The scream came again, less piercing and dwindling into a low persistent sigh. The engine of a Rover. A Rover he had once known.

At the back of the machine shop, the mass of stinging nettles and elders had been trodden down. There was a faint smell of gas. Stefan slid between the factory and the perimeter wall and shone his torch into the bruised and crushed stems, brushing them aside with his foot; until the beam of light found a series of boreholes dug into the earth, close together, as if the digger was thinking to strike an object under the ground and never quite finding it. Over the perimeter wall, the top of the gas works gleamed silver in the leaping sun. At the base of the machine block, a brick had been dislodged and pushed back, imperfectly so that the lower right corner of it jagged proud of the rest.

He went back through the broken nettles and elders, pulling them together after him, covering tracks.

'Found any good ones?' Jerome tapped the newspaper with the blunt end of his pencil.

'Tampering at the rear of the machine shop. There's a brick loose, sir, and signs of someone digging.'

The gatekeeper hung his gabardine on the hook behind the door. He tapped the newspaper again. 'That's a good one, Stef. Circled it for you. *Turn a blind eye.* You and I, sir, we're not paid to have eyes in the backs of our heads. Mr Arper says. Job's a what's it called. Sinecure.'

'I heard something.'

'You don't hear nothing neither, Stef. Last chap turned to the bottle as I says. You don't see nothing and you don't hear nothing.'

Does anyone run a Rover? The words were already half formed, but Jerome was still talking.

'Look ere, Stef, Mr Arper don't pay the likes of you and me to speculate. Speculate and a chap falls victim to the what's it called.'

Curiosity. A mild need to know. Walking back to Ludlow Gardens, Stefan Czerniak reflected on the few times he had been curious. On a morning not long after the end of the war when he had posted a small packet marked "fragile" to a girl who lived on the border of Nottinghamshire. Then a synapse of six years until the next access of curiosity. Yesterday, walking through his parents' home, observing the absence of things. A slight hiatus of a single night, and the sound of a Rover driving off, the counterpoint to all the mornings of his earlier life when Mr Beaumont set off for the office, racing the engine and sending a cloud of exhaust smoke over the hedges and into the front gardens, to rise and thin and dissipate among the branches of the horse chestnuts.

For the most part, he hadn't wondered: why he was so frequently absent from himself, coming back after the world had leapt forwards several minutes, several streets, several pages of a book by Sartre; why his life had been punctuated by letters, like a long black sentence, broken up by heavy commas and carrying the heady scent of fear; why the woman standing on the corner of Ludlow Gardens wouldn't let him be.

'Have you got a light, sir?'

She stood in front of him. He could smell her perfume, compounded of roses and perspiration. Her cigarette was dyed crimson with lipstick. He took a box of matches out of his pocket.

'Thank you, kind sir. Going to be a gentleman and light it for me?' She stood in his way so that he couldn't pass. 'Seen you before, haven't I?'

He struck a match and lit the cigarette between her lips, watching her face vanish behind the smoke, and return. 'You can have the box if you like.'

'Are you going to invite a lady in, sir?' Still she stood in front of him, slight in frame but blocking the whole pavement, blocking the whole sentient world with its sunlit sky and tall plane trees, and its daily music of wheels and voices. She touched him, suddenly, slightly, shamefully. 'Are you going to invite a lady in, sir?'

'No, I'm sorry, not today.'

'Another time then, sir.' She stood aside. She wasn't young.

'No, I'm sorry, not another time either.'

'Good are you, sir?' She turned and walked away.

Not good. Just not...curious.

*

He looked in the pocked and fly-blown mirror that hung on the wall of his room. His father looked back. A good man. And something else. A man of…there wasn't a word for it. Some indefinable grace he would never himself possess: laying, on an impoverished table at the dreg ends of a war, an armful of golden rod and Michaelmas daisies. He would never do that.

Stefan thought for the first time of the wife of the stranger his father had met. He could scarcely see her, only a glimpse of her light hair and a face marked by disappointment. Blessed with the gifts of the spirit though she didn't know it. She had passed quietly through the world and walked out of it, one night when there was no one there. Leaving a garrulous heroic widower. Leaving a daughter designated "fragile". And he knew beyond the shadow of a doubt that she had done as he had done, slipped the mooring and drifted off, anchorless and alone, but in her case never to return.

The pebbles had been peppering the windowpane for some time. He opened it and looked out. The woman was standing at the corner, leaning on the railings, smoking. She turned her head, caught his eye and winked. He closed the window.

He could hear the front door of the house opening and an altercation taking place. 'Not allowed to let no one in, sir.' Then there were footsteps. He went out into the hallway.

'Lad.'

'Sorry, old chap. May I step inside? Sorry and all that.'

'What for? Have a seat.'

'Got bed bugs?'

'Probably.'

'Smells like it. No offence. Came across worse in the war. I followed you, Stef, old chap. Pretty base, to follow a chap. Had any dealings with the skirt on the corner?'

'She's after me.'

'You're a dark horse. Reason I'm here, old chap, we had to part with the Rover.' Lad looked around the room. 'Seen worse during the war. Coping all right?'

'I think so. Thank you, Lad.'

'I mean…' Lad jerked his head in the general direction of the corner of the street.

'I told her not today and not another time either.'

'Not her. I mean the old grindstone. Had to let the Rover go. Decent chap. Still with the old…?' Lad played a few notes on an imaginary violin. 'Freda said she'd dug out the quartet. Dad never could get the hang of it. As I said, decent chap, Harper. Very decent chap. One of the best, remember that, Stef old boy. Just mind what you're getting into. Between you and me and the gatepost. Won't do him any favours to…you know.'

Then Lad had gone. Stefan watched him from the window as he approached the corner and gave the woman standing there a cigarette. He watched as Lad lit the cigarette for her, holding her wrist as he did so. He watched him through the intervening buildings, approaching the station and descending the dark well of the stairs. And as he emerged into the bright air again at Gant's Hill. As he reached the house in Golen Avenue and ran his hand over the gleaming black bonnet of a Rover that was no longer there.

Chapter VII

Lola sat on her own at the back until everyone else had gone.

There had been a great number of people, a multitude, more than Lilian Robertson had ever known in the whole of her life. If her mother had realised – and the thought came to Lola with a deafening clarity – if her mother had realised that today would be like this, that so many would be standing on the steps of the Methodist chapel wishing her well on the journey, she would have had no need to go. She would have remained in the breathing world, in the mere assurance that she had friends.

But her mother didn't know that. Her world had fallen inwards until it was a narrow oblong of a room populated only by her husband and the nurse and Alison Goody. Because her father suddenly wanted to cleave to his wife, as it said in the Bible, to the exclusion of nearly everyone. And her mother had slipped down in the bed and drowned when she was alone one night, thinking that the only three people she had in all her life had left her.

Lola could hear Mr Parnell approaching with the keys. Oh, Miss Robertson, I didn't know you was here. A fine woman, your mother. But Mr Parnell didn't notice her. He walked past, and went into the side room.

Lola slipped out, engulfed in the musty smell she had been aware of all through the service: someone else's underarm perspiration, mothballs, the fried breakfast to give someone else the strength to face a sad occasion. She hadn't looked at the costume properly before she put it on. There was a mark on the front of the skirt and a button was missing on the jacket. She put half a crown on the plate, burying it among the shillings and sixpences. People had given generously, unstintingly.

All at once, Pip Beaumont was there, standing in front of her in the porch. She had an absurd thought, that he would delve into his pocket and give her a new three-penny bit.

'You don't know I'm here, Pip.' She started to cry. Pip took the neatly ironed handkerchief out of the breast pocket of his demob suit and gave it to her. 'But it's yours, Pip.'

'I've got another. Abracadabra!' He pulled out another handkerchief, endlessly, from a trouser pocket.

She started to laugh. So much that she couldn't stop.

Then she was seated in the side room taking sips from the cloudy glass of water kept at the back of the chapel for when people felt faint.

Pip said, 'Now look what I've done.'

'Shouldn't we ought to…' Mr Parnell started and stopped. Fetch the young lady's mother.

'I'll be all right, Mr Parnell. Thank you, Pip. Have they all gone?'

The door opened a crack and a muttered sorry came through before it was quickly closed. Then someone knocked. Pip went to answer it. Lola could hear his dwindling voice from the other side of the door, engaged in some kind of negotiation, coming back. She knew before he said it. He would have to go.

Mr Parnell spread his hands. 'Now what do we do with you, young lady?'

'I'll be all right now, Mr Parnell. Thank you.' She looked down at the mark on her black skirt. 'I'm sorry about that. It was from a jumble sale and I didn't notice.' She stood up. 'I'll be all right now. Thank you, Mr Parnell.'

'My condolences, Miss Robertson.'

She couldn't remember if she had thanked Mr Parnell. She was outside the chapel at the top of the steps, looking down into the Market Square.

People were still standing around. Men holding their hats in their hands. Women dabbing their eyes. Anyone who had ever lost someone; before the war, during the war, since the war. Her father had gone.

Her mother had gone. They had driven her slowly out of the Market Square in a black car, and the crowd had parted, as had the waters of the Red Sea in the Bible when the children of Israel passed through. She had gone so recently that the rift in the crowd of people had not closed.

Barry Green was seated on the second to last step smoking. And another young man whose name she couldn't remember. And another, whose name she could. Nigel Chadwick, who had vanished on the day she left a diamond crease in the centre of the tablecloth. Alison Goody would never do such a thing, but her mother had still drowned. She started to cry again.

The chapel doors were closed and there was nowhere to hide. She sat down on the top step, pulling her stained skirt down over her knees. No one would see her. Maybe she wasn't there. Maybe the difficult rasping respiration on the edge of her consciousness wasn't there either.

But it was. She could hear it quite plainly. On a normal day, she would have sought out the patient suffering from difficulty in breathing and asked if she could help. Yet this wasn't a normal day. There would never be a normal day again. Ever. There might not even be another day, in the bright world with the late weak sun glancing across the Market Square and the rooks wheeling overhead. She also would vanish, as completely as her mother had done, and it might be today, and it wouldn't matter.

The painful breathing continued, moving around, sometimes nearly approaching where she was, sometimes farther away, as if the person were engaged in a bizarre form of blind man's buff. She continued to sit there on the step with her head in her hands until the breathing went away.

'Open yer eyes, Lola Robertson.' The voice bounced off the building behind her, circled the pillars, and rolled down the steps. 'Open yer eyes, Lola Robertson. What yer doing there anyroads?'

She opened her eyes. Barry Green and Nigel Chadwick were still at the foot of the steps. The crowd in the Market Square was breaking up, the men putting their hats on, the women in clusters. Talking about our sister Lilian who had followed in the footsteps of the Lord and had stood alongside those in need. Who had slipped down the bed one night and had drowned.

At the other side of the square she could see the two people who had been on the opposite side of the chapel, near the back and wrapped in the shadow of a pillar. They were standing in front of Fortesque's shop, looking bewildered. Still, she realised, searching for someone whom they hoped to meet.

She knew, from the spasmodic lift and fall of the man's shoulders, that it had been his rasping breath she had heard. He was wearing a long black coat and had a black scarf tied loosely round his neck. He held his hat, a kind of beret, in one hand. He was still wishing to express his condolences to the person he had not found. The woman with him was beautiful. Lola could see that, even from a distance. As tall as he was, with her grey hair drawn back into a pleat, wearing, as he did, a long black coat. He held her by the hand, a simple, foreign gesture, which was drawing the attention of people nearby.

They were engaged in conversation with another man, no doubt asking for the person for whom they had been so uselessly searching. It was Jozef Schmidt. The recognition hit her, hopelessly, painfully…joyfully.

She saw herself suddenly leaping down the remaining seven steps into the Market Square, threading through the crowd, arriving breathlessly at the other side, at the place where Jozef stood talking to the two foreign people. He would explain their presence, tell her their names because she had forgotten how to pronounce it, if she had ever known. They would walk to the railway station, would wave as the train left, stand watching until it went out of sight, until the steam appeared once more, and briefly, across the fields where the river turned to the west by the village of Marsh.

But she was still seated on the top step outside the chapel, enveloped in the aroma of someone else's perspiration, someone else's moth balls, in the sensible breakfast someone else had been encouraged to eat to shore them up against a desolate public occasion. Studying the mark on someone else's black skirt.

When she looked up, they had gone, the beautiful foreign people – and Jozef. Instead, it was the shadow of Nigel Chadwick that leaned over her. Barry Green was at the bottom of the steps, pulling faces, trying to make her laugh. She scrambled to her feet, struggling to keep the skirt down over her knees. Barry Green would be looking.

'Miss Robertson, I am sorry for your loss.' Nigel Chadwick blushed and offered a fistful of red knuckles. Lola said thank you.

Nigel Chadwick stood in front of her, the blush spreading up to the roots of his hair. 'A nice service,' he said.

'Yes,' she said. She couldn't remember which hymns had been sung or what Mr Jardine had said about her mother. She thought of the foreign people whose name she had forgotten how to pronounce, making their way to the station. Barry Green was still at the bottom of the steps pulling faces.

'Miss Robertson…'

'Yes, Mr Chadwick.'

'Mr Goody has heard that you are living at the—'

'Bawdy house,' Lola finished the sentence for him. 'He should have said boarding house.'

'Ma says to tell you…' The sentence trailed off into some wordless cul-de-sac.

She didn't want to. She didn't want to move in with Nigel Chadwick's mother. Her mind searched for a response to the offer that hadn't been made. She could see Mrs Chadwick, on the edge of the crowd, wearing a black that sat oddly with the auburn out-of-curls escaping at the back, and her pale face without rouge or lipstick. She couldn't go there, for a reason she could hardly explain. The same aroma, of the public house, hovered around Nigel Chadwick as if the sweet stale scent of yesterday's ale and the quiet breath of generosity were the same.

She couldn't. Not even if she were to find herself, with her suitcase, on the pavement. She couldn't go to the hospital each day with the aroma in her hair, and without knowing it was there.

But he hadn't asked. He wasn't going to.

'Ma says to tell you that she's sorry for your loss, Miss Robertson.'

'Thank you, Mr Chadwick.' She wanted to say something kind to make up for her lapse in charity. She blushed. 'Do you still go to the library?'

He said he was…But as soon as she heard she had forgotten. She said how pleased she was.

She could see Jozef entering the Market Square again. Looking for someone who was hidden in the public daylight on the top step of the Methodist chapel.

'Mr Chadwick, I'll have to go. They have come to take me back to the hospital.' She held out her hand. 'The man in the black coat down there. He's from the hospital.'

She went down the steps. Barry Green had gone. One or two people turned to look at her. One or two whispered. That's Lilian Robertson's daughter. Why wasn't she with her father?

Because she hadn't been asked.

Did she have to wait to be asked?

She didn't know the answer. Maybe she could have taken the empty place beside her father at the front of the chapel. Maybe he had been waiting for her. She didn't know. Maybe he would have looked down at her, wearing someone else's black jacket and someone else's marked skirt, wearing someone else's aroma, and edged imperceptibly away. Where were yer when yer ma needed yer, duck? She could no longer see Jozef.

Then, all at once, he was there, not far away from her, still not seeing her because she was wearing black, someone else's black, and the picture of her he was carrying in his mind was of someone different.

She looked towards the steps of the Methodist chapel. Nigel Chadwick had been joined by someone else whom she didn't recognise, who was offering him something, maybe a cigarette. She could see him shaking his head.

'Lulu.'

She blushed.

'*Wie geht es*?'

She started to cry. In the Market Square, in the sight of the Methodist chapel, Jozef Schmidt placed his hands on her shoulders and, brushing the hair from her forehead, kissed her.

'The people were looking for you.' Away from the hospital, Jozef's English was almost without an accent. 'They gave me this to give to you.' He took a brown envelope out of his pocket and gave it to her. It bore her name on the front, written in an old-fashioned copperplate she had seen before.

'Do I open it?'

'It's yours, Lulu. You may wish to read it in privacy.'

'I have no privacy.' And it was true. Since she had been locked out of her room in the boarding house and the door had been broken down to allow her to go back in, she had been unable to lock herself in anywhere; only in the WC, and there was invariably someone or other standing outside, banging on the door, demanding to know how long she would be. She could feel a sheet of writing paper inside the envelope.

She started crying again. People were moving away, observing from a distance the daughter of Lilian Robertson making an exhibition of herself in the company of the German man from the hospital on the day of her mother's funeral.

'We will go to the park, Lulu. You may sit and read your letter there.'

'I can't, Jozef.'

'Miss Taylor doesn't expect you back today, Lulu.' He took a folded handkerchief from his pocket and dried her eyes.

'I still can't, Jozef.' Because she was wearing someone else's black jacket with the morning of their grief still on it, the skirt of someone else who couldn't hold the cup of tea they were given and who had let it spill.

But she did go. And seated on a bench with the glimmering sun above her head and the worn out grass at her feet, she opened the letter. It was a letter of condolence, which honoured her loss as equal to that of her father, but different. It honoured her, simply, as a human being. It began, "Our dear Lola", and ended…the words melted in front of her eyes.

'How do you say that name?' She asked Jozef.

'Churnick.'

'But is has a zed.'

'The zed is qualified by the c. The sound is ch, as in Methodist chapel.'

'It is a beautiful letter. Where have the people gone?'

'Back to London.'

'Will I ever see them again?'

Jozef turned to face her, laying a hand on her arm, the right hand with the ring on the third finger.

'Lulu,' he said, 'there are many things we do not know in this life.'

She looked across the park to where they were collecting up deck chairs, collapsing them and loading them onto a cart. Taking away the summer. She thought of her mother, who had slipped down the bed into the sea and drowned when no one was looking; who had come back walking in the sunlight, young and pretty again.

'I had a dream about mother, Jozef.' She told him.

'Yes, Lulu, that happens. *Ich verstehe,*' he said.

Then he asked her, looking not at her but at the other side of the park where the doors of the pavilion had been closed on the last of the summer, if she could ever think of going to the pictures with him. She said yes.

Chapter VIII

Stefan put Bazal over the fence. He picked up the hoe and the rake, gathered the strings of nettles and couch grass into an armful, and took them to the bottom of the garden where the sycamore was already rusting and dropping leaves onto the sunless earth.

Bazal had come back, moving swiftly on his baggy legs to the remaining cabbages. The gardens of Golen Avenue were still full of cabbages, six years after the war. They invaded the air and informed the consciousness. While there were cabbages in the gardens, however malodorous and clothed in grey green rags, England was keeping her head above the northern sea. He had forgotten who had written about the northern sea. Someone.

'We thought everything would be all right after the war, and look what happened to us.'

Mrs Beaumont was in the garden next door. 'Just put Bazal over the fence if he's bothering you, dear.'

'I'll give you back the keys, Mrs Beaumont.'

'So you're not coming again, dear?' Her face crumpled in disappointment.

'Mother and father will be back.'

'Of course, Stefan dear. Shall I tell them you've been?'

But they would know. Even if they didn't go down the garden, and they probably wouldn't, they would know the moment they walked in the front door that he had been there. Some part of him – his spirit – would still be there, wandering from room to room, noting the absences; just as part of them was there when he went in, seated at the scrubbed kitchen table, a pot of tea between them and the paper still open at the vacancies.

He walked up Golen Avenue to Congreve Park, looking for them, his father back from the mines and his mother carrying flowers.

And then he saw them, seated on a bench at the other side of the pond, looking not in his direction but at the bandstand where the lower door was open and the last of the summer's deckchairs were being taken inside. He could hear the clatter as they were flattened and stacked and the iron shudder of the door as it was slammed shut. Two mallards rose from the pond, shaking diamonds into the quiet evening.

His father and mother were still there, his father opening his satchel and taking out a bag. Stefan could see him undoing it, offering it to his mother; boiled sweets, one for you and one for me; his father closing the bag and returning it to his satchel; saving the rest for later.

His mother had taken off her black church hat. She captured a wisp of hair and pinned it back, his father holding her hat while she did so. He could see every breath his father stole from the generous air around him.

They stood up, brushed down their coats and set off, hand in hand. His beautiful mother; his difficult father. Going back to a home without the measured walk of time. He saw his mother and father stop to speak to the men who had been clearing the deck chairs; he saw them go through the side door by the rose garden. He caught sight of them again at the bottom of the hill and saw them step over the luminous word in front of the gate. A new pavement would be laid and the word would go, but his parents would always step over it.

The shop was still open. Stefan went in, stumbling down the tiled ledge at the other side of the door.

'Mind the step, sir. How may I help you?'

'I'd like…' The interior of the shop was filled with the voice of clocks, like the steady pitter of rain. Their placid moon faces glimmered from the wall and from shelves and from behind glass cases.

'If you'd like a clock, sir, you could be in the right place, who knows?'

'For a mantelpiece, please.'

'Ah, now we're getting somewhere. And the price range, sir?'

Stefan didn't know. He turned out his pocket onto the counter. The assistant deftly separated the change into its component parts. He was terribly sorry, he couldn't help.

'Try the stores. Remember your money, sir. And mind the step.'

'Thank you.' Stefan saw his father's face reflected in the glass of the door as he left, a dark foreign looking man, the hair rattled by the wind and the flannel shirt undone at the neck. Some conchie left over from the war.

'Try the stores, sir. Mind how you go now. Got your money? That's the ticket.'

There was seventeen and sixpence: a ten-shilling note, two half crowns, a florin and two three-penny bits. An obscenity of riches.

He tucked the clock, wrapped in brown paper and string, under his arm.

It was ticking, counting each step he took to his parents' home, each reluctant breath he drew, every deafening beat of the blood running through the arteries in his head. He would have to ring the front door bell and wait. He would have to do that, in spite of the unsettling end of season scent carried on the chestnuts. Having rung the doorbell, he would have to wait until it was answered. But probably he wouldn't. He could ring the bell and leave the brown paper parcel on the shelf in the porch for his father to find. His father would not see it. He would instead go down the chequered path and look uselessly up and down Golen Avenue. Only when he got back to the porch would he hear the ticking and discover it.

He should unwrap it and silence it. But he didn't. He rang the bell and waited. The curtain was drawn back and his father was there, swimming on the surface of the glass, fumbling with the key, stooping down to push the draught guard aside. Opening the door.

'Stefan!'

'Hello, father. I saw you in the park. You and mother.' His father stood aside to let him in. 'No, I don't want to trouble you.'

Tears were running down his father's face.

'Who is it, darling?' The kitchen door opened and his mother was in the hall. 'We've put a cup out for you, Stefan. We saw you in the park and we didn't think you'd come, but we put a cup out. Your father always puts a cup out.'

'I saw you. You had a bag of sweets.'

'Potato crisps. Wonderful.' His father had suddenly found a voice. 'You have to try them. You'll help us finish them?'

Yes. Stefan didn't say the word. He wished he'd rung the doorbell and gone. He went inside, following his parents to the kitchen. Leaving himself outside, hesitating, in the porch. His parents must know, although they appeared not to, that he was nearly twenty-three. For them, he had remained as he was on the day that he left.

He poured out more tea. His parents were still seated at the kitchen table, admiring their clock, passing it between them, adjusting the time, trying the alarm. Thanking him, thanking him, thanking him, All at once, he had become their parent. Something happened inside his head, suddenly and painlessly, as if a synapse had been bridged and there had been a sudden leap into some other, surprising place.

'We must put it on the mantelpiece.'

But for the moment, it was there, on the table, measuring out each second until he had to leave.

'Where did you go?'

'Didn't Mrs Beaumont tell you when she gave you the keys?'

'Yes. Vaguely.'

'We didn't want to say too much to her, not after losing Ken. It was a funeral. The wife of the army corporal who intervened to stop some nastiness on the train when your father was returning from the mines. By a strange coincidence, the family live next door to Pip and Jean.'

'I remember. Father's sock.' His father got up and went to the satchel which was hanging on the peg behind the kitchen door.

'Your father's tired,' his mother mouthed. Then something like, 'Be patient with him.'

His father came back with the half-finished packet of crisps. He offered the bag to his mother, then to him.

'I nearly forgot these,' he said. The cuffs of his shirt sleeves had been turned in and hemmed. The same shirt belonging to his father, Stefan noticed, that his mother had brought to him to wear to the concert in the Albert Hall at the end of the war. 'Try them,' his father said. 'They're jolly good.'

'Darling,' his mother said, 'what kind of a word is that?'

'A jolly good one,' his father said.

The packet of crisps went round until only dust and grains of salt were left in the bottom. The clock continued to measure out long silences between their words.

'Stefan, how nice, it says *Tempus Fugit*,' his mother said.

'Did the old one break down?' He still couldn't think that its absence was ordinary.

'Your hand, if you would,' his father said, and tipped out the remaining contents of the crisp packet. 'Don't let your mother see. The truth is, Stefan...' His father stopped. 'Your mother will explain.'

'What can I say...your father is unable to work. He has a condition of the lungs, possibly from the mines, possibly from the white dust at the factory. He is able to teach a little, but few people can pay for tuition now. We thought after the war everything would be better.'

And now look what has happened to us all. Stefan didn't say it. He had heard the words, recently, set to a melody in E minor written by Smetana in his last years. The kitchen darkened and a gust of wind threw a fistful of raindrops against the window.

'We were managing,' his mother went on, 'until we heard about poor Mrs Robertson, and we had to make a journey on the railway. Without the corporal's intervention, your father might not be here. You won't remember, dear, you took a thank you letter to the post.'

Stefan said nothing. He couldn't ask. He couldn't find the words, or the reason. The gifts of the spirit and she didn't know it.

'But we didn't see the lovely girl,' his father said. 'We looked all over.'

'Your father's talking about their daughter,' his mother said. 'What was she called, darling?'

'Lola.'

'Are you sure? I thought the German gentleman referred to her as Lulu.'

Stefan felt himself reddening. The small incandescence in him guttered and died.

'Someone who knew her at the hospital,' his mother was saying. 'We never did find her and we wished to very much. In all likelihood our paths will never cross again.'

'Sweetheart, that's a cliché,' his father said. 'We must write to her.' Still nothing about the clock. His parents were justifying their poverty without mentioning the letters from Wickham Place. 'In short, Stefan, we were faced with a journey by railway and we had to use Bratley's.'

'The pawnbrokers,' his mother said.

'But we don't need to go back, sweetheart.' His father took a ticket from his shirt pocket and tore it up, scattering the pieces on the table and scooping them up into his hand. He drew a breath, sufficient for the tortured beginning of a sentence. 'You did rightly, Stefan. Your mother and I didn't understand at the time what had happened, but when…'

'When?'

'I'll tell him, darling. We didn't wish to search your room, Stefan. You were at an age when many young men leave home for various reasons. It was only when the bedroom ceiling needed attention that we found those dreadful letters. We considered the matter and came to the conclusion that you had acted with integrity.

You didn't wish to involve your parents. It is over now. They wrote to this address later. Your father didn't...you know. Do you still play Smetana, dear?'

He told his parents that he was sometimes called upon to play *The Blue Danube* and the *Vlatava* of Smetana in the public house, and watched the glance pass between them. His father said, 'Gee.' His mother said, 'Darling, not that word.'

Outside, stepping on the word that would one day no longer be there, Stefan tried to remember how he had made his exit. But he couldn't. There was nothing left of the time between his parents' brief exchange and his arrival under the whispering chestnuts in Golen Avenue. Only that the clock would still be measuring out the seconds step by step, its placid moon face turned on the ageing man and the beautiful woman seated at the kitchen table, on the chair left empty by the sudden departure of the guest, and beyond the window on the garden where Bazal wandered disconsolately between the hoed and weeded cabbages left there after the war.

He tried to reel in the time but he couldn't retrieve anything later than his father saying gee. It was something he must have said. Something better left unsaid, which for some reason he was unable to fathom. Something to do with...

Then he knew, with sudden clarity, that his father was an abstainer. And he knew, just as certainly, that his father would offer no word of blame if he himself chose otherwise. Or if he should be night watchman at a disused munitions factory. It would all be OK.

It was his night off. As far as he knew, the other chap wouldn't be there either. There would be no one. No one to go round to the back of the machine shop and examine the trodden vegetation, to search for an underground gas pipe, and bore holes in the wall.

They would be waiting for him at the public house. A draught of Strauss on a Friday night. Lehar. Offenbach. Suddenly, he was there in the dark gold and crimson smoke of it, playing Smetana's first movement from the quartet in E minor.

When he had finished, someone from the bar approached him.

'With respect, Mr Czerniak, that don't carry a melody. The fellows request a tune. With respect, Mr Czerniak.'

So he played *The Blue Danube*. He played it again, and again. He played it until his arm had turned to lead and the air had been drunk dry. He loosened his collar. 'I'm sorry, I'll have to call it a day.'

The man who had requested a melody opened the door, went out and came back in.

'It's gas, chaps.'

'Wrong war, Eric.' A few of the men laughed.

'Mr Czerniak, sir.' The man called Eric pressed some coins into his hand. One and nine-pence.

'I don't need it, sir.'

'Mr Czerniak, sir, for a rainy day. A chap needs to plan for a rainy day. With respect, sir. Mind how you go. Don't have to tell a clever chap like you, Mr Czerniak, but close your windows, sir. Never known it so strong. The weather, that's what it is. Heavy. You won't see many folks out tonight.'

Eric peered at him through round health service spectacles.

'Thank you, sir.'

'You're welcome, Mr Czerniak. Mind how you go now. Got to look after chaps like you. Not many chaps that can spin a fine melody.'

A blanket had come down on the night, dense and breathless and reeking of gas. People were hurrying home, their hands over their faces. The woman at the corner of Ludlow Gardens was engaged in an altercation with the driver of a taxi.

'No, miss, I'm not taking you nowhere, not till you put the fag out.'

She threw it down and climbed into the taxi. The cigarette still smouldered on the pavement, glowing red and orange, and sputtering into life. Stefan stamped on it, knocking into another man who had stepped forwards for the same purpose. The man raised his hat and turned away, still with his hand over his face. Someone over the road vomited into the gutter.

Inside the house the smell of gas was stronger, as if everyone entering had let in a consignment of it and now it was trapped there, on the landings and stairs and in the rooms. Stefan closed the window and looked out at the bilious sky over East Ham.

He could hear the unmistakable purr of a Rover's engine. He went to the window, waiting for the car to pass by. But it didn't. There were no vehicles in Ludlow Gardens. Yet the sound of the engine was still there ticking over interminably outside his window in the empty street. He stood by the window, listening.

By now, it would have reached its destination. He was certain of that. He saw it, stopping in front of the factory gates, the driver getting out and using his own key to enter, because the watchman had a night off. He had made sure of that. He had neglected to appoint a chap to stand in. He drove forwards, got out of the car and dropped the keys into a side pocket of his jacket.

Stefan Czerniak laid his violin on the table and went out.

Simon Harper, he saw in his mind's eye, was now making his way nonchalantly across the yard of the munitions plant picking up the scattered pages of a newspaper. The racing section. *Turn a blind eye* circled heavily in dark pencil. Filling in for the night watchman. Leaving it tidy. Peeling off the mask on his face because there was no one to see. The gas would in all likelihood sting the raw flesh, but it didn't matter.

Stefan quickened his pace. He noticed that Simon Harper had returned to the lodge and was running water into a cup. He swallowed the water in gulps, and something else, which he transferred deftly into the cavern of his mouth from the other hand. Stefan began to run. Mr Harper had left the lodge and was walking slowly towards the machine shop, pulling on a cigarette. It could have been still light, or dark. Stefan no longer knew. There was no one to ask. Everyone had gone home and closed their windows because that's what they did when the gas works were bad.

Simon Harper walked round to the back, to the area between the machine shop and the perimeter wall of the plant. He examined the exposed piping. Everything was as it should be. The narrow gauge tubing remained in situ, feeding in through the brickwork. He looked at his watch and made his way to the first fire hydrant, took a spanner from his pocket and disabled it. Then the second, and the third. The fourth and final one.

Stefan Czerniak had been listening for some time to the hoarse rasping breaths somewhere near him. He caught sight of his father in the plate glass of a passing window. Simon Harper was apparently in no hurry. He continued, unsteadily, to the front of the machine shop, the workers' entrance, and unlocked the door using a key of his own. He sat down on the floor, leaning back against the wall. He was feeling for something in his pocket. Something necessary which he couldn't find. Stefan noticed the expression of anguish pass over Mr Harper's expressionless face.

He continued running, round the gas works, until the munitions factory rose up before him, sudden and silent under the cover of the bilious night.

The gate would be locked. Simon Harper continued to search through his pockets, emptying their contents onto the stone floor at his side: a handkerchief, a fountain pen, a toothbrush, a packet of Craven A. A box of matches. The anguish melted from his face. He patted his pockets again. A frown flickered across the taut flesh of his forehead and went. He struck a match.

Stefan tried the gate. It gave slightly on its hinges.

A dull glow rose behind the grimed glass of the east windows of the machine shop, reddening as it rose through the panes. All the blank orifices of a face that had served Simon Harper in the years after the war had sealed and he slumped sideways, hitting the ground and trying to right himself.

Stefan shouldered the gate. It gave a few inches, sufficiently for him to slide in. Mr Harper had stopped struggling and was lying awkwardly on his side, only his head bouncing slightly each time as it made contact with the floor.

From the lodge, Stefan Czerniak searched for an expression on Simon Harper's face, but there was none. He listened for the sound of Simon Harper's voice, but heard nothing. He picked up the telephone and dialled.

'There is a letter.'

'Read it to us, sir. Stand well back.'

But he wouldn't. He would run. If it was the last thing he did. Round to the back of the plant where a red glow rose up through the tiers of windows of the machine shop and into the roof space. The smell of gas was overpowering. It coursed through what remained of the air passages of the man slumped on the floor. It filled the cavern of his mouth, his eyes, his lungs, until the head sank for the last time onto the floor.

The letter swam in front of Stefan Czerniak's eyes. He had scarcely folded it back into his creases and returned it to the envelope when the machine shop went up. He was still there with the letter in his hand when the pressing room went up, the drawing office, purchasing, sales, the finishing shop, each link of the chain. Until all of the plant was reduced to a cloud of fiery particles riding on the night sky over the Roding Valley.

Chapter IX

She shouldn't have worn a hat. Lola knew that now, taking it off in front of the tin lid that did as a mirror. Apart from the inappropriateness of it, when only one other woman in the whole of the cinema was wearing one, it had obliged Jozef to take her to the back so that she wouldn't obscure anyone else's view. He stood aside to let her go in first.

Next to her, two people were kissing in the darkness.

'I can't sit here, Jozef.'

'You do not have to, Lulu.' He changed places with her, brushing against her as he did so. In the darkness, she blushed.

Afterwards, in the foyer, he asked her if she had enjoyed the picture. She had, very much. Anna Neagle was beautiful and she imagined that the hospital at Scutari would have been exactly like that. She was suddenly aware of Jozef's hand on her arm, holding her back.

'Lulu, is it Miss Taylor?'

It was, with another lady who must surely have been her mother. Miss Taylor hadn't seen them. She was helping her companion down the steps, carrying her handbag for her. She looked round, to make sure they weren't holding anyone else up. Neither she nor her mother wore a hat.

Lola shook out her hair and looked at herself in the tin lid. The imprint of Jozef's lips should rightly still have been there, visible to her, and the touch of his hands on her arms, on her neck, on her…front. The colour flooded her face. She couldn't think the other word. She started to cry.

Someone was knocking on her door with a metallic object, a key or a knife. But she couldn't answer it. She couldn't let anyone see how she was in her shame and delirium, and for all she knew her mouth still bruised from the recent farewell on the corner. She saw that an envelope was being slid under her door and heard the footsteps of someone retreating along the corridor, letting the door at the end close with a bang, and clattering down the staircase.

There was no one she could ask what she most wanted to know. Had she done anything wrong? Had she, finding herself on the brink, looked down into some abyss that she, Lola Robertson from Barratt's Place, knew nothing about? Her body still burned with a need she could hardly identify.

She took off her clothes, standing in front of the tin lid, and looked at the whole of herself, angling it to slide down her chest, her abdomen, the shadow between her legs, down the flesh of her thighs to her knees, her ankles, her bare feet on the linoleum.

She thought of the bones of the lower limb, chaste and white. And she thought of Miss Taylor, holding her mother's handbag and helping her down the steps of the cinema. Whose life was virtuous, who had never experienced the fire that smouldered behind the triangle at the base of the pelvis.

The footsteps returned. They stopped outside her door. She saw that the envelope was being nudged farther into her room until the whole of it lay there, an odd rhomboid with her name written approximately on it in pencil. It said Miss L Rob – son, as if the writer, having set off with her name in their head, had lost the middle of it on the way up the stairs and couldn't remember whether it was Robertson or Robinson.

She picked it up and opened it. Her rent book fell out and landed at her feet, open at the current week. She could see that the subsequent dates on the same page had been crossed through. The accompanying letter informed her that the term of her tenancy had expired with effect as from Monday (the date hadn't been completed) inst and that she was required to vacate the room at her earliest convenience.

She washed in cold water and put on her clothes again, the same ones she had worn to go to the pictures with Jozef. The same panties with the lace trim, the brassiere he had unaccountably known how to unfasten, the straight grey skirt with the kick pleat at the back, the twinset and glass beads. Everything that might have defined her as a good-living chapel-going girl.

But she wasn't thinking of the chapel. She was, she realised, constructing in her mind a conversation with Miss Taylor in the staff room the following day.

She pulled her suitcase out from under the bed and began to pack: her undies and her other skirt, her dress, her slippers and her work shoes; her brush and comb and her sponge bag; two pairs of stockings, a tin of shoe polish, a box of sanitary towels and a belt. She stripped the bed and left the folded sheets and pillow slips on top, over the stain on the mattress which was there when she arrived. She looked around, and drew the curtains back.

There were still two days on the rent but it didn't matter. She left the book on the counter in reception with the letter she had received addressed to Miss L Robertson or Robinson and made her way to the exit, wearing her hat because it was easier to wear than carry. It was ten minutes to twelve by the clock on the back wall.

Someone coming in held the door for her. 'Need a hand, duck?'

She made her way to the Market Square and sat down on the top step of the Methodist chapel. There were voices in the distance, attenuated nighttime voices. Someone shouted. She fell asleep leaning against a pillar.

When she woke the clock of the parish church was chiming half past the hour. 'Lola Robertson,' she said, but no one had asked. The night voices were still there, and, carried on the darkness, the plash of water. They were throwing ropes out onto the surface of the river. She lodged her suitcase and hat behind the pillar and ran.

Someone had gone in. A man passing by with a dog had raised the alarm. The dog was still there, whining on the bank. A policeman picked up a pair of shoes and took them away. People were standing on the bridge looking down. A fire engine arrived, its lights turned onto the water. An arc lamp was being manhandled onto the parapet of the bridge. No one had seen anything, only the pair of shoes left there, side by side, as if they would be required again.

Lola looked down at the seething river. The tide was on the turn.

'With any luck the feller ull get hooked up on them willows yonder of boat yard,' a man near her said. 'Aye, aren't you the young lass from x-ray? Thought it was you, duck.'

Then, suddenly, she saw her father, on the wharf side, near the fire engine, wearing his corporal's hat. The policeman touched his hat. Their voices rose up to her on the shimmering night.

'Chap overboard, constable?'

'Could say that, corporal. Maybe, maybe not. All we've got to go on is a pair of shoes.'

'Shoes, eh?'

'Any ideas, corporal?'

She didn't hear what her father said in reply. On the bridge, they continued to shine the light onto the oily surface, where the ropes flashed and writhed and gained no purchase. She should leave, before her father discovered her, with the fire of the evening still in her, and, for all she knew, vestiges of rouge and lipstick still on her face. But she had nowhere to go.

Someone touched her arm. 'Lola.'

She turned round. 'Alison!'

'Your father's down there, Lola.'

'Has he seen me?'

'I don't know.' Alison Goody hesitated. 'You look nice.'

'I've been to the pictures and I put the same outfit back on again.' Which was true to an extent. In the scattered light of the arc lamp, Lola blushed. It was true, she thought unaccountably, to the extent that a sock with a hole in the heel is true, sound for the most part but certain areas of it missing. 'Do you know what happened?'

'No one saw. There was a pair of shoes as if someone had gone in. They rang your father. We can't do anything, Lola.' Alison touched her arm again. 'Come home with me, dear. They won't let you in when you go back...there.'

'To the bawdy house, you mean? They won't let me in ever. I've been evicted, Alison.'

'Then come back with me.' Alison took her arm. She smelt of Pond's cream and Vick. The bedtime smells of home. Lola noticed that under her coat she was wearing her nightdress. She had no stockings on. 'Please, Lola. Your father would want you to.'

'I have to go to the hospital.'

'Surely not at this time of night?'

'In case Miss Taylor's called out.' The hole in the imaginary sock was becoming larger. Soon it would be too extensive to mend. 'I mean, she isn't usually, but it could happen.' She never had been called out for someone in the river to Lola's knowledge.

Alison said, 'Oh dear.'

Lola felt the tears gather behind her eyes. Alison believed her. Everything she had said.

'Well, if that's the case, Lola, your duty at the hospital comes first. God bless you, darling.'

She watched Alison go down the steps, one at a time, the fitful light picking out her head and shoulders, and the hand extended to hold onto the railing.

Nothing different was happening at the water's edge. Her father was still there talking to the other men. Lola saw him take off his corporal's hat and scratch his head. He would put it on again, in front of some non-existent mirror, taking care with the angle of it, pulling it sideways and forwards until it was right.

But he didn't. He kept the hat in his hands, his eye focused on some distant place downstream where the edge of the light had picked out an object caught on the turn of the tide. She saw her father gesture towards the men operating the arc lamp, that they should send the beam as far as possible downstream. For an instant, she thought her father's eyes met hers. She ducked into the shade.

Her father was directing the ropes. 'Take them down yonder.' She could hear his voice clearly, flickering in and out of the glancing lights of the lamp. Down yonder. Down yonder. Down yonder.

She watched as they went down, the men with the ropes, her father, the policeman, dwindling into the distance. The men with the arc lamp manhandled it down the steps and followed.

Several people from the bridge had gone down.

Lola stood leaning on the parapet, looking at the receding procession until she could see no longer; only, a long way off, the sporadic flash of the lamp. Then, on the quiet night, she heard her father's voice.

'Hats off, gentlemen. Please.'

So the deception she had, in her desperation, practised on Alison Goody was, by some dark alchemy, about to become the truth. She went back to the Market Square and collected her suitcase and hat from behind the pillar.

The hospital was already awake, the main gates pulled back to admit vehicles and the doors of the casualty department standing open. Everyone had been called in. Miss Taylor's bicycle was in the cycle stand.

The x-ray department was unlocked. Jozef must have arrived already and wheeled the domiciliary machine round the corner.

Lola left her suitcase in the film store and took off her hat and coat. She looked in the mirror in the staff room and tried to remove the last vestiges of lipstick and rouge with the corner of her handkerchief. An expression of remorse passed over the face, her own and not her own. Alison would have noticed. Miss Taylor's voice was coming along the corridor and into the staff room.

'Lola! Thank goodness you're here. Would you mind giving me a hand, dear. You don't have to do anything, just pass me the plates. The gentleman will be covered. It's the same as any other patient, dear.'

Lola nodded. She noticed, absurdly, that Miss Taylor had left a curler in, clinging tenuously to a wisp of hair at the front.

She noticed, also, that the patient in casualty was wearing shoes, the laces still tied and dripping river water and strands of the kind of weed that rippled at the water's edge. Someone handed her a pair of gloves and a facemask. Miss Taylor wheeled the machine to the side of the trolley.

'Lola, a plate, please. Will someone lift the patient's head. Thank you, sister. Could you hold his head straight, please; hold his chin, if you would.'

Not Jozef then. He wasn't there. No one mentioned his absence.

Lola stood at the developing tank, inspecting the films one by one. She could hear Miss Taylor's voice discussing last night's film at the pictures with someone, coming through the light trap.

'Have we got anything yet, Lola?'

'Two have come out, Miss Taylor. I think the other might be blank.'

Miss Taylor said damn. 'You didn't hear that, Lola.'

'No Miss Taylor.'

'What do they look like?'

Lola took the x-ray out of the developer and put them in the wash tank. 'They're good, Miss Taylor. Maybe you don't need the other one. What time is it?'

'Half past six. I don't know why Jozef isn't here. We wouldn't have had a blank if he'd been here, but we can't do anything about it now. Shall we have a look, dear?'

Lola switched on the light box. She held the x-rays up, the one from the front and the one from the side and the third, with only the ghostly outline of the back of the skull on it.

'Do you see what I see?'

'Yes, Miss Taylor. A fracture of the frontal bone. And the mandible. Will they need a repeat of the mandible?'

She could hear the x-ray machine being wheeled back. 'I've left it outside, Gwen.' Sister's voice.

Lola went back to casualty to wind up the extension cable. The night nurse was finishing a bandage on the patient's head, fastening it with a safety pin. His eyes were open. He looked, she thought, as he would have looked when he set out for the bridge on the previous evening. How everyone looked at the beginning of the second half of the twentieth century: unsurprised, and disinterested in the flat grey leavings of the war. His clothes had been placed in a pile at the end of the trolley with the shoes on top, dribbling water onto the floor. A policeman stood in the corner, holding his helmet in his hands.

'We'll let you know, sister,' he said, addressing the night nurse. She didn't answer.

Everyone looked white and hollow-eyed in the breaking dawn of the next day. Lola thought of the girl she had seen, who was herself, with the remains of lipstick and rouge on her face. Let you know what? But she couldn't ask.

Miss Taylor said she would go home for an hour to "titivate" and see that her mother had her breakfast. She asked Lola if she would like to come with her. She didn't say anything about the suitcase in the film store, although she must have seen it.

'You'll need some breakfast, dear. We'll do a round of toast and marmalade.'

Suddenly, Miss Taylor's life in the difficult world, with a white-haired mother at one end and the x-ray department at the other, separated only by a chain of cigarettes and a short cycle ride, seemed endlessly reassuring.

'Thank you, Miss Taylor.' She hadn't said yes.

'Then you will, dear. I'm so pleased. I've told mother so much about you.'

It was still only twenty past seven. An early frost was whitening the pavements as the day lightened. Miss Taylor continued to talk: about the picture she and her mother had seen the previous evening, how they tried to go once a month if they could, about the difference Mr Bevan had made. Lola felt unaccountably cold. She put her hands in her pockets. Her gloves must be somewhere at the pictures where she dropped them when she stood up to change places with Jozef.

Jozef.

All at once, Miss Taylor was talking about him. She had had to unlock the department herself and wheel Hercules round to casualty. Jozef had never missed a day. She was worried.

'Yes, Miss Taylor.' Lola didn't know if that was an appropriate response. Her teeth were chattering and she could hardly speak.

'Lola, my dear, you must forgive me. You're suffering from shock.'

'I believe so, Miss Taylor.'

'It's natural, dear. You hadn't seen that kind of patient before.'

'No, Miss Taylor.' She wanted Miss Taylor to continue speaking. She wanted her to say something about the shoes left side by side on the riverbank. Shoes left there by someone who had been a soldier. Or a prisoner. Everyone had been either one or the other. Sent to fight or sent to prison because they wished not to fight. Or sent to the mines. From nowhere a vision of her former self came back to her. A day not long after the end of the war when a stranger had arrived at the door of their house in Barratt's Place. A dark, foreign looking man who had brought golden rod and Michaelmas daisies for her mother, who had dressed the suppurating wound on her father's leg. Who had come to say thank you. Whose sock she had mended.

It was when she was walking home at the end of the day, neither to Salisbury House, nor to Miss Taylor's home, but to the residence of Nigel Chadwick and his mother, that Lola saw the headlines. Body found in river. The man, believed to be from Yorkshire, had been identified by his brother who lived locally. A post mortem would take place. Foul play was not suspected.

And lower down on the same page, inset, a grainy picture of Jozef Schmidt: hospital orderly. Missing. No mention of the finding of a pair of shoes.

She picked up her suitcase and went to the address in Beacon Street.

Chapter X

Stefan placed the envelope on the table in the gatehouse. He looked out of the window at the ear-splitting clouds of smoke and at the fire that rolled across the yard as if buckets of flame had been emptied out of every window of the munitions plant simultaneously.

He watched as the burning tide divided and swept round the gatehouse like the boiling waters of some sudden sea, and left a single path leading to the machine shop. The voice still echoed on the line. 'If it is safe to leave, do so. If it is not, stay where you are and an engine will be at the location presently.' He poured the cold water left in the kettle onto the tea cloth and, winding it round his head, went out into the burning night. Somewhere in his head a bell clanged. A tongue of flame licked the toe of his shoe. He stamped it out and continued running. The bell crashed down on his head.

'No, sir, leave that to us. Not as if there's blokes inside. Bloody place is empty and has been for years. Escort this gentleman off the premises, Bill. Reckons there's a bloke inside.'

But there is. There was.

'Did you see him go in, sir?'

'Not in so many words. It was more in the imagination.'

'Imagination, eh?'

'He drove up in a black Rover.'

'See him driving up in a black Rover? No? More in the imagination?' A sudden peal of thunder split the night. 'That'll be the petrol tank, eh?'

The rain fell in sheets, and fell and fell, until the previous night was drowned in it, and the next day dawned, grey, aghast and absent.

Stefan Czerniak was still there, seated in the gatehouse drinking tea out of a tin mug, waiting, as were the firemen, for the rain to complete the task begun the night before.

The letter lay on the table, still in its envelope.

'You'd better show us where your imaginary bloke is, young man. The rain looks as if it's lifting. Here, used one of these fellows before?'

'They taught us gas masks at school, sir.'

'That's the ticket. If you think it's going to smother you, it ain't. Smoke smothers a chap. A mask don't. Might not have been washed out since the last chap but don't mind that.'

A dense hood of smoke lay over the plant. Tongues of flame lived briefly and expired. Far off an exploding canister. The sustained sigh as the ruins sank into the ground.

'Just two of you chaps. We don't want an army.'

The man's name was Bill. Or it might not have been. Inside the malodorous confines of the mask Stefan felt a sudden compulsion to know the officer's name. He started to gasp, gulping down the scarce black air. Any moment and he would have to tear the mask from his face and take in great gulps of the poisoned daylight.

'No need to rush, young man. Your imaginary fellow's not going anywhere.'

The machine shop lay where it had fallen, only the door and a window and the supporting struts left standing.

Stefan Czerniak was still on his knees in the rubble, digging with his bare hands, wiping the dust from the shoe. A black shoe, polished to go out that evening, a sock that had been clean on. Half the lace blown away, the other half alight, frayed and guttering like the wick of a dying candle. He was on his own, digging, searching for anything other belonging to the polished shoe with the flame of a lace. There wasn't room, he knew that, between the shoe and the door heaped with rubble. But still he was digging, watching the handfuls of masonry fall in as soon as he had cleared them.

He looked up. The whole dome of the sky hovered above his head like some wan helmet set there to protect him from the diminishing shots of fire raining down. The munitions plant was spread out in front of him, heaving and sinking into the earth. A wall of the finishing shop remained standing, the windows vacant, the door an absence, open-mouthed and silent. The gatehouse, intact.

He continued digging, finding nothing more than the polished shoe and the clean black sock. He redoubled his efforts. There must be a leg, a knee, a body thrown against the door, trapped by falling masonry. Breathing in a pocket of air. But he knew there wasn't enough room.

'You won't find nothing more, young sir.' The man called Bill and the other man were lifting him to his feet. 'We've located your imaginary fellow, over yonder.' He indicated the place with a broad sweep of his arm.

'Can I see him, sir?'

'Not at this point in time, young man. Maybe later, depending on who else comes forward. In the interim, we'll ask you to furnish us with a few details. There's a chap called Gerry here. Just turned up for work, poor bastard. Fortunately Gerald found the list of personnel for us.'

'Any reason for thinking Mr Harper was giving the correct name, Mr Czerniak?'

Stefan hadn't thought. 'I hadn't considered any alternative, sir.'

'Drink your tea, Mr Czerniak. In what capacity were you employed?'

'Night-watchman, sir.'

'Know much about Gerald, the other chap?'

'I understood his name to be Jerome, sir.'

'Ah, know much about him?'

'No sir.'

'Drink up, please, Mr Czerniak. We're dealing with a case of shock here.'

'Sir?'

'You're deemed to be in shock, Mr Czerniak. Know anything about the chap Gerald?'

'No sir.'

'Anything about the chap called Simon Harper?'

'He was my employer, sir.'

'Tell me about him.' The officer laid down his pen. One in a line of officers in various capacities he had encountered in his life; laying down their respective pens, searching his face, seeing his father. An objector.

'Mr Harper's face was badly disfigured, sir.'

'Tell you how?'

'No sir.'

'What did you make of him?'

'A very decent chap, sir.'

'Gave you a job. Had many jobs? Ever heard of Wickham Place?'

'Yes sir.'

'Tell me about Wickham Place.'

'I applied for a clerical vacancy and believed the location to be Wickham Place. I began to receive letters asking for sums of money on the supposition that I had been in breach of contract.'

The officer nodded. 'Present address?'

'Mine sir?'

'Yours, Mr Czerniak.'

'Ludlow Gardens.'

'Father's name Paul. Mother's name Ruth.'

'Yes sir.'

'Father: professor of mathematics, mother: industrial chemist.'

'Some time ago, sir.'

'Know a chap called Aveling?'

'Yes sir.'

'Context?'

Stefan said nothing.

'One word, Mr Czerniak.'

Still he said nothing. He couldn't think of a word.

'We're chaps together, Mr Czerniak.'

A word was slowly assembling somewhere behind his eyes. A word he had never used. Latinate.

'Virgilante, sir.'

'Vigilante, Mr Czerniak. No r in it. Do you…? No, forget that.' The officer picked up his pen. 'We have more on you than on Simon Harper. The bottom line, Mr Czerniak, is that we have nothing on Simon Aloysius Harper. A chap of that name went out on a raid in 1944 and failed to return. You know what that means?'

'Yes sir. No sir.'

'What do you understand by the expression "failed to return"?'

'He didn't come back, sir.'

The officer tapped his pen on the table. 'Thankfully, Mr Czerniak, the other chap, Gerald…'

'Begging your pardon, sir, Jerome.'

'The other chap, Jerome Cousins, corroborates what you have told us. Namely that a fellow by the name of Simon Harper was in post here and employed others. I'd like you to say all you can of the chap you knew as Simon Harper. Even if you're under the impression you've supplied the information before.'

The gifts of the spirit. But he didn't say it. He thought he hadn't said it.

'You a religious man, Mr Czerniak?'

'No sir.'

'Physical appearance of the chap you knew as Simon Harper.'

Stefan looked down at the pen, poised, ready to write. Its physical appearance.

'Was he a well-built chap, for instance?'

'No sir.'

'Not well-built. A tall chap?'

'About average, sir.'

'Facial expression, Mr Czerniak. Was he the type of chap you would confide in, or the type of chap you'd cross over the street to avoid?'

'No sir.'

'Neither.'

'The former, sir.'

'Mr Czerniak, look back on your life. Have you ever held a poor opinion of anyone?'

'I don't remember.'

'Chap called Aveling, for instance. As good as tried to kill you on the steps of the underground, and you had to search in your mind for some bloody euphemism. I put it to you, Mr Czerniak, that the chap so called Simon Harper didn't have a facial expression.' The officer slid a photograph across the table. It showed the head and shoulders of a young man wearing RAF uniform. 'That him?'

'I don't know, sir.'

Another photograph. That him? And another. And another.

I don't know...I don't know...I don't know. There was nothing left of the face of the man he knew as Simon Harper to suggest what he had once looked like.

Neither did Stefan Czerniak know anything of the journey home. The space in minutes and miles between the munitions plant and the corner of Ludlow Gardens had closed to nothingness.

It was late in the day. The shadow of the woman standing there lay tall along the pavement. He stepped to the side of it to avoid treading on her legs, her skirt, her head, any part of her. She was saying something that he couldn't quite hear. Aware of him, backing off, her hand over her mouth. Asking for a cigarette. Or not asking for a cigarette.

A faint sense of her perfume followed him, and was still there as he glanced at the letters on the table in the hall: Abrahams, Golland, Beech, Birkin, Tasker, Ferencic, Bates. Czerniak. He placed the others in alphabetical order and picked up the envelope addressed to himself, the smell of perfume swimming in his head. Maybe the woman on the corner had been inside.

But she wouldn't. Stefan knew that. He knew it as an undeniable fact. He knew it, suddenly and blindingly, that she was as he was. She didn't think enough of herself to suppose that she would be welcomed, even in a squalid lodging house with its odours of drains, and sweat, and bed bugs. And perfume.

He took the letter into his room. He thought they had stopped, and here was another. Handwritten. Exquisitely written. Personally delivered. Unobtrusively, so that he had stepped over it when he went out the previous night, and left it to be found by Abrahams, Golland, Beech, Birkin, Tasker, Ferencic or Bates, and placed on the table. Who, no doubt, any one of them, after leaving the letter, had looked up and inspected himself in the mirror, his head framed against a background of peeling Jacobean wallpaper. Not quite believing that he was he, still half alive and washed up in some corner of a straitened post war city.

Stefan sat on the bed and opened the envelope. The letter was folded in such a way that the script couldn't be seen. He would have to take the page out of the envelope and extract it from its folds. But he wouldn't. He could hardly touch it. He tore the contents into pieces and returned them to the envelope. He would flush it away when the knocking on his door had stopped.

'Sorry, old chap. Another fellow let us in.' Lad's voice was in the corridor. 'May we step inside for a moment?' The door opened a chink.

We.

Lad continued to talk as the door opened. 'I've brought...' Avril or Rose or Betty...Stefan forgot the name as soon as it was said.

'Come in, Lad.' He shook hands. 'Will you sit down.' There was only one chair, and the bed.

'Not for long, Stef, old chap. You look done in.' Lad's eyes drifted towards the envelope on the table. 'In short, Stef, I've come about the Rover. Changed hands, you know. Official requirement to divulge and so on. Last known movements. This good lady saw it. The chap inside stopped to ask if a young man of foreign appearance and courteous manners lived in the vicinity.'

'What was he like?'

'As I say, Stef, of foreign appearance and courteous manners. Remind you of anyone?'

'I meant the driver of the car, Lad.'

'Binny?' So not Avril or Rose or Betty. The name of the woman who stood on the corner was Binny.

She was looking down at her hands, examining her fingernails. She wasn't wearing a hat and Stefan saw that the thin hair on the crown of her head was already grey.

'Binny,' Lad said again.

The woman looked up. The corners of her mouth drooped in misery and tears were running down her face. She shook her head.

Lad said, 'There, there,' and gave her the handkerchief from the breast pocket of his jacket. 'I'll answer for her, Stef. Shot down in the war, poor bugger. Don't see many of them around these days.' Binny nodded. Her shoulders were heaving with sobs now. 'The chap wanted to deliver a letter, Stef. Binny doesn't remember seeing him do same.'

Stefan indicated the envelope lying on the table. A harmonic on the E string keened in his head until every other sound had gone. He could see Lad talking, and Binny crying, dabbing at her eyes with the still folded linen handkerchief embroidered in the corner with the letter L. He saw the question on Lad's face, to which he must have answered in the affirmative, because the envelope was now in Lad's hands, being opened, the contents falling to the floor like a rain of white fire.

He saw Binny on her hands and knees gathering up the pieces, and Lad restoring them to the envelope, and the envelope to an inside pocket of his jacket. 'May I, Stef, old chap?'

Chapter XI

The room was high in the house and had sloping ceilings.

Looking down, Lola could see Mrs Chadwick in the garden handing articles from the laundry basket to Nigel, who was pegging them on the line, meticulously, shaking out folds and arranging the pegs symmetrically: two sheets turned sides into middle, pillowcases, towels, greyed and thin and stained from long use. Washed through and freshened, put on for another month.

In the distance, on top of the only hill in miles, she could see the beacon.

In the room, rose curtains, rose wallpaper, a rose counterpane on the bed, and roses on the carpet. All different roses. Mrs Chadwick had provided her with the best out of the little she had. She had given her a mirror with a rose frame. A crucifix on the wall over the bed. She hadn't yet asked for any rent.

Lola's gaze followed the movements of the woman in the yard below: a slight woman with long auburn hair coming out of curl, with a sideways tilt of the spine and one brown laced shoe built up making the thick lisle stocking wrinkle as if the foot sat uncomfortably; a cigarette in her mouth which she took out from time to time, and exhaled a long stream of smoke into the cold grey air.

A low fire burned in the grate in the room. Nora Chadwick couldn't afford it, Lola was certain. She would let it die down and then say she didn't feel the cold and could manage without any more coals.

She watched as the last item took its place and as Nigel propped up the line, as the washing settled into the breeze and sparks of water showered down onto the tiled yard. A pail of slops for the pigs stood by the back gate, waiting to be collected. A broom leaned against the wall, a string mop standing on its handle weeping humble tears.

She buttoned up her cardigan, put on her coat and hat and looked in the mirror: Lola Robertson with the terrible secret which would go with her every day for the rest of her life. A secret written on her face for all the world to see, in the circles drawn under her eyes and in the downward curve of her mouth.

It wasn't her. It was surely some other girl, left over from the war. There would have been many such girls, and she hadn't realised. She closed the door of the room and went down the stairs.

Nigel Chadwick was in the hall, waiting for her. He was wearing a gabardine belted at the waist, left behind by his father, frayed at the wrists and collar. He took a cap down from the hook in the front hall. He asked her if she was comfortable in her room. He told her he had received his call-up papers. 'May I walk with you, Miss Robertson?'

She said yet. She heard, somewhere far away, a door slam shut. But it didn't seem to matter. Not now.

'I've got my call-up papers,' Nigel Chadwick said again. 'Mother thinks the holy angels have sent you to her, Miss Robertson.' They carried on walking in silence to the end of Beacon Street and through the alley to London Road. 'I'll have to tell them at work. They don't know yet.'

Nigel darted round the back of her so that he was walking on the outside. They went along by the park railings, trailing through the fallen leaves. A lost glove had been lodged on one of the spikes. Lola's hands were cold and she put them in her pockets. She didn't know what to say.

'I'll have to go for a test.'

'Yes, I suppose so, Nigel.' She asked when the test would be and he said it was the next week, and did she think he would get through.

'Then I'll be in the army,' he said. 'You need to turn off here, Miss Robertson. Mother said to tell you tea's at six. She said she hopes you like spam. Here.'

Lola looked with dismay at the brown paper parcel he'd pulled out of his pocket. 'But I can't, Nigel. Really I can't.'

'You can, Miss Robertson.' He took a similar parcel from the other pocket. 'We've both got one, see.'

Miss Taylor was standing in front of the mirror in the staff room doing her hair. Lola waited as she made a new parting and tucked in the dark brown wisps. She could see that Miss Taylor had noticed her standing in the door. Miss Taylor would surely know, from the smell that clung to her, a smell compounded of mothballs, rose scent, cigarette smoke and strong drink, that she had moved to Beacon Street.

Is Jozef in? Lola didn't say the words but Miss Taylor answered her.

'If you're wondering if Jozef's in, Lola, I'm afraid he isn't. Make yourself a cup of tea, dear. This has upset everyone. He was all right the day before, wasn't he? I'm losing track of time and I forget which day it was.'

'Yes, Miss Taylor.'

'He seemed cheerful in fact. But you could never tell with Jozef.' Could never tell. In the past tense. 'No one knew anything about him.'

Was he a good man? Lola didn't say it. But it suddenly seemed terribly important. Not, was he a married man, but was he a good man.

'Well, we might never know.' Miss Taylor extracted stray hairs from the teeth of her comb and put them in the waste paper basket. 'Are you settled in Beacon Street, dear?' So she did know.

'They're very kind.'

'Yes, I'm sure they are, dear. I only wonder what happens when the young man receives his papers. He'll need to know his mother is being watched over.'

'Yes, Miss Taylor.'

'You are too innocent and trusting to have thought of that, dear. You'll have to stop for two years, or longer if the young man finds he takes to the army and decides to stay in, whether you like it or not.'

'I suppose so.'

'I only mention it because it happened to me, dear. A broken engagement. Home to mother. There for life. Don't let it happen to you, dear. Of course, I love my mother dearly…' Her voice trailed off. 'Would you like to see to the first patient, dear. There are rumours going around that Jozef has returned to Germany.'

Lola stood in the staff room doorway. 'Germany?'

'That's what people are saying.'

'Who?'

'I don't know, dear. It's something going around.'

Lola closed the staff room door and went back in. 'I don't think he has, Miss Taylor.'

'I'm not saying one thing or the other, dear. You must admit that he was rather enigmatic. Anything could have happened.'

'Yes, Miss Taylor.' She was on the point of describing the dark night and the arc lamp and ropes, and her father's arrival at the wharf. A pair of shoes. The bell in the waiting room rang for a second time. She went to answer it.

Mrs Jardine was there. Lola blushed. She would have to ask Miss Taylor to see her. But Mrs Jardine had already taken her by the hand and was saying to her how nice and that she would tell Mr Jardine that she had been attended by Miss Robertson.

'Your dear mother would be so proud of you, Lola.' The tears shone behind Mrs Jardine's glasses. 'But I mustn't detain you, darling. I'm not here on a professional visit. There's a letter, you see.' She let go of Lola and took a brown envelope out of her handbag. 'Is that not beautiful writing? If Mr Jardine's was like that I would have no trouble typing his sermons. You will come and see us, won't you, Lola? I keep asking Mrs Beaumont if she's seen you. But of course, they've had their sorrows as well, as you know.'

Lola didn't know. She hadn't seen Pip since they day she started crying in the chapel and he suddenly had to go home.

Mrs Jardine looked over her shoulder. There was no one else in the waiting room. 'I'm all right for another minute, am I?' She lowered her voice. 'Jean would like to see you, Lola. She and Pip think the world of you, you know.'

Lola didn't know that either.

A gleamy sun filtered through the staff room window, throwing the shadow of a chimney onto the table and spilling down onto the linoleum. Mrs Chadwick's spam sandwich lay beside the shadow chimney, uneaten. It was new white bread and the crusts had been cut off.

'Eat up, dear.' Miss Taylor didn't look up from her crossword. 'It's been a shock to us all. I can't do the crossword today. Damn.' She put down the pencil. 'Have you read your letter?'

'No.' Lola took it out of her pocket, crumpled and still unopened. 'Will you read it for me, please, Miss Taylor? I find I can't.' She put the letter on the table.

'There are very few circumstances in which a person might read a letter addressed to someone else,' Miss Taylor said. 'It's not the done thing.'

'Please.'

'If you're absolutely sure, dear. Shall I read it all out or tell you the gist of it?' Miss Taylor had already got up and found a knife to open the envelope. 'I'll read all of it. It isn't very long. Are you ready? It says,

'"Our dear Lola, please forgive us. We tried to find you, but in spite of the tireless assistance of a good gentleman from the hospital we failed utterly. We pray that our paths may yet cross again in this life. Until then we send our best love and lasting esteem to a dear girl who mended a wayfarer's sock one evening at the end of the war. The road to heaven is indeed paved with such acts of mercy. May God bless you always. Yours affectionately, Ruth and Paul Czerniak".'

Miss Taylor handed the letter to Lola.

'I should have written. The people left a letter with Jozef to give me and I didn't write back.' She started to cry.

Miss Taylor silently wrapped Mrs Chadwick's sandwich in its greaseproof paper and returned it to the brown bag. 'You will write now, dear.' She went out and came back with a sheet of plain paper. It need only be an acknowledgement, to thank them and explain the delay. Say you'll write again later.'

'They'll think Jozef didn't give me the letter.'

Lola saw a look of surprise flicker across Miss Taylor's face. 'Then tell them he did.' She hadn't asked who the people with the foreign name were, only commented that she had never had a name like that in the files.

Lola wrote the letter in the office, not knowing how to begin it, or how to end it, or what to put in the middle. These people had known Jozef Schmidt, however briefly, as someone like themselves: a stranger in a strange land. As he had known them, and recognised their confusion and their searching. They may have done what no one at the hospital had presumed to do, and asked him how he found himself there, in a small town on the borders of Nottinghamshire, with its uneventful sun-paved streets and its inclination to leave him to himself.

Suddenly Lola knew, as she sat in the x-ray office, that by some miracle she would one day find the people with the name spelt with a silent z.

Miss Taylor knocked and came in with a stamped envelope and Mrs Chadwick's sandwich, in its brown wrapping. 'You will post it, dear, won't you?'

'Yes, Miss Taylor.' She thought of the sandwich, and of persuading its well-meant bulk into the open mouth of the letterbox on the way back to Beacon Street.

'You will eat it up, won't you, dear?'

*

The day was closing down. Lights glimmered through the branches of the trees, picking out the diamonds suspended from the ends of twigs. The remains of the sandwich were still in her bag. She sat down on a bench and took another bite. Absent-mindedly she removed the leftover spam and put it down for the dog snuffling around her feet.

She'd walked past the box and forgotten about the letter. She would have to go back. The dog was still there, at her feet, whimpering.

'I haven't got any more. All gone…Watson! Dear Watson!' The dog pushed his soft head into her hands and circled the bench in ecstasy. 'Watson! I can't believe my luck!'

'Nor can we.'

Suddenly, she was no longer alone. Jean was seated on one side of her and Pip on the other. Jean looked pale and haggard under the yellow evening lights. Lola hadn't seen her, not since…she tried to remember. It must have been when she'd taken Lilian to the hospital.

Jean took her hand. 'We had a sudden change of plan, Lola. You'll know more about these things than Pip and I do, working in the hospital.' All at once, Jean was talking to her as if she were an infinitely wise adult. 'I lost the baby at six and a half months. I don't know what I did wrong, dear.' The tears ran down her face, glittering in the lamplight. 'I can't have loved her enough. We were going to call her Lilian. Your dear mother said it was going to be a girl by the way I looked.' Jean took a handkerchief out of her pocket and dabbed at her eyes. 'But how about you, Lola? You are still a good girl and eating up your spam.' Suddenly, she was a child again.

'I gave some of it to Watson,' she said. 'It wasn't anything you did wrong, Jean.'

'Wasn't it, dear?' A pale smile lit Jean's face. 'Are you sure?'

'Yes, I am certain, Jean.'

'You know best, Lola, darling.' Jean started to cry again. 'I've been so worried. I haven't even said so to Pip but I thought I was a murderer.'

'No, no, Jean. It sometimes happens with the first baby.' Lola didn't know if that was true or not. Pip had got up and was kicking small pebbles about with the toe of his shoe.

'Will you say a prayer for us, Lola?' Under the thin light Lola felt herself blush. Jean didn't expect an answer. 'I feel much better now, dear. But what about you? What are you doing here at this time of night? Watson, get Pip.'

Then Lola was telling Pip about the letter, still in her bag, unposted. How the people with the foreign name, Pip's mother's neighbours, had taken the trouble to travel up for Lilian's funeral, and how she knew the gentleman was looking for her but she couldn't face anyone because she was wearing a skirt and jacket from the jumble sale and the skirt was marked and the jacket smelt.

'They wouldn't have minded, Lola,' Pip said.

'That's not the point, Pip,' Jean said. 'Lola minded.'

Then Lola said she had seen them asking someone from the hospital. She started to cry, trying to say what Jean and Pip surely knew, that the colleague from the hospital was now missing.

'I saw his shoes.' Suddenly, the words were out, running across the darkening grass and springing up into the branches of the trees.

'Let's slow down a bit,' Pip said.

'Pip...'

'We're talking about two things here...'

'You'll have to excuse him, Lola. You've interrupted her, Pip.'

'It's all right, really, Jean. I'd finished, I think. I'd better post this.'

'Whose shoes did you see, Lola?'

'Pip! She's upset, can't you see?'

'I'm sure they were his.'

The German chap's? The missing chap? Pip had said nothing but Lola could see the words as clearly as if she'd heard them, unfolding into the collapsing world, letter by letter, falling to the ground. Being trampled underfoot. Pip was giving her a linen handkerchief. She buried her face in it, inhaling its flat iron smell. Jean was saying there, there. Lola could feel her thin arm round her shoulders.

'You're freezing, Jean.'

'No, Lola, I'm not. Probably Pip's right, though don't tell him I said so. Part of the time, it's me who's right. It's more than an unposted letter isn't it, darling? We can take that down when we go. We can take you with us, Lola. Would you like to go to London? It's so exciting. We can take Lola, can't we, Pip?'

Lola didn't hear Pip's answer, if he gave one. He was occupied in untangling the lead from around Watson's paws and pulling leaves from his thick coat; telling him he'd really done it this time and was going to have to answer for his unruly behaviour at the police station.

Not now?

Yes, better now, Lola.

There would be an article in next day's final. She could visualise it. New lead, it would say, which would have nothing to do with Watson. There would be the same picture of Jozef, grainy, straight-faced. And somehow already fading. Was that how it would be, that he would fade away, that he was already doing so, and would continue to do so until she couldn't remember how he looked? She tried to visualise his face and failed, seeing only the gloomy newspaper image, no doubt taken from some official papers. And she realised she didn't know anything about him. She didn't even know where he lived. Or how he had come to be the only German in the small town on the borders of Nottinghamshire. Or if he was married.

She decided not to read the next day's paper. She decided that, before it went to the newsstands, before it came off the press, still warm and smelling of musty black ink, even before the night reporter was summoned from his sleep and informed that there was a story.

You've got to go to the police now.

Now?

Yes, now. We'll come with you.

Chapter XII

In the light of the next day, Stefan looked in the mirror. Not particularly at himself but at the figure of the man who stood there facing him, with the wallpaper of all Ludlow Gardens at his back. A grimy face with blood seeping from a recent laceration. Someone he recognised from a long time ago; someone walking down Golen Avenue in the company of his mother, someone he could hardly look at. He continued to scrub at the word, CONSHY, written on the pavement, but it wouldn't come off. The more he scrubbed the brighter the word became, the nearer the footsteps of the man with the insignia of the mines still on his face, who was approaching with his mother. Then his father was saying something, something he might have said to a silent student whose voice he had driven away. 'Where is Stefan Czerniak? I haven't seen him yet.' Something like that.

And, standing in front of the mirror in the room in Ludlow Gardens, Stefan could remember no more, not until he was in the kitchen seated at the circular table, where a place had always been laid for this stranger, his father. Not until his father was telling the story of the corporal who had intervened to prevent him from being thrown out of a moving train, how he had gone in search of the corporal to thank him, finding him in a dwelling poor beyond telling with the tiles broken on the floor and the blackout curtains drawn against the sun. How he had laid golden rod and Michaelmas daisies on the table for the unhappy wife, how the corporal had developed what looked like an intractable infection in the bone of his leg, how a dear girl had been enlisted to mend a sock. All of them possessing nothing but the gifts of the spirit and they didn't know it.

The violin was still lying on the table where he had left it. Stefan lifted it out of its case and plucked the strings, each one in turn, and tightened them until they were in tune.

He tried to remember a sequence of events that had slipped his memory: the sound of a car engine in the street outside, a suffocating night. But it was no use. Everything had gone. There was nothing remaining from the time he placed the violin on the table in his room to the recent vision of the man facing him in the mirror with all the appearance of his father returning from the mines with a story to tell at the end of the war.

The mirror would continue to observe him. It would see that Stefan Czerniak, with the perplexity of lost time still written on his face, had noticed a fragment of paper lying on the floor, lodged in a lifted thread of the worn rug in front of the fireplace. The mirror would see, as he stooped to pick it up, that his hair wasn't brushed and that his shirt was untucked and that he wore a general mantle of heedlessness – that of a man who had found himself face to face with mortality, who had dug with his bare hands in the rubble, looking, without reason, for anything to suggest that the leg and foot he had found might not be alone, that the remains of Simon Harper might be there in an absurdly small space.

He looked at the piece of paper. The writing was Mr Harper's: a single word framed in elaborate brackets – "{post.}". Stefan didn't know what it meant. Only that it was something of importance to the poor woman Binny, whose frantic efforts to recover the torn fragments were still present in the room, fluttering the curtains, rattling the window panes and setting the light bulb swinging.

Suddenly, she was there in person. She stood in the open doorway, dressed too thinly for the chill that came in with her. She looked around the room.

'The other gentleman's not here then?'

'No.' Stefan didn't know what else to say. He thought of the kitchen in Golen Avenue, with a place perpetually laid for whoever was absent. 'Would you like a cup of tea?'

Binny said no. Her eyes lighted on the fragment of paper on the table with the unfathomable word written on it, "{post.}".

'What's that?'

'It was on the floor.'

'Was it? I thought…' She picked it up.

'Do you know what it means?'

She said no. Her eyes clouded with tears and her mouth trembled. 'No, I don't know. Is Leonard coming?' The scent she was wearing was suddenly overpowering.

'Leonard?'

'The other gentleman. Your friend. He told me his name's Leonard. He said he was coming. Can you play that? It's a viola, isn't it?'

'A little. It's a violin. Please sit down, Mrs…' She was wearing a narrow gold ring.

'Call me Binny. Will you give me a tune while we're waiting?'
Stefan lifted the violin and put it down again.

'Please.'

'The bow's gone slack.'

'Can't you wind it up? That's what they do, isn't it?'

'What shall I play?'

'Eternal Father would be very nice, dear.'

'You'll have to sing it first. Please.'

Binny's plaintive voice accompanied the notes of the violin. Stefan continued playing, verse after verse, then for a second time until she had come to the end and was beginning it all over again, her lipstick smudged by the tears rolling down her face.

Lad had come in and was standing by the door, his arms by his side. 'Didn't know you were a religious chap, Stef.'

'I'm not.'

'It was me,' Binny said. 'I asked for a tune. Your friend can play anything if he hears it once.'

'Blow me, Stef. I didn't know that. Can you?'

'I told you he can,' Binny said. She handed Lad the fragment of paper. 'That was on the floor, Leonard. Your friend doesn't understand what it means. Have you…you know?'

'I have, Binny.' Lad spread Simon Harper's letter on the table. 'Done it as best as poss, Stef.' The torn fragments had been glued onto a sheet of foolscap. Meticulously. 'You'd better read it, old chap. Here.' He fitted in the remaining fragment, like the last piece of a jigsaw.

'Leonard, your friend isn't quite well.'

'I'm all right, Binny, thank you.' He had said her name.

'I know it's ridiculous,' she said. 'Whoever's called Belinda these days?' A hint of her perfume had settled on the air in the room. 'He isn't well, Leonard.' She whispered a word. 'Didn't you know?'

For some reason, he was seated at the table, a cup of tea in front of him.

'We took the liberty, Stef, old chap,' Lad said, indicating the tea.

'Make one for yourselves, Lad.'

Binny was still there, seated on the bed. She had taken her shoes off. The toes of her stockings were darned. A stray thought arrived in Stefan's mind and went again.

The letter was on the table, upside down, lifting in the draught coming in from under the door. He started to read, beginning at the top of the page with the puzzling word.

Simon Harper had been decorated. The letters were there, followed by the elaborate brackets. Stefan looked up. Lad nodded.

'Does it mean…?'

'Yes, old chap. It means that?'

'Why?'

Lad shrugged. 'Your guess is as good as mine. Have you read the letter?'

'Only that.'

'Read the rest, old chap.'

'I can't make it out, Lad.'

'No?' Lad bent over the page. 'It's clear enough to me. Might help if you turned it the right way up, of course.'

'It's just…a letter.' Stefan pushed the envelope away. 'I don't want it, Lad.'

'Might help to set you up, Stef, old chap.'

'I can't. I'm going to hand it in.'

'Good chap. That's the noble thing to do. Just playing devil's advocate.'

'The noble thing to do,' Binny's voice echoed. 'Your friend's made the right decision, Leonard.' She had drawn her legs up under her and an inch of torn lace appeared below the hem of her skirt. Stefan looked away. A wave of shame washed over him. Shame for her that she was shameless. Shame for himself that he had noticed.

'You can read the letter, Binny.' Her name again.

'Thank you, dear. Forgive me, I seem to be a cry baby today.'

'Binny won't mind me telling you. She lost someone in the war, you see.' Lad gave her his handkerchief.

'I do mind, Leonard. It's a secret.' Binny's sobs redoubled. 'Now your friend knows.'

'I won't tell anyone.' Stefan took the letter back and read it: a brief expression of valediction. Gratitude. Fare you well. Simon Harper. The letters of the decoration had run into each other "{post.}". Enc, draft to the value of £…sterling in lieu of wages owing. Fare you well. 'How are you going to give an account of your chap?' Somewhere in the room, Lad was still talking.

Stefan didn't know. The face of Simon Harper had gone from his mind as completely as had the night of his exit. There would be nothing left of it, were it not for the taste of smoke he continued to take in with every breath and the flash of fire every time he blinked his eyes.

'It's gone, Lad.'

'Come on, Stef.' Lad was writing words on the envelope.

'Stop it, Leonard.' Binny caught hold of his hand and took away the pencil. 'I told you, your friend isn't quite well.'

Then he remembered. Simon Harper had enquired after his health, sitting across from him at a desk in some kind of office. The masked face began to reassemble. The face without the mask. The eyes, as if he were looking into them for the first time, eyes of incredible kindness. Fare you well.

'His people have never mentioned anything, Binny.'

'Possibly they didn't know, Leonard. We had other things to think of in the war. Now Mr Bevan is looking after us all and we don't have to pay for a doctor. I'm not saying your friend has seizures exactly, but that he goes away for short periods of time.'

Stefan looked from one to the other. They had forgotten he was there.

'It's quite possible that your friend is in shock also, Leonard.' There was no end to Binny's opinions. 'The fire, you know, and seeing…' She was about to cry again.

'You can call me Stefan.'

'May I really? You don't mind? Why, thank you, dear.' She pulled her skirt down over her knees.

But she didn't call him Stefan. There was something about him. He had always known. Something that rendered him unapproachable. Some negative polarity that drove people away. *Noli me tangere.*

She merely asked for another verse of Eternal Father and made to go away. He realised he didn't know why she had been there in the first place. He watched as she slipped into the jacket that hung forlornly from her shoulders, as she pulled on her gloves and tucked a slack curl under her hat. She held out her hand.

'Good-bye, dear.'

Lad lit a cigarette for her.

In a few minutes, she was back, carrying a paper bag. 'Don't take offence, dear, but when we were making the tea we couldn't help noticing that your cupboard was nearly empty. Do you like rock cakes?' She looked up hopefully. 'Has your friend an income now, do you think, Leonard?'

'Working on it, Binny. Working on it. Don't you worry your pretty head about it.'

'Not any longer, Leonard.' Binny turned to Stefan. 'I used to be…pretty, you know, dear. In the war we were all pretty.'

Her perfume was still in the room, even after she had left.

Lad was pacing around, waiting until the ring of the segs on her shoes had dwindled to nothing in the street outside. The sun had climbed above the rooftops opposite, covering the window with grime and finding every worn thread on the rug.

'Did I thank her, Lad?'

'What's that, old chap?'

'Did I thank her for the rock cakes?'

'You did, old chap. Now, a word with you if you please, Stef. How's the old…you know. You know, old chap. Half hoped you'd…you know. Cupboard bare and all that.' Lad paced backwards and forwards in front of the window. 'She's gone. In a word, Stef, old chap, the old spondulicks.'

'It's all right, Lad, thank you.'

'Cupboard empty, old chap.'

'Probably. I haven't looked recently. I don't use it much.'

'I can tell that, old chap. What am I getting at? This, that's what. Saw it this morning. Take a look.' Lad pulled a scrap of paper from his pocket. 'Just a thought. Don't wish to interfere and all that. Just a thought, as I say.'

'Thank you, Lad. I have to hand that in first.' The envelope containing Simon Harper's letter was still on the table.

'Painless, Stef, painless.'

So painless that the event had already entered a recent and disappearing history compounded of rain and fire, and a torn letter, reassembled, lying on the table. A woman singing in a lost and watery voice. Thank you, sir. I'll see this is passed on to the right quarters. Leave your name and address if you would in case we need to talk to you again. How does a fellow enunciate that, sir? Churnick. Thank you, sir. On the fiddle, ha? Nodding at the violin.

Stefan Czerniak stood outside the stage door of the palais. The notice was still there, tacked down with rusted drawing pins. First violin required. Apply within. Genuine enquiries only.

He tried the door. It opened, releasing a wave of dark breath compounded of cigarettes, the lees of last night's ale, and black serge shiny at the knees and elbows.

'Come in, young sir. Are you any good?'

Stefan felt himself blushing.

'No, sir.'

'You'd better prove it then, young man.'

'Sir?'

'Prove that you're no good. Give us a tune. A round of applause for the young maestro, gentlemen.' Elsewhere in the building a door opened and closed. Someone sneezed. 'Anything'll do, young man. Among friends, you see. That's what you are, among friends.'

'I'll need to hear it first.'

'Someone fetch Miss what's er name. You going for her, Titch? Mercy boco. Get her to give us a rendering of the Queen of the Night. If the young maestro can do that he's in.

And at the end of the day, back in the room in Ludlow Gardens, Stefan Czerniak saw in the mirror, as he slowly realised, a travelling companion. Not his father, but himself, framed there against the dingy wall at his back, the cupboard, empty but for a paper bag of rock cakes, and the window, beyond which a woman called Binny came and went, travelling with the verses of Eternal Father in her head. Wary of him for a reason he knew only too well. And that was how it would be.

Chapter XIII

The wet sheet flapped in Lola's face and drenched her hair and collar. She tried to unravel it, feeling for the edge and not finding it, until the whole of her was enveloped in its cold suffocating hug.

'Dear me, Miss Robertson,' Mrs Chadwick's voice sounded, muffled, from the outside world. Lola could see the shape of her, standing patiently by the line, the basket of laundry at her feet. 'Dear me, I hope this isn't making you late for work, Miss Robertson. God bless you.'

The sheet suddenly released her and she was in the garden at Beacon Street, pegging washing on the line. Mrs Chadwick continued to talk. 'I do hope Nigel will do well. What do you think, Miss Robertson? Do you think he'll be accepted?'

'I don't know, Mrs Chadwick. I don't know what they look for in the medical test.' Inside the white tent again she wondered why the washing had to be done on a day when Nigel was leaving early. Probably Miss Taylor had been right and this was how it would be. At the time it didn't matter, but now, in the cold garden with the washing dripping down on the tiles and the grey clouds racing overhead it suddenly did.

'Miss Robertson, I'm so pleased you've come to live here,' Mrs Chadwick continued. 'I wanted to ask you, my dear, if Nigel goes into the National Service, will you...I don't know how to say this. It's a lot to ask of a young woman your age, but Nigel and I think very highly of you. It would be two years, darling. Are you...walking out with anyone? In which case, of course, we couldn't presume to ask.'

Lola dropped the edge of the sheet she was holding. Suddenly, everything, the grey clouds, the plain garden and the tops of the rows of houses over the wall tilted until the floundering sky was under her feet and the solid ground was on top of her, crushing her under its weight. So Mrs Chadwick didn't know. Probably no one knew. Probably everyone knew and didn't talk about it in her presence. Probably it was all round the town, being talked about over shop counters, at street corners, and in the back room of the Methodist Chapel.

The question hung in the air. Mrs Chadwick stood in front of her, a look of dismay on her face.

'My dear, I've upset you. May the Lord forgive me. What is it, darling?'

Lola picked up the sheet.

'Don't worry about that, dear.'

The words were still there, hovering in the space between them. Unanswered.

'What is it, darling?'

'I don't know.'

It was still early, eight o'clock by the clock on the wall and not properly light. Lola sat at the table in Mrs Chadwick's kitchen. A half full bottle of some honey coloured liquid had been removed to the top of the dresser. A crucifix hung above the fireplace. Mrs Chadwick sat opposite. 'Let me make you a cup of tea, dear.'

Lola shook her head.

'You know, darling, when Nigel suggested that you might stay here while he's away doing his National Service, I had my doubts. I couldn't say so to Nigel, but I said it to myself, "That young lady has the look of a loved woman". Could I have been right, darling?

Lola nodded. She hadn't thought anyone else would see.

'Now, what is it, darling?'

As Lola went in, Miss Taylor quickly slipped a newspaper into the middle of a pile of x-ray packets. A corner of it remained visible.

'We'll file these later, dear, after lunch.' Then she asked Lola to take the domiciliary machine to the ward and do a chest x-ray on Mr Palfrey. 'Get someone to help you, dear. You won't be able to manage him on your own. And put a pillowcase over the plate, dear.'

Miss Taylor continued to talk, telling Lola that she had been at school with the Palfrey twins and they were no different now, in fact more the same than ever; and that there was a patient in the waiting room whom she would attend to herself while Lola was looking after Mr Palfrey.

The patient, Lola knew from the double ring on the waiting room bell, was her father. A newspaper badly concealed under a pile of x-ray packets and her father announcing his presence in the waiting room; and she was being sent away.

The door of the visitors' room closed quietly as she walked past; the screens were round Mr Palfrey's bed. There was no one in sister's office. The other patients were silent, waiting for any sound that might reach them from the bed with the screens.

Lola opened the case at the end of the ward and started to assemble the machine. She plugged it into the large socket and pressed the button a few times to warm it up. She had forgotten the lead apron. Shapes of people pressed against the fabric of the screens round Mr Palfrey's bed. A gap appeared and closed again, but in the brief interval of its opening revealed the recumbent figure of Mr Palfrey, drowned, washed up without breath and peaceful on the white island of his hospital bed. His oxygen mask had been taken away and the intravenous needle was being removed. Sister O'Hara appeared, shaking her head, mouthing something. 'Sorry, dear.'

Lola packed up the machine. Her heart sank. It was surely her fault. If she had been earlier it might not have happened.

From behind the closed door of the visitors' room there were voices. On an impulse, she knocked. A voice from inside said, 'Come in.' She would ask if Mr Palfrey's daughters would like a cup of tea. But everything was there: china cups, sugar lumps, a plate of shortbreads, a jug of hot water. She could still ask. Sister wondered if you would like more hot water.

Yet someone was saying something quite different.

'Marjorie, look, it's Lilian Robertson's daughter. Lola, isn't it?'

'Yes.' Lola felt herself blushing. The words she had prepared were already slipping away.

'We were so sorry to hear about your mother, Lola. Our dad, he was eighty-five. Can you imagine that? But your mum was only…'

'Forty-seven.'

'Oh dear. You poor darling.'

The sister was called Dorothy. 'We were expecting the minister, but he hasn't come. Do you think we just get up and go? They must be terribly busy.'

'Have you…seen your dad?' The question, even the word, sounded over familiar.

'No, we didn't like to ask.'

'They must be terribly busy.'

Her father was still there when she got back to the department, talking to Miss Taylor in the x-ray room. Lola could hear his voice negotiating the double right angle of the light trap when she went into the dark room. Two plates lay on the bench, unprocessed. She switched off the overhead light and reached up for two large frames, bringing the whole rack clattering to the floor. The voices next door stopped. She heard the x-ray room door open and her father's unequal footsteps go out. She switched off the light and began to develop his x-rays.

'We'll have to get that rack seen to.' Miss Taylor had come in noiselessly and was disentangling the frames. 'How did you get on with Mr Palfrey, dear?'

'I didn't. He died.'

Miss Taylor swore. 'I've told the ward not to ask for x-rays when patients are so close. It's not…helpful. That was your father,' she added.

'How is he?'

'About the same. You'll see what the x-rays look like. Not much difference, is there?'

'No.'

'Your father was asking questions, Lola. I had to tell him I don't discuss my staff. I hope I was kind to him.'

Miss Taylor propped her father's x-rays in front of the light box. 'I can't really tell you what he was saying, Lola.'

'I wasn't going to ask, Miss Taylor.'

'No, I know you weren't, dear. He was talking about Jozef.'

'Yes.'

'There's something in the paper. I didn't want you to come across it without being warned, dear. That's why I sent you to see poor Mr Palfrey. I hid the paper in the pile of x-rays. Mother would be ashamed of me. It's in casualty now. Or pharmacy,' she added.

What does it say? But Lola didn't ask. She knew what it would say: that a pair of shoes had been found at the side of the river on the occasion of the recent tragedy and the shoes had become part of the investigation into the disappearance of the hospital orderly, Jozef Schmidt.

'If you'd like to see it…'

Lola didn't. She already knew.

'What about young Mr Chadwick, dear?' Miss Taylor was passing her father's x-rays through the rinse, draining the surplus water and transferring them to the drying cabinet.

'He was going for his medical today.' Lola hadn't thought of Nigel Chadwick. He might be finished now, waiting in some bleak official room for the verdict, his coat so big on him that the belt went round twice.

'It could go either way,' Miss Taylor said. Then, 'You need to take some holiday, dear, just in case…you know.' Just in case

269

you're going to be trapped for the rest of your life. 'Is there anywhere you'd like to go? How about a nice day in Lincoln or Sheffield? You're a pretty young woman. You could look round the shops. Mawer and Collingham and Bainbridge are very nice. You could see the lights.'

Somewhere in a hospital staff room a newspaper lay on a table, folded inwards, concealing the fading straight-faced picture of Jozef Schmidt, whose whereabouts were unknown; where he had come from and where he had gone.

'Thank you, Miss Taylor,' she said. She couldn't leave, not even for one day.

Yet now, she couldn't imagine Jozef, not how he had been, only as he was now, a difficult image folded inwards, passed from hand to hand, discussed in low voices, hidden in a stack of x-rays waiting for filing. Always something strange about him.

And there would be another paper, on the stands when she left work with the same picture but receding farther and farther into some irretrievable past. She wouldn't read it. She wouldn't go within hearing of the Scottish man they called Jock who stood in the Market Square calling "Late Night Final".

'Late Ni…' The words broke off suddenly. Something was going on. Loud voices. An expression she had never heard before. As Lola turned the corner into the Market Square she saw the paper seller pinned against the front of Fortesque's, face to face with two other men and trying to back away from them, except that he could go no farther because of the wall.

As she approached, the two men stood aside. There was a smell of strong liquor.

'I'd like a paper, please. Is it threepence?' She had never bought one before. The men were still there, waiting for her to go. 'Is there any more news, Jock?'

'Aye, ye mean the hospital fellow? Aye. New lead. Is that what it says, young lady? I havena me glasses.'

'Yes, it does.' The heavy black words ran into one another. She could hear the double footsteps of two constables on the beat at the other side of the Market Square. The argumentative men had gone. She would pay for the paper and leave it in the nearest litterbin.

'To tell ye the truth, young lady, I canna read na write. Yon blokes calling me a Nazzi an all. I sez to them Jock Dork's nobbut the messenger and ye dunna shoot the messenger. Thanking ye kindly, miss. Here, tek yer thruppence.'

But my mother's not here to give it to. Jock Dork was still standing in front of her holding out his hand with the shiny three-penny bit planted imploringly in the middle of it.

'No really, Mr Dork. I'm grateful for the paper, thank you. I'll read it tonight.'

Lola Robertson didn't know if that represented a promise.

She went back to Beacon Street and took the paper to her room. She could hear the voice of Nigel Chadwick in conversation with his mother, and the background sound of the saucepan as he drained the cabbage.

The face of Jozef looked at her from the front page, blurred and grainy, an enlarged version of the same official photograph. Along the side were some odd words in German, hand-written in heavy black ink. She tried again to remember Jozef as he was the last time she had seen him, but she couldn't.

"MISSING HOSPITAL ORDERLY – NEW LEAD"

A pair of shoes found by the side of the river on the night of the recent tragedy had been identified as being of German manufacture. The police were not divulging any further information. However, a townsman walking a dog along the wharf late that night had reported to this publication hearing sounds of mayhem near the town bridge. Readers were invited to draw their own conclusions.

"The missing hospital orderly, Joseph Shmit, was, it is believed, at one time a prisoner of war. The privacy of Mr Shmit's colleagues is being respected."

Nigel Chadwick was calling from downstairs. Would Miss Robertson prefer to dine in her room or join his mother and himself downstairs?

Lola went down. A place had been set for her and a tureen of steaming vegetables was already on the table. Nigel was dishing up fishcakes, two to each plate. Mrs Chadwick was seated, her head covered, ready for the grace.

'Miss Robertson, would you mind, dear?'

Lola blushed. Nigel was looking down at his plate.

Mrs Chadwick was looking at her expectantly. 'It doesn't have to be anything much, dear. As long as we return thanks in some way.'

'ForthefoodweareabouttoreceivemaytheLordmakeustrulythank fulamen.'

'God bless you, dear. Nigel has something to tell you, but we'll finish our meal first. Did you pick up your letter, dear? Your father put it through earlier. He said you might be going on holiday to London. That would be nice, wouldn't it?'

Nigel hadn't passed his medical test. Tears stood in Mrs Chadwick's eyes. 'It's my fault, Miss Robertson. If I'd known a long time ago there might have been an operation to correct his back, but we had other things to think about in the war.'

Chapter XIV

The letter was lying on the hall table, addressed to Miss Lola Robertson, c/o Salisbury House, in Jean Beaumont's neat square capitals and looking as it if had been opened and closed again.

Lola took it up to her room.

"Dear Lola", it said. "We are sending this with your father. We hope you don't mind. Pip and I are going to London. For Christmas! Would you be able to come with us? Pip is of the opinion that you have 7 days and 4 hours owing (I don't know how he worked that out!).

"Darling, we do hope you will say yes. We'll go down Regent Street and see the lights. Isn't that so exciting!

"Yours ever

"Jean Beaumont xx

"PS Watson's coming too. Now are you persuaded!

"PPS Enc From your father."

The room swam in front of Lola's eyes. She looked out of the window towards Holister Road where the lights in the back windows of the houses shimmered in the fragile evening. A wind had got up, rattling the clothes line. A dog barked far away. Downstairs, Mrs Chadwick and Nigel were listening to something on the Light Programme.

Her father's letter was written on formal paper; folded inwards so that she couldn't see what it said. She would have to open it out, and then she would have seen the whole of it. She only wanted to see the beginning. She took it downstairs and knocked on the kitchen door.

There was a sound from inside of the bottle of honey-coloured liquid being moved. Nigel answered. 'Miss Robertson, come in, come in. We're making the Christmas trimmings. Is it mother you're requiring?'

A fire burned in the grate. The table was covered with paper chains.

'Either of you, if you would be so kind,' Lola said. 'It's a letter from my father and I'd like to know how it begins before I read the rest of it.'

Mrs Chadwick and Nigel exchanged glances. She wasn't making sense. Mrs Chadwick started another chain.

'Nigel will read it, Miss Robertson. He's always in the library looking at books. His father would have been proud of him.' She took a sip from the tumbler in front of her.

'Mother, not while Miss Robertson's here, please. Yes, I'll read it.' Lola gave Nigel the letter. 'Do I have to open it out?'

'Yes please.'

'It might be private, Miss Robertson. What if I see more than the beginning of it by mistake, I mean?'

'It wouldn't matter, Nigel.'

Nigel Chadwick began to open the letter and dropped it on the floor. He picked it up, wiped it on his sleeve and began again, turning it this way and that until he found the beginning.

'It says, "Lola, my dear".' He blushed, folded the letter, and handed it back.

'Thank you, Nigel.'

'You must ask Miss Robertson if you may help her with anything else, Nigel.' The tumbler of honey-coloured liquid was empty and Mrs Chadwick was dabbing at the corners of her mouth with a pocket handkerchief.

Nigel Chadwick had been reduced to speechlessness.

'Nigel, please.' Mrs Chadwick replaced the handkerchief in her pocket and folded her hands on the table. 'I've done my best to bring him up with nice manners, Miss Robertson, and now look.'

'Mrs Chadwick, it's all right, really. Nigel has helped a lot.' It suddenly came to Lola that she could say anything in this room, bright with firelight and the jumble of paper chains on the table and the taste honey-coloured liquid hanging on the air. 'It's a letter from my father and I had to know how it starts before I read the rest. We haven't always been on good terms.'

Nigel continued to blush. Mrs Chadwick nodded. 'Nigel has always worried that his departure from Salisbury House led to you being blamed and having to leave, Miss Robertson.'

'Mother!' Nigel took the empty tumbler away and returned the bottle of honey-coloured liquid to the sideboard.

'It is so, Nigel. It's crippling your life, dear. Miss Robertson knows that you came here when your father passed away.'

Lola didn't know. 'I had to leave Salisbury House because National Insurance came in, or something like that. I was going to have to be paid wages.' She could hardly remember the sequence of events, only that the police came and she had sensed her parents' anxiety, that there was something the government wouldn't like about her situation. It all seemed so long ago.

Mrs Chadwick was still talking. 'There you are, Nigel. I told you it would be something like that.'

"Lola, my dear", her father's letter began, in a precise, scholarly hand she didn't recognise. "By the time you return from the metropolis, your father will be a married man again. The lucky lady is Mrs Betty Palmer, a respectable widow, of the parish of Retford. You are a kind girl, Lola, and will want to wish your father happiness and good fortune.

"Yours,

"Cyril Robertson (Corporal)

"Post script: Mrs Alison Goody is in agreement and has been found an alternative situation."

Lola gazed at the letter until the words ran into one another. The clock on the church was chiming eight. She put on her coat and went out, the letter still in her hand and the words of it sounding in her head.

The river flowed swiftly downstream, oily and dark. She could hear the lap of it against the wall, and on the other side the ripple of it among the willows. Far off, she could hear the engine of a barge, going slowly, negotiating the double bend.

She went down to the wharf, half sliding, holding onto the railing. She walked the short distance to the place where Jozef's shoes had been left, and looked down into the sightless water.

But she wasn't alone.

The dog was tugging at the hem of her coat. Running feet were beating the pavement of the wharf, a man's voice shouting.

'Lola!' Pip Beaumont stood facing her. 'What on earth are you doing?'

'I don't know. I think I was going to throw this in.' She gave Pip the letter.

'May I?'

'Yes.'

Pip read it and handed it back to her. 'This isn't your dad's writing.'

'No, I don't know whose it is. Is it…real?'

'Probably. Might be some solicitor's clerk. All the more reason for you to come to London. Did you hear from Jean?'

'Yes.'

'Well?'

'Yes, Pip.'

'Does that mean you'll come with us?'

She said yes.

She looked out of the window, half expecting to see the plain garden at Beacon Street with its clothes line and sheets turned sides into middle; the rows of similar gardens at either side and over the back wall, with similar flying sheets.

But it wasn't Beacon Street. It was Golen Avenue and she was in the house of Pip's mother, whom she didn't know whether to address as Mrs Beaumont or Freda. Nor did she know how she was going to find out.

Early morning sunlight was filtering through the branches of the sycamores at the bottom of the garden making intricate patterns on the grass and among the broken sticks of sprouts and overblown cabbages. There was a birdbath, and a rusted roller at one side, and, walking drunkenly towards the dividing fence, a tortoise.

'Basil!' The voice reached Lola before the sight of its owner, a man wearing a red bandana round his neck and a long black coat, who reached over the fence and scooped up the small creature. He stood up to recover his breath. And she was suddenly back in the Market Square at home, sitting on the chapel steps on the day of her mother's funeral, wearing a black jacket carrying the aroma of someone else's breakfast, and a skirt with a stain on the front. Hiding from whoever it was who was looking for her.

The man had meanwhile appeared in Mrs Beaumont's garden and was occupied in burying the tortoise. She couldn't see his face, only his hands and arms as he hollowed out a space. As if he were digging coal.

Someone knocked.

'Come in.'

'May I? Isn't it too early?' The door opened slowly and Jean came in, her face still smeared with cream. 'Gosh, you're dressed already, Lola. And you've made the bed! May I?' She sat down on the bed.

'I like your twinset. Is it…?'

'I've been saving up.' Lola blushed.

'The colour suits you. How would you describe it?'

'It said deep rose in the bazaar, but I think it could be pink. Or red.'

'I wanted to say something, Lola, before you find out. Pip's gone to the park with Watson.' Jean hesitated. 'I don't hit it off with Mrs B. I never have done. There's nothing wrong with her. It's just me.' Jean burst into tears. 'I'm so pleased you're here.' The flood of tears finished as suddenly as it had started. 'You won't notice anything. We're quite civilised about it. I won't mention it again, but as long as you know. There now. What can I do for you, dear? There must be something.'

'You could tell me if I call Mrs Beaumont Freda or Mrs Beaumont, please, Jean.'

'Call her Mrs Beaumont, dear, and she'll ask you to call her Freda. She's a sweet soul. It's me. I still feel responsible for...you know. Oh dear.' The scent of bacon and eggs crept under the door. 'I should be helping.'

'Should I go?'

Jean shook her head. 'I wouldn't, dear. That's the mistake I made, invading Freda's kitchen. You have to wait to be invited. You can't just walk in there. However...' she rubbed her face. 'Do I look a sight?'

'You look nice, Jean.'

'Do I look as if I've been crying?'

'No, not now.'

'Any other questions, dear?'

How do you say that name? But Lola didn't ask.

In the event, there was no need. Mrs Beaumont started a long way off, with the tortoise Bazal, restored to his place of hibernation by her dear neighbour. She turned to Lola. 'After Mr Bazalgette, you know. We found him in the foul drain. Now dear...' She took Lola's hand. 'I know all this is very new and unfamiliar to you, but could you possibly bear to meet him?'

'You're not going to dig him up again, mum.'

'Pip, don't be absurd. I meant Paul. And Ruth. They're not complicated, Lola dear. They still take their tea black without sugar. We thought everything would be better after the war, and...'

Watson heaved a great sigh from under the table.

'Now look what we've done, mum. I'll fetch the Czerniaks.'

Lola went hot and cold. She couldn't. She searched her mind for an excuse; anything, if only to take her out of the room before they came. She felt the years of her life dissolving around her, draining away, as surely as the rain she could hear falling from the guttering on the outside of the house.

She was in Barratt's Place again, bent over a sock she was mending. She could see herself, as if she were back once more in the room, outside herself, and looking at a girl called Lola Robertson who was wearing a skirt with a lumpy hem from the jumble sale and a cardigan that scarcely met across her front. Doing her best sewing because there was a visitor under their roof, who had brought Michaelmas daisies and golden rod for her mother; the strangeness of whose presence caused all the shoeless children in the neighbourhood to follow after him as he went away, when all anyone had was the hope of magic and the grey beginning of the peace.

Pip's voice was already outside, in the company of other footsteps. She stood up.

Then, suddenly, she was seated at the table again with a cup of black tea in front of her, and face to face with these unusual, delighted people, who could scarcely believe their eyes; the gentleman saying, 'The dear girl,' over and over again, and the lady 'Darling, you'll embarrass her.' Over and over again. 'God bless her.'

'Darling, you'll embarrass her!' Over and over again.

He was pitifully short of breath. His wife was beautiful, with her grey hair drawn into a knot behind her neck. They wore their threadbare black coats with…a word came to her from nowhere…grace.

They introduced themselves as Ruth and Paul Czerniak, pronouncing the name as if it were only three letters long, all consonants. She said she was Lola Robertson. As if they had never seen each other before. She thanked them for going all the way to attend her mother's funeral. She stopped. And blushed. The tears gathered, hot and imminent, at the backs of her eyes. They would ask about the German gentleman from the hospital who had tried to help them.

But they didn't. They told her how they had been objectors during the war, how Mr Czerniak had been sent to the mines and Mrs Czerniak to the laundry; how Freda and Ken – that was dear Freda's husband – had given them a print of a picture by John Constable so that Ruth appeared to be patriotic when people came to question her.

'But what about you, my dear?' Mrs Czerniak took her hand. 'Tell us about yourself.' Her eyes were brown, kind, unconditional, questioning. Tired.

Lola blushed, 'I…'

And Mr Czerniak said, 'Sweetheart, the dear girl isn't used to being asked to give an account of herself.'

And Mrs Beaumont, 'Ken and I were so simple in those days. That picture by Constable, you know. As if…'

And Mrs Czerniak, 'Lola, forgive me. How tactless I am.'

'No, really, I'll tell you. It isn't very much. I work in the dark room in the hospital.' She looked down into her cup of tea and caught sight of herself, her wide eyes, brimming with words. She would tell everyone: Mr and Mrs Czerniak, Mrs Beaumont, Pip, Jean, and Watson lying at her feet. 'The German gentleman who helped you when you came to my mother's funeral was called Jozef Schmidt. I was…' she hesitated, trying to find an expression…'he was…I was…sorry. We had been to the pictures earlier the same evening that a poor man drowned in the river. Jozef hasn't been seen since then. A pair of shoes…' She stopped. Watson sighed. 'They thought at first that the shoes belonged to the drowned gentleman, but he was wearing his own when he was brought into casualty. I think…'

She didn't think. She knew. No one said anything.

Jean whispered something to Pip, 'Tell them.'

Lola continued to look down into her cup of tea. Someone was speaking to her and she hadn't heard what they said.

'What do you think, Lola dear?' Mrs Czerniak's question came again.

'No, sweetheart…'

'I think Jozef took off his shoes and jumped in the river to try and save the gentleman.'

It had been said. She heard Mr Czerniak saying, 'The dear girl, the dear girl…'

Mrs Beaumont came over and kissed her. 'We will always be proud of your good young man, Lola dear.'

When Lola looked up, her words had gone far away. Back to the borders of Nottinghamshire, to the wharf and the brown river, the flat fields over the other side, to the space where Barratt's Place had been.

'I'm better now,' she said. 'Thank you.' She started to cry. 'I've spoilt your day.' The rain continued to clatter down from the overflowing gutter outside.

Mrs Beaumont had gone away, saying she would make more tea and bring the biscuit tin.

'We'd like you to choose one, Lola darling,' she said. She took the lid off.

Lola hesitated. There were pieces of paper folded up inside.

'One of mum's ideas for wet days in the school holidays,' Pip said. 'Not biscuits.'

'Now don't spoil it, Pip.'

Lola took a piece of paper out of the tin and put in on the table in front of her.

'Now another,' Mrs Beaumont said.

She took out another.

'Two more, dear. Open them up, darling, and maybe you could tell us what they say.'

'Mum, she's not a child.'

'That'll do, Pip. What does the first one say, dear?'

'A musical concert at the palais with Ruth, Paul, Jean, Pip and Freda.'

'And the second?'

'Window shopping in Regent Street with Jean, Ruth and Freda.'

'And the third?'

'A turbine exhibition with Paul, Pip and Watson.'

'And finally…'

'A walk in Congreve Park with Watson.'

'Now tell us which one you fancy, darling. It's your holiday.'

Lola looked at the pieces of paper again.

'Mum, she's not a child.'

'Leave her be, Pip. She's arriving at a wise decision.'

Lola picked up the first slip of paper. 'This one's nice because it's with everyone,' she said.

Pip was mouthing something she couldn't understand.

'And because you have chosen wisely, my dear, you will be given them all,' Mrs Beaumont said. 'We'll fit them all in somehow while you're here.'

'Oh, thank you!' Lola could hear her own voice somehow filling the room, nudging at the ceiling and the French windows, and flying out into the drenched winter garden where the leavings of the wartime vegetables leaned drunkenly against each other. She didn't know if she was crying or not, but probably it didn't matter. She could hear Pip's voice, 'Now look what we've done.'

Chapter XV

'Whatever next.' Mrs Beaumont was trying to attract Jean's attention but Jean was lost in the scene unfolding at the front of the theatre: the heavy crimson curtains being drawn back and the orchestra arriving, taking their seats at the desks and arranging sheets of music.

'Lola dear,' Mrs Beaumont nudged her arm. 'The gentleman in the grey suit just now walking up with the lady is Pip's brother.' Then, under her breath, 'Whatever next. They're going right to the front. Pip, do you see that?'

But Pip didn't. He was also occupied in watching the orchestra.

'Ruth and Paul didn't like to be near the front, dear,' Mrs Beaumont continued. 'They're afraid they'll be an embarrassment to Stefan, but between you and me I think it's the other way round. Something seemed to go wrong at the end of the war. We never did know what it was. There he is, dear. He's so much as his father was.'

The heads of two tall people moving into the row in front came between Lola and the orchestra. The lights were going down, leaving the stage, which she couldn't see, in an imaginary brilliance. Cigarette smoke hung in the air. Coughs were being swallowed.

'Do you know the *Méditation* from *Thaïs*, dear? It's very beautiful.'

Lola said she didn't know it.

'I'll be quiet now, darling,' Mrs Beaumont said, 'otherwise you never will hear it. The lady with Lad...' she nudged Lola's arm again. 'Oh dear, do be quiet, Freda. He's a grown man and he can do what he likes. There's no one to tell me that now, so I have to keep telling myself.'

At the end of the day, Lola Robertson stood at the window looking at the sycamores in the garden with the full moon caught in their branches. The same that hovered over the late night theatre where the caretaker was locking the doors and picking up cigarette ends on the steps; the same that shed its quiet light on the gardens of Golen Avenue, on Bazal and Watson and on all sleeping creatures; on a woman called Binny returning to a street corner; on a violinist called

Stefan Czerniak who had forgotten playing the *Méditation* from *Thaïs* by the time she was introduced to him, whose eyes had lightened with surprise, who had held out his hand and said her name: Lola.

The same moon that shed its silence on the town near the border of Nottinghamshire: on Miss Taylor, carrying Ovaltine up the stairs to her mother; on the x-ray department, where, at the back of a high shelf labelled "Deceased", the records of Lilian Robertson had come to rest. On the cold river with its burning secrets winding slowly out to Marsh.

Blessing, for as long as she stood at the window cloaked in the velvet night, even that.